THE LAST TSAR

D1508131

THE LAST TSAR

Emperor Michael II

DONALD CRAWFORD

By the same author
Michael & Natasha
WEIDENFELD & NICOLSON, LONDON; SCRIBNERS, NEW YORK;
PIPER, MUNICH; ÉDITIONS DES SYTRES, PARIS,
JAVIER VERGARA, BARCELONA; ZHAKAROV, MOSCOW

`All rights reserved. No part of this publication may be
reproduced, stored in a retrieval system, or transmitted in any form
or by any means, electronic, mechanical, photocopying, recording,
or otherwise, without the prior permission of the copyright owner.

Donald Crawford has asserted the moral right
to be identified as the author of this work.

ISBN13: 978-1466445000

For Rosemary

The war and all the great horror it involves cannot help inspiring sadness in every sensible person; for example, I feel greatly embittered...and most of all towards those who are at the top, who hold power and allow all that horror to happen. If the question of war were decided by the people at large, I would not be so passionately averse to that great calamity; but...nobody ever asks the nation, the country at large, what course of action they would choose.

Grand Duke Michael Aleksandrovich, from the front line to his wife Natasha, January 22, 1915

I am deeply concerned and worried by what is happening around us. There has been a shocking alteration in the mood of the most loyal people...the public hatred for certain people who allegedly are close to you and who are forming part of the present government...and this hatred, along with demands for changes, are already openly expressed at every opportunity... I have come to the conviction that we are standing on a volcano and that the least spark, the least incorrect step could provoke a catastrophe for you, for us all, and for Russia...I cannot help feeling that if anything happens inside Russia, it will be echoed with a catastrophe as regards the war.

Grand Duke Michael, in a warning letter to his brother Nicholas II, November 11, 1916

To His Majesty the Emperor Michael: Recent events have forced me to decide irrevocably to take this extreme step. Forgive me if it grieves you and also for no warning — there was no time. Shall always remain a faithful and devoted brother. Now returning to HQ where hope to come back shortly to Tsarskoe Selo. Fervently pray God to help you and our country. Your Nicky.

Telegram from ex-TsarNicholas II to his brother after abdicating in his favour, March 3, 1917

CONTENTS

MAPS:

ILLUSTRATIONS

Grand Duke Michael, Blue Cuirassiers
Natasha 1910,
Sergei Mamontov
24 Nikolaevskay Street
The Fighting General, 1915
— *Leeds Russian Archive, University of Leeds*
Princess Patricia of Connaught
— *By kind permission of HM The Queen*
Vladimir Wulfert
— *School of Slavonic and East European Studies, London*
Michael, Savage Division HQ 1915
— *Washburn, Russian Campaign 1915*
'Prisoner of Perm', April 1918
— *M Zagulaev, Perm*
Executioners
— *Central Archive, Russian Federal Security Service*

MAPs by Chris Duggan

DATES

Until February 1918 the Russian 'Julian' calendar differed from the 'Gregorian' in use elsewhere. In the nineteenth centry the Russian calendar was twelve days behind and in the twentieth century, thirteeen days behind. As example, January 1, 1914 in Russia was January 14 elsewhere. Throughout this book, the Russian calendar is used, unless otherwise stated.

MONEY

It is impossible, because of fluctuating currency values, to give the precise present-date equivalent for monies quoted in the book. Where such figures are given they are those effective at October 1, 2011 as quoted by the Bank of England. The following short table may be helpful. The sterling and $ figures are for the 1914 value and the italic figures below are for 2011 equivalent values.

Rouble	Sterling	US dollar
1,000	110	512
	9,900	*15,500*
5,000	550	2,560
	49,500	*77,500*
20,000	2,200	10,250
	198,000	*310,000*
30,000	3,300	15,400
	297,000	*466,000*

Source: Conversion rates sterling: Bank of England.
£1 in 1914 = £89.98 in 2011; £/$ exchange rate at 1.57
£/$ rates for roubles as quoted in *Baedeker's Russia* 1914

INTRODUCTION

THE life of Grand Duke Michael Aleksandrovich, younger brother of Tsar Nicholas II, is not one which hitherto has easily fitted into the history books. His affair with the beautiful double divorcée daughter of a Moscow lawyer, was conducted in secrecy. When she gave birth to his illegitimate son, the official world refused to accept that he was the father. His runaway marriage under the eyes of the Tsar's trailing secret police was so carefully concealed that they never found out how he had done it without their knowing. On becoming Emperor, in succession to his brother Nicholas, it was said that he had immediately abdicated, though he never did. And when the Bolsheviks put a bullet in his head, they pretended for their own good reasons that he had escaped. It is small wonder, therefore, that Grand Duke Michael, hidden away by the Soviets, has been something of a mystery man in the story of modern Russia. Even in 1951, when his widow — 'the last uncrowned Empress' — died penniless in a Paris charity hospital, they did not know who she was.

In fact, the real story of Michael is that of the one Romanov whom Russia could least afford to lose. It is also the story of the one Romanov whom Russia in coming years could yet rediscover to its advantage.

PART 1
Before The Storm

1. LOVE AND DUTY

FOR Grand Duke Michael Aleksandrovich, younger brother of Tsar Nicholas II, the only place he would ever think of as his real home was the little garrison town of Gatchina, 29 miles north-west of St Petersburg. Although born in the Anichkov Palace on the Nevsky Prospekt in St Petersburg on November 22, 1878, it was the immense, 600-roomed palace at Gatchina where he had been brought up, and he would ever think of that and its parks and adjoining town as the place where he belonged and to which he would always want to return. He was just three years old when his father, Alexander III, retreated there with his Danish-born wife Marie and their five children after the assassination of his 63-year-old grandfather Alexander II, ambushed by terrorists on his way back to the Winter Palace on Sunday March 1, 1881.

The bomb, thrown at his feet as he climbed down from his carriage to inspect the wounded from another bomb thrown a few minutes earlier, almost ripped him apart — his right leg torn away, his left leg shattered, his stomach, chest and face mutilated. He remained conscious only long enough to moan, 'back to the palace…to die there.'[1] There was nothing anyone could do for him after they carried his mangled body into his first-floor study at the palace; forty-five minutes later his eldest son, standing grimly at the window, was the new Tsar.

Alexander II, dubbed the 'Tsar-Liberator' because he had freed the peasants from serfdom, had that very morning signed a new constitutional order which would have introduced a measure of representative government into Russia; his murder ensured that the order died with him. His massively-built son was not the kind of man to offer concessions to the terrorists who threatened to kill him as they had killed his father. However, Russia could not afford to lose two Tsars in a row and Alexander III, furious that 'I must retreat now before those skunks',[2] took himself and his family off to the security of Gatchina. It was the only retreat he would make. Once there, he stamped down hard on the anarchists, terrorists and revolutionaries who thought they could overthrow the Romanovs.*

Thirty-six when he became Tsar, Alexander III did not claim to know what was best for liberal Britain, republican France, or the new thrusting German empire fashioned by Bismarck, but he thought he knew what was best for Russia: not muddle-headed constitutional government but the stern hand of a loving father. Under this Alexander, the country would begin to catch up with the industrialised West, the huge bureaucratic machine would begin to tick over more smoothly, and Russian prosperity would increase as never before.

Favouring peasant dress of blouse and boots, and wearing patched shirts,[3] Alexander had barked the orders in Gatchina which had transmitted his rule from the Baltic to the Pacific, and in so doing he had made Russia respected in every chancellery in Europe and beyond. An intimidating figure, standing six feet four inches tall, his physical strength was as awesome as it was legendary.

When, in the middle of a Balkan crisis, the Austrian ambassador was rash enough to hint at a state dinner that his country might mobilise two or three army corps, the Tsar's reaction was to pick up a silver fork, bend it into a knot, and toss it contemptuously in the direction of a now discomfited ambassador. 'That', said Alexander, 'is what I am going to do to your two or three army corps.'[4] However, after only thirteen years as Tsar, and at the age of only forty-nine, Alexander fell ill, and although his doctors

---

*Among them would be a young student, Aleksandr Ulyanov, hanged in 1888 for attempted assassination. His brother, Vladimir, would become better known as Lenin.

believed that all he needed was a long rest and reviving sunshine, his condition rapidly deteriorated. He was suffering from a kidney complaint which, long undiagnosed, had developed into nephritis. On October 20, 1894, he died at his holiday home at Livadia, in the Crimea, and at the age of twenty-six his son Nicholas became Emperor in his place.

At the moment he found himself Tsar, Nicholas had cried out: 'What am I going to do...I am not prepared to be a Tsar. I never wanted to become one. I know nothing of the business of ruling...' [5]

But help was at hand. One of those present in the death-chamber at Livadia was his 22-year-old fiancée of six months, Princess Alix of Hesse-Darmstadt. Unable to speak a word of Russian, she had watched the bustle of the past days in silence. However, she became increasingly dismayed that her husband-to-be seemed to be ignored entirely by the crush around the dying Tsar's bed. So she went to his study, opened his diary, and penned a note to him in English which would be the first of many such notes to come. *'Be firm and make the doctors come to you every day and tell you how they find him...so that you are always the first to know. Don't let others be put first and you left out...Show your own mind and don't let others forget who you are.'* [6]

It was the message she would still be sending him twenty-three years later as their world collapsed around them.

MICHAEL was not quite sixteen when his father died and it marked the end of his childhood as it marked the end of an era for Russia. Three months earlier his elder sister Xenia had married a second cousin, Grand Duke Alexander Mikhailovich — known in the family as 'Sandro' — and one week after his father's funeral in November 1894 his brother Nicholas married Princess Alix, now to be styled the Empress Alexandra Fedorovna. His other brother George, two years his senior and suffering from tuberculosis, was living in the high air of the Caucasus in the hope that it would save his life. His distracted mother, now the Dowager Empress, and trying to come to terms with the loss of her husband, moved back to the Anichkov Palace, taking with her Michael and his younger sister Olga, aged twelve. The new emperor Nicholas would make his family home in the Alexander Palace at Tsarskoe Selo, fifteen miles north of the capital, and reign from there not the Winter Palace, which after the assassination of Alexander II was used only for ceremonial and official purposes. With that, Gatchina palace become a place visited only occasionally until seven years later when Michael found himself back there as a soldier, and able to make it his home again.

For a young Grand Duke there were few choices when it came to a career, so Michael at eighteen followed the traditional path into the military. In the army he found himself for the first time among young men of his own age, free to make friendships of his own choosing, and to follow his own pursuits — and certainly, in sporting terms, more than able to compete with his fellow officers. Standing well over six feet tall — his brother Nicholas was barely five foot seven — he swiftly became a crack shot, a skilled swordsman, and so excellent a rider he won prizes steeplechasing.

After a spell at artillery school he first joined the Horse Guards Artillery, serving with them until June 1902 when, aged twenty-three, he was transferred to the élite Guards cavalry regiment, the Blue Cuirassiers, garrisoned in Gatchina, and of which his mother was colonel-in-chief.[7] Michael, who took his soldiering seriously, was appointed a squadron commander. With that he moved back into his old apartment.

Gatchina palace, designed by the celebrated Italian architect Antonio Rinaldi, was deliberately unlike any of the other Romanov palaces in and around St Petersburg. Commissioned by Grigory Orlov, Catherine the Great's lover, who had been given Gatchina as reward for helping her to depose and then dispose of her husband Peter III — strangled in 1762 to clear the way for her seizing his throne — it was built in mellowed limestone in what the Russians regarded as the 'English style'. This meant it was on austere, simple lines, with walls left in natural stone colour rather than painted yellow, blue, or Venetian red as was the case with the other more classically-styled Romanov palaces. Surrounded by a drawbridged moat, it was said by its detractors to look more like a barracks than a royal palace, though that was one good reason for Alexander III going there. No terrorist would ever breach its security, though that may have been because no terrorist ever thought there was any chance of doing so.

Alexander III had housed his family not in the palace itself but in the adjoining quadrangle, known as the Arsenal, a place originally intended for staff, not their masters. Michael's three-roomed apartment there was off the vaulted, low-ceilinged corridor on the mezzanine floor of the three-storey building. He had a bedroom with a single brass bed, a sitting room furnished with button-backed sofa and armchairs, a study with a desk and mahogany desk-chair, and a bathroom with a tin bath, albeit linked to hot-and-cold running water, and shelves filled with his shaving tackle and pomades.

The rooms were cluttered, as all rooms were in the style of the day, with the walls covered in family photographs and military prints. In the display cabinet in his sitting room there were sets of painted lead soldiers as well as his collection of crystal ornaments, and throughout the suite, on side tables and chairs, there could be found the *bric-a-brac* to be expected in any apartment occupied by a well-off but not overly fussy young bachelor.

What his apartment noticeably did not have was a kitchen. When he wanted something, day or night, he ordered whatever it was from the main palace, still swarming with uniformed servants, many of them in the dress of the eighteenth-century. For even though the palace no longer had a place in the official business of empire, it continued to function as before, with sailors manning boats on the lake, soldiers on guard at the doors, and important functionaries issuing orders to gardeners, footmen, cooks, maids and liveried menservants. Sometimes his mother would return for a week or so and then the palace would bustle around the business of luncheon and dinner parties and in opening shutters on rooms closed for most of the year. But otherwise the vast palace primarily served the needs of those who worked there, the kitchens cooking meals for the staff, not for its imperial master, the maids cleaning rooms which from day-to-day only they would walk through.

Thus, modest though his own private apartments were, Michael needed no more. He could entertain whenever he wished in the main palace, or under the magnificent painted ceilings of the eighteenth-century Pavilion of Venus in the great park outside.

His fellow officers were free to boat on its lakes, stroll in its gardens, take girls for winter sleigh rides, shoot in its woods, and on occasion dance in its ballroom. So although only Michael could call it home, the palace was full of life throughout the year, and a vibrant part of the social world both within the Blue Cuirassiers and the town itself.

Gatchina, founded in 1796, was a graceful place to live. There were houses painted primrose-yellow, standing in large country-style gardens, elegant apartment blocks, imposing public buildings, and two great churches, the Cathedral of St Paul and the Church of the Intercession of Our Lady, which lay at the head of the main boulevard. Although its usual population was only 18,000, in the summer that greatly expanded as the trains from St Petersburg, just an hour away, pulled into the town's two railway stations and disgorged families, servants, dogs and the mounds of luggage which marked the annual exodus from the capital to the summer *dachas* in and around Gatchina. There were evening concerts in the palace park, sailing on the two great lakes around the town, and leisurely dinners in the crowded restaurants on the tree-lined boulevards. And always and everywhere the delicious murmur of scandals, real or imagined.

Michael, as the town's own Grand Duke, was rarely the subject of critical gossip and woe betide anyone from the capital who thought of doing so in earshot of any resident of Gatchina. He was popular, greatly admired, and the Grand Duke whom the town was proud to think of as its own. He was never accompanied by guards or officials or courtiers and he never exhibited any signs of rank. Walking openly through the streets he would stop and cheerfully chat to the locals, patting their children, and often quietly helping those in need — though sometimes he was known to be too trusting for his own good, giving aid where none was deserved.

This approval of Grand Duke Michael Aleksandrovich was echoed well beyond the narrow world of Gatchina itself. His brother-in-law Sandro wrote of him that 'he fascinated everybody by the wholehearted simplicity of his manner. A favourite with his family, with his fellow officers, and with all his countless friends, he possessed a well-organised mind and would have succeeded in any branch of the service.'[8]

His cousin and close friend, Prince Nicholas of Greece, observed that 'he was a very keen soldier and a real sportsman; his jovial nature endeared him to all. He was a fine, athletic young man, and went in for physical training, which he practised like a professional gymnast'.[9]

Yet there was much more to him than that. He spoke French and English fluently and was a competent musician on piano, flute, balalaika and guitar, composing several of his own pieces. He enjoyed the theatre, ballet and opera, and was widely-read. In one letter he listed the books he was then reading; they included *A History of the French Revolution*, a biography of Robespierre, Dostoevsky's *Crime and Punishment,* as well as a couple of other literary novels.

Polovtsov, a member of the state Council, and head of the Imperial Russian Historical Society, which had published several of Michael's academic papers on the Napoleonic War,[10] judged that Michael 'has an extraordinary strong will and once he has taken an aim in his sights he will achieve it without haste, and with undeviating firmness.'[11]

Sergei Witte, who had been Alexander III's chief advisor and who twelve years later became Russia's first prime minister after the convulsions of the 1905 Revolution forced Nicholas to agree to the formation of an elected Duma, or parliament, was another who spoke highly of Michael. He had taught him political science and economics,[12] and he had long made little secret of his view that Michael was to be preferred to Nicholas. One senior courtier observed that Witte 'never tired of praising his straightforwardness.'[13] Grand Duke Konstantin Konstantinovich wrote that 'Witte sees in him a clear mind, an unshakeable conviction in his opinions, and a crystalline moral purity.'[14]

Dr E. J. Dillon, the widely-respected correspondent of the London *Daily Telegraph*, quoted Witte as saying that 'if Alexander III had lived, or if his son Michael had succeeded him or were yet to come to the throne, much might be changed for the better, and Russia's international position strengthened.'[15]

Comments such as this were taken seriously at the time, for in 1899 Michael's elder brother George had been found dying beside his overturned motorcycle near his home in the Caucasus, and with that Michael, still only twenty, had become heir to the throne, for although Nicholas had daughters he had as yet no son to succeed him.

In eighteenth-century Russia there had been empresses reigning in their own right — the widow of Peter the Great, his daughter Elizabeth, and Catherine the Great — but after Paul I succeeded his mother, whom he hated, he ruled that henceforth no woman was eligible to take the crown; that law had been accepted as binding ever since.

Six weeks before Michael found himself heir, Alexandra had been delivered of her third child, Marie, and after that it was noticed that Nicholas 'set off on a long solitary walk', although when he came back he seemed as 'outwardly unruffled as ever.'[16] Obsessed with her need to produce a male heir, Alexandra quickly became pregnant again in the autumn of 1900, though it seemed that it might be too late, for Nicholas had fallen gravely ill on holiday in the Crimea and there were fears that he might die. He had intestinal typhus, a disease which in those days often proved fatal. In that event, Michael would automatically succeed his brother as Emperor.

Alexandra refused to accept that, insisting to gathering ministers that even if Nicholas died, the posthumously-born child, if a boy, should be declared Tsar and that in the meantime she should rule Russia as Regent on behalf of her womb. The ailing Nicholas 'sided with his wife'. Court minister Baron Fredericks reported that Nicholas thought Michael 'will get everything into a mess — he is so easily imposed upon.'[17] Witte strongly disagreed. At an impromptu conference of ministers in a Yalta hotel he 'succeeded in winning over to my side all the members of the improvised conference. It was decided that in the event of the Emperor's death we should immediately take an oath of allegiance to Michael Aleksandrovich.'[18]

Witte, dismissed as prime minister in 1906, dated his becoming 'the object of Alexandra's particular enmity' from his stand at Yalta, which she interpreted as 'an underhand intrigue on my part against her.'[19] As it happened, it was all for nothing anyway: the Tsar recovered and when Alexandra did give birth to her fourth child, it was another girl, Anastasia. It would not be for another four years — in August 1904 — that Alexandra finally and triumphantly produced the long-awaited son and heir, named Alexis. Tragically, he would be found to be suffering from the 'bleeding disease' haemophilia, with any bump or bruise a threat to his life.

Six months earlier, in Germany, her sister Irene, married to the Kaiser's brother Prince Henry, had lost her own haemophilic son to the 'terrible illness of the English family'; years earlier, Alexandra's own little brother had also died after he fell and bumped his head in Darmstadt. The threat was clear and terrible: Alexis's chances of surviving childhood, or even living long into manhood, were not great.

However, that Alexis was so inflicted was not immediately apparent and in the manifesto produced on his birth Nicholas declared that in the event of his own death before Alexis was old enough to reign in his own right — 1920 — Michael was appointed Regent. Characteristically, Alexandra succeeded in adding her name as co-Regent, meaning that she and Michael would rule in tandem. With that, Michael had especial reason to pray for his brother's well-being.

GIVEN that the life of the infant Tsarevich was at constant risk, there were very good reasons why Michael's mother the Dowager Empress should be anxious that he married the right woman. The immediate imperial family relied upon him to be able to step in, should anything terrible happen, as it could do in those dangerous times. He was the insurance policy for the throne of his father.

There were plenty of other Grand Dukes in the line of succession, to be sure, as descendants of Alexander II or his predecessor Nicholas I, but the Dowager Empress was chiefly interested in keeping the crown in the hands of her late husband's direct descendants, not passing elsewhere. In her mind, Michael properly married was the best hope of ensuring that future. Moreover, when she looked at the other Romanovs, there were none with the qualities she saw in her son Michael.

The family which ranked immediately behind him was headed by her brother-in-law Vladimir, who for his own reasons had always thought that he would have proved a better Tsar than his elder brother Alexander, though no one else outside his own circle shared his conviction. He had been briefly banished by Alexander after a disgraceful scene in a St Petersburg restaurant, in which he drunkenly tried to throttle a French actor whom he thought had made a pass at his wife[20], but in 1908, aged sixty-one, he was the senior Grand Duke after Michael, and stood third-in-line to the throne.

His wife Maria Pavlovna was a German princess from Mecklenberg-Schwerin who had steadfastly refused to convert to Russian Orthodoxy, notwithstanding the imperial law which made that a condition of marriage to a Romanov. Since they had married in Lutheran Germany, there was nothing the Russian church could do about that, but purists questioned whether in consequence he remained eligible for the throne — and indeed, whether therefore any of his three sons were in turn fit to succeed. A towering figure as huge as his brother Alexander, Vladimir's answer to that was to smash his fist down and damn the rules. The Romanovs made the law, not the Church, and the priests could go hang.

It was an understandable stance, for *fourth in line* was his eldest son Kirill, who had broken church law by marrying his first cousin 'Ducky'. Although it was common enough for royals to marry first cousins in Europe — Queen Victoria married her first cousin — the Russian Orthodox Church prohibited marriages of that kind. Since he had defied the law, Kirill had been banished for that in 1905, though for Empress Alexandra at Tsarskoe Selo his greater crime was that Ducky had divorced Alexandra's brother Ernst, Grand Duke of Hesse-Darmstadt, swopping one first cousin for another. That was family rift not church law, though Ducky excused herself by saying that Ernst was a homosexual: 'no boy was safe, from the stable hands to the kitchen help. He slept quite openly with them all', she would tell a niece.[21] Ducky and Alexandra hated each other ever after.

Fifth in line was Kirill's brother Boris, a year younger than Michael; like Michael he was still unmarried, but unlike Michael he had led a notorious life, frequenting prostitutes as well as being involved in a number of scandalous affairs, including one with Ducky's sister Marie, the future Queen of Romania. It was an open secret that the father of her daughter was not her husband but Boris — though for the sake of the Romanian crown, that was hushed up and her cuckolded husband acknowledged the baby girl Marie as his.[22] It was just as well, since she ultimately became the Queen of Yugoslavia.

Boris was also involved in another scandal when he bedded a young woman in St Petersburg on the eve of her wedding. Sadly for the bride-to-be the bridegroom found out and the wedding was cancelled.[23] Of all the Grand Dukes, Boris could be said to be the one more likely to be shot by a husband than by a terrorist.

Sixth in line was Andrew, Kirill's youngest brother, who was living contentedly with the prima ballerina Mathilde Kschessinska, seven years his senior. They had an illegitimate son, Vovo — though Vovo himself was never sure whether his father was Andrew, who acknowledged him, or her previous lover Grand Duke Serge Mikhailovich.[24] However, what was recognised was that Andrew would never give up Kschessinska, and never marry anyone else.

Seventh in line at the beginning of 1908 was Vladimir's younger brother Alexis. Officially a bachelor, it was widely known that Alexis had secretly married a commoner but whom he subsequently abandoned for a French actress. Sometime in charge of the navy, he was widely blamed for the disasters of the 1904 war with Japan —'fast women, slow ships', was the popular comment on him. Such was public scorn that his actress mistress had been booed off stage when she appeared in St Petersburg, and had fled back to Paris; Alexis followed her. In November 1908, aged fifty-eight, he would die there in her arms.[25]

Eighth in line was Vladimir's youngest brother Paul, who after the death of his first wife, Princess Alexandra of Greece, had also fled to Paris where he married a divorcée commoner, Olga Pistolkors.[26] Olga's mistake, when his mistress, had been to wear jewels given to Paul's mother the Empress Marie at a palace ball; the Dowager Empress recognised them, and ordered her out. A crimson-faced Olga crept away and next day left the country. Paul followed her, leaving behind his two young children Dimitri and Marie by his first wife — a niece of the Dowager Empress. With Paul banished because of his marriage, the two children would be brought up at Tsarskoe Selo by Nicholas and Alexandra.

Ninth in line was Paul's only son Dimitri, and the one bright spot in the line, since he was still at seventeen too young to have blotted his own book — mercifully, no one could then foresee that one day he would be also banished abroad, in his case for murder.

Tenth in line was Nicholas Konstantinovich, a nephew of Alexander II, who had been banished after a scandalous affair with an American actress, Fanny Lear, daughter of an Ohio preacher. Then still too young to have access to his own funds, he had been caught stealing imperial jewellery to fund the affair, and banished to Tashkent. There he had married a policeman's daughter. Calling himself 'Nicholas Romanov' and declaring that he was a republican, he was an unlikely successor.[27]

In short, there were scant grounds for reassurance when the Dowager Empress looked at those who, other than Michael, might follow him. However, whatever the misdeed, no Tsar had the power to remove any Romanov from the line of succession. What she saw was what they had.

Five years earlier, after his Uncle Paul had vanished abroad with three million roubles and his divorcée mistress, Nicholas had sent a letter to his mother which seemed depressingly prophetic: *How painful and distressing it all is and how ashamed one feels for the sake of our family before the world...in the end, I fear, a whole colony of members of the Russian Imperial Family will be established in Paris with their semi-legitimate and illegitimate wives! God alone knows what times we are living in, when undisguised selfishness stifles all feelings of conscience, duty or even ordinary decency'.*[28]

His younger sister Olga would later agree that he was absolutely right about 'the appalling marital mess in which the last generation of my family involved themselves. That chain of domestic scandals could not but shock the nation but did any of them care for the impression they created? Never.'[29]

When she pronounced that hypocritical verdict on her family, she was clearly not thinking of herself and her lover Captain Kulikovsky, later her husband after she divorced her first husband, Duke Peter of Oldenburg. But certainly, she had a point. The Romanovs had an awful lot of skeletons in their cupboard

Michael was about to add another.

THE girl whom both his mother and her sister in London, Queen Alexandra, wife of King Edward VII, hoped he would marry was Her Royal Highness Princess Patricia of Connaught. Indeed that seemed to be what was to happen in September 1906 when the British Sunday newspapers announced their engagement. The London *Observer* was flattering about Michael. 'Like his bride he is exceedingly fond of horses, and has taken part in a good many officers' races. He is also adept at boxing, wrestling, riding, dancing, and swimming. He has always enjoyed the reputation of being a stronger character than the Emperor.'[30]

Like his bride? Within hours of the newspapers landing on British breakfast tables, a flustered Buckingham Palace was issuing denials, prodded by an indignant Connaught family which knew that the reports of a betrothal were wholly baseless.

The source of this non-betrothal lay in Denmark, where the Dowager Empress and her sister Queen Alexandra had as usual holidayed together that summer in the house they jointly owned at Hvidore. Eavesdropping courtiers, listening to their eager talk about Michael's marital prospects, had somehow translated hope into fact, telling the Reuters agency in St Petersburg that what the sisters intended had already happened. Wisely, the Dowager Empress and Queen Alexandra kept silent, pretending to be as baffled as everyone else.

Two years later, in October 1908, they tried again, sending Michael to London, where the Queen 'paired' him off with Princess Patricia for a weekend at the British royal family's country home at Sandringham, 100 miles from London.[31] Michael was polite, but disinterested. The only woman he was then interested in — or ever would be again — lived in Gatchina, and was married to a fellow officer in his regiment. Her name was Madame Nathalie Wulfert. Five years later it would be why he would find himself an exile in England.

2. SCANDALOUS EXILE

MADAME Nathalie Wulfert — known as Natasha — was five foot six inches tall, slender, fair-haired and possessed of deep-set velvety blue eyes which once seen would be rarely forgotten. In December 1907, when Michael first set eyes on her, she was twenty-seven, elegant, poised, and very beautiful, with a way of holding herself, a look about her which turned eyes wherever she went. Her taste was impeccable, she had immense charm, she was unquestionably clever and at the dinner table she could converse easily and knowledgeably about books, theatre, ballet and opera. Her friends included the young composer Sergei Rachmaninov and the famed basso Fedor Chaliapin, and she could claim acquaintance with some of the best-known sculptors and painters in Russia. That was more than could be said of the conventional Guards wife in small-town yet snobbish Gatchina, where salon conversation rarely rose above the trite. However, these same salons had something to talk about when Natasha arrived — a divorcée with a four-year old daughter from her first marriage to a Moscow pianist, Sergei Mamontov, who worked at the Bolshoi opera.

Although divorce had become more common in recent years, it still came with a considerable stigma in conservative circles, and that included the narrow world of Gatchina. The Dowager Empress, like her London sister Queen Alexandra, frowned on divorce and would not entertain anyone who had parted in that way. Since the Blue Cuirassiers was her regiment, divorcées could expect a cold reception from the wives of senior officers.

As Natasha would swiftly find out, she was not welcome in the higher salons, and as the wife of a mere lieutenant it was doubtful if she ever would be.

Natasha had been born in a rented summer *dacha* in Petrova, on the outskirts of Moscow, on June 27, 1880, some eighteen months after Michael. Over the next twenty years her father, Sergei Aleksandrovich Sheremetevsky, had built up a successful law practice, employing eleven lawyers in all, and for a time was a deputy in the Moscow City Duma.[1] Well-known in Moscow, he lived comfortably in a spacious apartment, No 52, at 6 Vozdvizhenkan, close to the Kremlin.[2] Of his three daughters, Olga married a promising lawyer Aleksei Matveev — destined to play an important role in Michael's life — Vera a successful businessman, and Natasha, the pianist Mamontov who hoped one day to be a conductor, which in time he would be.

Unfortunately, one score he could never conduct harmoniously was his marriage. Inevitably other admirers stepped into his place, and after five years Natasha was divorced and had become wife of Lieutenant Vladimir Wulfert, with an apartment home at 7 Baggout Street, close by Gatchina's Warsaw railway station. She and her daughter Tata had been there only a few months when Michael first set eyes on her in early December, 1907, in the regimental riding school;[3] having introduced himself, he would never look at another woman ever again. In his case, it was love at first sight.

Michael was very correct, and although local society gossiped inevitably about the way he danced attendance on Natasha, her husband made no complaint, seemingly flattered that he had found himself in a Grand Duke's inner circle, dining in the palace, a welcome guest at every function at which Michael played host, and in his own mind with prospects of unexpected advancement in a regiment where otherwise he might spend years trying to get on the next rung of the ladder. However, as months passed, the public face of the marriage concealed its failure behind the closed doors of Baggout Street. Wulfert was a violent man, prone to rages, and an indifferent step-father to Natasha's daughter Tata. By June, 1909, the marriage collapsed, and Natasha walked out never to return. After that the new man in her life became the adoring Grand Duke Michael. The scandal struck when Wulfert, blaming Michael for the break-up, challenged him to a duel.[4] When news of that reached Tsarskoe Selo in July 1909 a furious Nicholas immediately despatched Michael to command a provincial cavalry regiment, the Chernigov Hussars, in faraway Orel, 240 miles south of Moscow. Wulfert was also removed from the regiment, and given a staff job in the Kremlin.

However, Michael was not giving up on Natasha. By November 1909 he had installed her in a house in Moscow, which he treated as his weekend home, swearing never to 'leave or abandon' her. Within weeks she discovered she was pregnant and on July 24, 1910 she gave birth to an illegitimate son to be named George, after Michael's elder brother who had died so young in the Caucasus. Although subsequently Natasha was granted a divorce from Wulfert — but only after Michael paid him 200,000 roubles to go away[5]* — her prospects remained that of being Michael's mistress and never his wife. There could be no Marriage No 3; she accepted that as did Michael. He regarded her as 'his true wife', but both knew that could never be written on a marriage certificate in Russia. All they could hope for was that they should be allowed to live quietly, and privately, away from the public gaze.

That seemed to be the resigned response of Nicholas, and even Empress Alexandra, after the birth of baby George. Natasha was banned from joining Michael in Orel, but she was allowed to stay at his nearby country estate, Brasovo. Michael was also allowed to take her abroad on holiday, provided that they travelled *incognito*. However, in 1911, two years after Michael's banishment to Orel, Nicholas decided that it was time for him to return to public duties in the capital, as colonel and commandant of the Chevalier

*The equivalent of almost £2m and more than $3m in today's monies. Wulfert's marriage to Natasha had lasted only two years.

Gardes, the premier cavalry regiment in Russia. Michael pleaded that he would prefer to go on serving quietly in Orel, with his family close by, than be back in the limelight of St. Petersburg, but Nicholas would not hear of it. In consequence, and dreading it, in January 1912, Michael and Natasha found themselves back in the capital, but apart.

MICHAEL had been told by Tsarskoe Selo that if he brought Natasha to the capital he would not be allowed to see her publicly, set up home with her, or move back into the Anichkov Palace on the Nevsky Prospekt, his mother's home and the place where he had been born; instead, he would have to live in modest quarters at the regimental headquarters. Given that choice, he took the quarters.[6]

For Natasha and the two children he rented a huge 28-roomed apartment at 16 Liteiny, in the fashionable heart of the capital. Natasha protested, saying that it was far too big — 'I don't even have the furniture', she told him. 'To live on my own in an empty house is very depressing'.[7] Nevertheless she moved in, and tackled the business of turning the echoing apartment into a comfortable home, though it was one few would ever visit.

Michael's determination to be seen openly supporting her did not, however, greatly help matters, 'for the whole of society turned its back on her as it had done before. To please the Court no one wanted either to recognise her or to receive her at their home.'[8] St. Petersburg was always going to be a disaster for Michael and Natasha, which is why neither had wanted to be there. Moscow had been a different story, since that was Natasha's home and she had family and a wide circle of supportive friends there; but she had never lived in St. Petersburg, and other than the few who stood by her, or rather stood by Michael, she knew almost no one.

Unfortunately, everyone knew her. Eyes stared through her when she walked in the street, and even in the Chevalier Gardes, Michael's own regiment, the officers shunned Natasha; none would ever dine in her apartment, and none 'would bow to her' if they encountered her in public.[9]

In the hope of making her life more tolerable, Michael decided to move her back to Gatchina, the town where they had met, and which he preferred anyway. He bought her a villa at 24 Nikolaevskaya Street, 'a charming, simple, pleasant two-storeyed wood house, sunk in a verdant garden',[10] but it was also an illusion of tranquillity. So long as the capital delighted in its slights and backbiting, there could be no hiding place in Gatchina, which took its lead from the capital and whose salons simply repeated what was being said there.

Moreover, the Blue Cuirassiers, which dominated local society, had neither forgotten nor forgiven that she had been the price of their losing Grand Duke Michael and the favour of their colonel-in-chief the Dowager Empress. The rule in the regiment — and obeyed by officers' wives no less — was that no one who encountered Natasha in the street or elsewhere should acknowledge her, or even utter her name, and one young lieutenant who broke that commandment, was drummed out of the regiment. The charge against him, a meeting of senior officers was told, was that he had appeared in a theatre box 'among a small company which included a certain lady who is well known to you'.[11]

The Blue Cuirassiers also took their war against Natasha into the capital. Remembering the fate of that young cashiered lieutenant, a drunken Cuirassier went up to Natasha during the interval in another theatre, and loudly berated her for having 'compromised' the Grand Duke.[12] It was the worst kind of public scene, and Natasha, cheeks red, was left fighting back her tears.

She could not go on like that, and neither, when he found out about it, could Michael. Absent on manoeuvres he wrote to her immediately, telling her that he had reached the end of the road. He had given his word not to marry Natasha, but the *quid pro quo* was that she should be treated with respect, as the woman he loved, and as the mother of his son. In his mind therefore the contract had been broken. He would marry her, because he had been given no other choice.

ONE concession which had not been taken away from Michael was his right to go abroad with Natasha *incognito*. Nicholas had agreed to that in 1910, while insisting that Michael and Natasha did not appear together in public in Russia — for example, at a theatre. However, without telling his brother, Nicholas had ordered the secret police, the *Okhrana*, to trail them wherever they went, and to make sure that Michael did not sneak off and marry 'that woman'. Alexandra was sure he would if he could; the *Okhrana's* job was to make certain that even if he would, he couldn't.

The *Okhrana* chief, Major-General Aleksandr Gerasimov, had been given a Top Secret order on the authority of Nicholas himself, charging him with the task 'of taking all reasonable measures to prevent the marriage of Madame Brasova (Wulfert) to Grand Duke Michael abroad; all Russian embassies, missions and consulates shall render Major-General Gerasimov every reasonable assistance that he might need to accomplish the task and, should necessity arise, to put under arrest any persons at the discretion of Major-General Gerasimov'.[13]

A year earlier, when they had gone to Paris and Cannes, the *Okhrana* had followed them and watched them day and night. There had been nothing to arouse their suspicions, but their trail had been ludicrously obvious, their car blundering hopelessly in the wake of Michael's grey open Opel tourer. The *Okhrana* therefore decided to change tactics: in future their agents were instructed to follow the baggage and Michael's staff and servants as they journeyed from place to place by train, whether or not Michael was with them or travelling separately by car. Their purpose was to prevent a marriage, not watch them having a picnic.[14]

This year they were going first to Berlin. They set off on September 12, 1912, leaving two-year-old George and nine-year-old Tata to be looked after by their staff in Gatchina. In itself, that seemed evidence that they would be back, since they were hardly likely to run away without their children, and knowing the consequences of any marriage abroad.

Although the order authorised the 'arrest of any persons' the *Okhrana* thought complicit in any marriage attempt, in practical terms that was hardly feasible abroad where Russian law did not apply. However, what the *Okhrana* could do was to warn the priests in any Russian church — whether Berlin, Paris or Nice — that they faced serious punishment if they agreed to any marriage, and to intimidate the two formal witnesses required to make a marriage valid by threatening their interests in Russia. The *Okhrana* would have plenty of notice of any such attempted marriage since the banns would have to be called in the preceding three weeks.

Michael had no chance, it seemed. The *Okhrana* would always be one step ahead of him. Whatever ideas he might have, he would return to Russia a bachelor.

Senior Agent Bint, the man entrusted with the task of watching Michael, was satisfied that all was well in Berlin, for no banns were called there in the Russian church and in any case on September 23 Michael and Natasha left and took the train to Bad Kissingen, where both signed into to a health sanatorium, Michael 'drinking the waters and taking baths' as he jovially noted on a postcard to his brother.[15] With Michael holed up in the sanatorium it would be three weeks before the bored *Okhrana* needed to stir themselves again.

Bint, a practised hand at bribing telegraph clerks and hotel porters, was quickly tipped off on Sunday October 14 that Michael and his staff were heading for Paris, and then almost immediately that he had cancelled his rail tickets and instead was going to Cannes, though he would be driving there separately via Switzerland and Italy, leaving his staff to take the train with the baggage.

There was no doubt about Michael's intentions, for on that

same Sunday he sent a second postcard to his brother telling him that 'having now completed my treatment, I am setting out in the car towards Cannes, where I expect to be on Saturday'.[16] Since the *Okhrana* read that postcard, having paid their informants to make sure they could, they duly boarded the train, following the baggage, but confident that Michael would turn up when he said he would — on Saturday, in Cannes.

What they did not know, however, was that Michael, wise to their ways, intended that they should read his postcard, as he had intended that they should read his first. Addressing them to 'His Imperial Majesty,' what he meant to do was to address them to the *Okhrana*.

What the *Okhrana* also did not know, and would not find out until some time later, when it was too late, was that on the way to Cannes, Michael's chauffeur-driven Opel tourer had gone only 30 miles, before the chauffeur put the car on a train to Cannes, while Michael and Natasha caught an overnight express to Munich, Salzburg and their intended destination, Vienna. They were going to get married there, but it would not be in a Russian church, but in a backstreet Serbian church.

What the *Okhrana* forgot, but Michael remembered, was that Serbian Orthodox marriages were as valid as Russian ones; while he and Natasha had been in the sanatorium for three weeks, the banns had been duly called in the Serbian church — the first on September 30, the last on October 14 — without anyone tipping off the *Okhrana* that they were his.[17] The man who arranged all this while the *Okhrana* was asleep in Bad Kissingen was undoubtedly the redoubtable Matveev, Natasha's lawyer brother-in-law, though he left no calling-cards. Given the level of secrecy required, he was the only man competent enough and trusted enough to arrange a marriage the *Okhrana* would not think a possibility.

The Church of St. Savva, on the ground floor of a modest three-storey building at Veithgasse 3, was hardly known outside the world of the émigré Serbs living in Vienna. The bearded priest-in-charge, Father Misitsch, was a worldly man greatly impressed by the enormous fee he was being offered for an hour or so on a quiet Tuesday afternoon — 1,000 Austrian crowns*, according to informed gossip afterwards.[18] To make it even better business, the two witnesses were members of his own family, including his wife Vrikosova.[19]

None were vulnerable to any threat from the *Okhrana*; as for the banns, the names mumbled each Sunday morning were stripped of any rank, and meant nothing to the half-attentive Serbs in his congregation. Nobody of importance married at St. Savva; whoever Michael Romanov might be — or *Rom'nov* in the mumbled mouth of Father Misitsch — he was no one of any interest.

Matveev also arranged the necessary residential qualification for Michael and Natasha, even though they were not there. Officially, for the purposes of the marriage register, they would be said to be living at Johannesgasse 23, which thus disguised the fact that it was actually a modest hotel, the *Tegetthof* — a hotel was not sufficient for residential qualification — managed by one of Father Misitsch's Serbian flock, and a man more than agreeable to the good business Matveev had on offer for 'borrowing' his private flat in the hotel.[20] After all, Michael and Natasha were not going to live there, and would not be in the hotel for more than an hour or so, while they freshened up after their journey.

Since Michael was fully briefed on the arrangements, and knew precisely where he was to be and at what time, Matveev was clearly in telegraphic contact with someone other than Michael, given that any cable to him ran an unacceptable risk of being intercepted by a paid *Okhrana* informant.

Michael's valet and chauffeur were both absolutely trustworthy, and his chauffeur certainly knew what was afoot when he took over the car at Wurzburg, and put it on a train. It can be assumed, therefore, that one or both were party to the plan, and key to

*Equivalent to some £3,500 or around $5,000 in today's monies — so it is hardly surprising that the worldly Father Misitisch was so accommodating...

its success, though there is no trace of their complicity —or of anyone else's.

Suffice that at 4 p.m. on Tuesday, October 16, 1912, when Michael and Natasha arrived at the church to be greeted by Father Misitsch and his two witnesses but no one else, it was exactly as they expected it to be.[21] Shortly afterwards they were married and signing the register in their full and proper names. With that done, they left Vienna immediately and caught the train to Venice. The *Okhrana* had been outwitted and made to look like fools.

It was the briefest of honeymoons: next day they were in Vienna, three days later they were in Milan, and then a week after their marriage, on Tuesday, October 22, 1912,[22] they turned up at the lavish *Hotel du Parc,* a little later than they had 'promised' the *Okhrana,* but not so much later that the *Okhrana* were in any way troubled. They had been out of sight for only a week; nothing could have happened in that time.

Within the next week, Matveev — now Michael's brother-in-law —turned up at the hotel with his wife Olga, bringing with them little George and Tata. The Gatchina house had been locked up and secured; the children were safely out of Russia.

Michael and Natasha were free. *Farewell, Gatchina. Farewell Russia.* They would live in England.

AT the Alexander Palace in Tsarskoe Selo, the news of his marriage produced consternation. There was no doubt in Nicholas's mind about where the blame lay —'that woman' as his wife Empress Alexandra sneeringly described Natasha. Nicholas was no less condemning: 'She's such a cunning, wicked beast that it's disgusting even to talk about her', he wrote to his mother after Michael's runaway marriage.[23]

The marriage itself had come as shock enough when Michael confessed it afterwards, but what added to the fury of Nicholas and Alexandra, and their court at Tsarskoe Selo, was that it was sprung upon them shortly before the long-planned celebrations marking the tercentenary of the Romanov dynasty in 1913 — and more to the point, to demonstrate that the Romanovs, who had faced ruin eight years earlier in the 1905 Revolution, were back on top. A scandal involving the brother of the Tsar was hardly a welcome prelude to a year intended to boost the prestige of the imperial family across the nation. That fact in itself dictated what the response would be.

At first there had been hopes that the runaway marriage could be kept a secret, thus avoiding public humiliation, at least until after the tercentenary celebrations, scheduled to end in June. That was the immediate response of Michael's mother, the Dowager Empress Marie, when she received Michael's letter on November 4, 1912, at her holiday home in Denmark.

As she wrote at once to Nicholas: 'I only ask that it should remain a secret, so there shouldn't be another scandal, there have been other marriages in secret, which everyone pretended not to know about. I think it's really the only thing that can be done now, otherwise I won't be able to show myself any more, it's such a shame and disgrace .'[24]

Nicholas, as appalled as his mother, agreed with her — 'My first thought was also to keep the news quiet'— though he doubted that it could remain a secret. 'Sooner or later everyone here will find out.'[25] Nevertheless, the hope persisted that somehow the marriage could be covered up. In a ten-point memorandum drawn up at Tsarskoe Selo by the elderly court minister Baron Fredericks, but with a nagging and vindictive Empress Alexandra at his elbow, the idea was that Michael would be granted eleven months' leave of absence — keeping him out of the way until after Nicholas had basked in the applause of the nation — and then, if he had still not divorced Natasha, he could expect very severe punishment. Meanwhile, to ensure that she could not get her hands on his money, his estates would be put under guardianship. The view of the inner circle was that Michael had acted unconsciously 'under the hypnotic influence of a malicious vamp' who was now to be banned 'from Russia forever …as somebody who has demonstrated criminal disregard for the Head of State and publicly injured the dignity and status of a member of the Imperial House.'[26]

With this hasty and desperate response in place, Michael's former trusted ADC Captain A. A. Mordvinov, a man who had come to hate Natasha as much as she despised him, was swiftly despatched in early November 1912 to Cannes and the *Hotel du Parc* which Michael had made his family base for the past three weeks — still under surveillance by the complacent agents of the Tsar's secret police, the *Okhrana,* as yet wholly unaware that the marriage they were there to prevent had already taken place, and that their mission had failed utterly.

Mordvinov's was no more successful. Michael found him 'difficult to understand for he was nervous' — hardly surprising given his task of delivering the Tsarskoe Selo ultimatum of 'divorce her or else'.

The Tsar had appointed 'the good Mordvinov' as one of his own ADCs and that switch of loyalties was enough to ensure an uneasy audience. Michael, who felt betrayed by him, told him brusquely to go away and not come back. 'We are no longer on good terms', Michael wrote to Nicholas. He then set out his own settlement of the issue: that he and Natasha should return to Russia to live quietly outside the public gaze, that she should be given the title of Countess, and that — despite the threats passed on by messenger Mordvinov — he was to retain full control 'of his personal fortune and property'.[27]

By the time Nicholas read that in his study at Tsarskoe Selo it was already too late to hope that the marriage could be kept secret. As he wrote to his mother on November 21: 'By now everybody knows…In Moscow it is the same; probably the news came from her relations.'[28]

The gossip had also spread far beyond Russia: all Europe was agog, and in England Michael's cousin King George V was as concerned as anyone else, writing to Nicholas that 'I am so fond of him that I am in despair that he should have done this foolish thing & I know how miserable you must be about it. What a lot of worries & anxieties there are in this world.[29]

At Tsarskoe Selo it was now clear that there was no choice left but to impose the severest punishment on Michael and quickly before the start of the official tercentenary celebrations, scheduled to begin with a great choral *Te Deum* in the Cathedral of Our Lady of Kazan on the Nevsky Prospekt on February 21. Michael was to be swept away, as a reminder that no one, however high, could defy the Emperor of All the Russias, and think that they could be excused.

On December 15, 1912, two months after Michael's marriage, the Tsar issued at Tsarskoe Selo an imperial ukase or edict to the Ruling Senate. It read:

Deeming it expedient to establish a guardianship over the person, estate and affairs of the Grand Duke Michael Aleksandrovich, we have considered it advisable to take upon ourselves the chief control of the guardianship and to entrust to the Central Administration of the Imperial Duma the direct control of all estate, personal and real, and also funds possessed by the Grand Duke Michael Aleksandrovich.[30]

Two weeks later, on December 30, he issued an imperial manifesto removing Michael from the Regency.

By our Manifesto given on the first day of August 1904, we, in the event of our decease before the attainment of his majority by our beloved son, his Imperial Highness and Heir, the Tsarevich and Grand Duke Alexis Nikolaevich, appointed our brother the Grand Duke Michael Aleksandrovich, to be Regent of the state until our son should come of age. Now, we have deemed it advisable to divest his Imperial Highness, the Grand Duke Michael Aleksandrovich of the obligations laid upon him by our Manifesto...[31]

Both the ukase and the manifesto were published for the world to see in the Official Messenger No 2 of January 3, 1913. Two days earlier the same official gazette had announced that 'Grand Duke Michael Aleksandrovich, Colonel and Commandant of the Chevalier Gardes Regiment of the Empress Marie Fedorovna...is relieved of his command.'[32]

These series of official statements caused a considerable stir, within the diplomatic world as well as in society at large. Sir George Buchanan, the British ambassador, telegraphed the news at once to the British foreign secretary Sir Edward Grey, adding that 'in the event of no one being specially appointed to act as Regent in place of the Grand Duke Michael the Regency would, as I am informed, devolve by law on the Empress'.[33]

In effect, if Nicholas died, it would be Alexandra who would rule Russia. That was a prospect which even in 1913 was unwelcome; Alexandra and her clique at Tsarskoe Selo were not yet hated as they would be, but there was little liking for her in society or in the political classes. When her mother-in-law had been empress, she had 'considered her chief function was to charm those who came into contact with her; she had every quality needed for doing so and was venerated at court and by the great mass of the people'.[34]

In contrast, Alexandra had no interest in charming anyone: her 'chief function' was in badgering Nicholas to 'be firm' and to show them 'who is master'. That would bring both of them down in the end, but it was not the end in 1913, though she hoped it would be the end of 'that woman' Natasha.

In St Petersburg, even hardened members of society were astonished at the severity of the punishment which, as one observer put it, was 'as unfortunate as it was unwarrantable'.[35] And because Alexandra was judged to be behind this humiliation, sympathy in some quarters swung to Michael rather than to Nicholas. Given the choice between condemning the well-liked Michael and condemning Alexandra, society was more than ready to forgive him if only to have more reason to denigrate her.

At the same time, few could think of anything which would be to the credit of Natasha. Society had cut her dead when she had arrived in the capital eleven months earlier. The runaway marriage seemed its own proof that they had been right to do so. He had been foolish; among those who followed the lead of the the smartest salons, she was unspeakable.

The princess his family hoped would be his wife, and the woman he ran away to marry

Princess Patricia of Connaught (above), the bride-to-be who never was, and Natasha, the double-divorcée he promised never to 'leave nor abandon'

Two failed marriages and a scandal...

Natasha, and above second husband Lieut. Vladimir Wulfert, who stole her from her first husband, and father of her daughter Tata, pianist Sergei Mamontov in Moscow *below*.

TWO weeks after his runaway marriage, Michael had written to his brother to tell him what he had done and concluded by saying that 'I know that punishment awaits me for this act and I am ready to bear it.'[36] He expected to be banished, relieved of his command of the Chevalier Gardes, and to have his assets frozen, perhaps for a year or so until the storm had abated. He was by no means the first Grand Duke to have married in breach of the imperial statutes — uncle Paul and cousin Kirill were just two examples of that — and there was always a price to pay, but no other Grand Duke had found himself subject to the kind of public humiliation inflicted on Michael. High society would always know when a Grand Duke had been banished and the reasons for it, but officially these were matters kept within the imperial family, and not something which the ordinary Russian should know about. Romanov prestige was not to be damaged by its private scandals becoming street gossip.

Yet that was precisely what had happened in Michael's case, and in particular with open publication of the fact that his assets had been placed under guardianship, a step normally reserved for situations where someone was adjudged to be no longer mentally capable of managing their assets themselves. Michael, the order implied, had lost his mind — the fevered view at Tsarskoe Selo in blaming Natasha for it all, but not a view which ought to have been promoted across the whole of Europe.

Understandably, Michael was appalled by that more than by anything else. Indeed, after reading newspaper reports of Nicholas's actions against him he was so incensed that he could not bring himself to write to his brother even in protest.

When he did so a month later, he explained that 'it took me some time to get over the guardianship decision, which you had announced for all the world to know. I will never believe that it was your own idea and it is painful to know that you listened to those people who wished to discredit me in public opinion.' Knowing what was being said, he added: 'It has already done a lot of harm'.[37] The people he had in mind, in particular, were

Alexandra and Mordvinov — and what added to his sense of outrage was that it was Mordvinov who had now been appointed to oversee his guardianship, thereby adding insult to injury.

That order, and Mordvinov's role of servant turned master, continued to enrage him. There would be repeated protests that he did not want 'this man anywhere near me or my affairs'[38] and that he was not competent to exercise powers which he ought never to have been given in the first place. As Michael said in one of his letters to his brother:

The combination of trusteeship over my estate with the guardianship over my person, without doing anything to protect my fortune, has put me in the position of an imbecile or madman and made my situation totally unbearable. As things are, even a short visit to Russia is impossible for me, for I shall be seen as a man who has been subjected to a humiliating punishment.[39]

Michael's assets were very considerable. The inheritance and savings accumulated by his original trustees until he was twenty-five had provided him with a capital of several million roubles; from the imperial purse he also drew, as did all Grand Dukes, an annual allowance of 280,000 gold roubles, a huge sum in those days. In addition he had substantial earnings, rising to a further one million roubles a year, from farms and factories owned by him across Russia, including, in the Ukraine, the country's largest sugar refinery. As one measure of the value of all that, a six-seater Rolls-Royce Silver Ghost he had bought in August 1911 had cost him £1,367 or the equivalent of just over 12,000 roubles — petty cash when set against his overall income.*

But he was worth a great deal more than that. His other assets included a palace on the English Embankment facing the Neva in St Petersburg — though he never chose to live there — a vast country estate, which he ran at a substantial profit, at Brasovo, near Orel, as well as another in Poland, then part of the Russian

---

*As the money table at the front of the book demonstrates, his annual income of 1.28 million roubles would be worth in today's money some £12.8 million or $20 million.

Empire. To this could be added his 'invisible' assets — his homes in both the Gatchina and Anichkov palaces, as well as the elegant imperial yacht *Zarnista*, with a crew of 120 men, ten officers and a priest, and his own blue-and-gold imperial railway carriage, lavishly furnished, which would be hooked onto any express train whenever he wanted to travel by rail — all now lost to him as they would have been anyway by his leaving Russia as he did.

Nonetheless, Michael had no immediate cause for financial worry. In preparation for his runaway marriage, and the certainty of enforced exile thereafter, in the summer of 1912 he had transferred a large amount of cash to the Crédit Lyonnais on the Boulevard des Italiens in Paris — the Russian rouble was then an international currency, freely traded — ostensibly for the purpose of buying a large estate in France,[40] so there was no need to be unduly concerned about cash in the short-term; nor was it in the power of the Tsar to stop payment of the imperial allowance to any Grand Duke — a figure of just over 23,000 roubles a month, the equivalent of £2,500, or almost $12,000 in the values of the day.

At the same time, his costs were considerable. He was paid as a Grand Duke, and not surprisingly he spent as a Grand Duke. He had not booked rooms at the *Hotel du Parc*, he had booked a whole floor to house not only himself and Natasha in a grand suite, but the children, nanny and governess, maids, chauffeurs, and a new secretary, Nikolai Johnson who, despite his surname, was a Russian. Johnson, a shortish, round-faced young man who spoke three languages — though his English was heavily-accented[41] — was a more than competent pianist, his mother who also joined the household having been a court music teacher; Johnson's keyboard talent was one reason why he and Michael got on so well, playing duets together — indeed, it was why he had been hired in the first place. In the end, it would be a post which would cost Johnson his life.

3. A BRIEF PEACE

A YEAR after his runaway marriage, Michael moved Natasha and his extensive retinue to England, preferring to make his home there rather than in Paris, or anywhere else in Europe. After all, he knew the country well and spoke English as well as any Englishman. His first cousin George was its king; his beloved aunt, the Dowager Queen Alexandra — sister of his mother the Dowager Empress Marie — had her own court at Marlborough House, a stroll from Buckingham Palace. Michael had known Queen Victoria and had spent a holiday at her Scottish home, Balmoral. She had thought his father Alexander III 'a boor' — in turn, he had described her as 'a nasty interfering old woman'.[1] But she had liked Michael, writing afterwards that he 'is remarkably nice & pleasing & pleasing looking.'[2] Michael had represented Russia at her funeral in 1901, as he had done at the coronation of her successor, her eldest son King Edward VII, after which 'Uncle Bertie' had made Michael a Knight of the Garter, a member of Britain's most illustrious order, with his own standard to hang in the chapel at Windsor Castle.

Natasha's introduction to England came in July 1913 when she and Michael arrived at the Ritz Hotel on London's Piccadilly. It was not a happy experience, for they had gone there in the hope of some sort of reconciliation with Michael's mother, who was staying with her sister at Marlborough House. The meeting had been arranged by Michael's sister Xenia — 'she so wants to see him!' Her husband Sandro had sent Michael a telegram 'saying that he must come.'[3]

Michael went to the first meeting on his own, leaving a very nervous Natasha to pace up and down their suite at the Ritz, dreading what might happen. His mother had been 'very agitated at the prospect of seeing him' and had been 'completely unable to sleep — she was so excited and upset', Xenia wrote in her diary. At last he arrived and 'they disappeared into the next room for a minute, but returned looking quite calm! Thank God it went all right. I was so anxious for Mama...'[4]

That evening Michael returned to Marlborough House, this time with Natasha, and he and his mother 'had a good quiet talk, thank God, and he was happy to be able to speak.'[5] Then it was Natasha's turn to face the Dowager Empress and the tongue-lashing that inevitably awaited her. There was no hope of 'a good quiet talk' now and all Natasha could do was to keep her head up and allow the anger to wash over her. As Xenia recorded it later, the Dowager Empress 'saw his wife and told her a few home truths in front of Misha...in general it was terribly *penible* (unpleasant) on all sides.'[6]

Afterwards the Dowager Empress wrote to Nicholas to give him her account of her meeting. *I was happy to see that he has remained the same; just as nice and good and even kinder than ever. We talked everything over quite frankly and all was said so nicely and quietly without a bitter word, that for the first time after all these dreadful worries my heart felt relieved and so, I think, did his...*[7]

She made no mention at all of Natasha. The next time they would meet it would again be at Marlborough House, but by then the world would have changed for ever and both would have more to worry about than either could have imagined in that summer of 1913.

What Michael and Natasha did imagine was that they could remake their lives in England and live there happily ever after. Notwithstanding her bruising encounter with the Dowager Empress, Natasha was excited at the prospect of actually having a home not a hotel suite as had been the case for the past year. Looking around, they found a house some 20 miles north of London, near

Stevenage in Hertfordshire. It was a magnificent stately home with an oak banqueting hall, four-poster bedrooms, state drawing room, picture gallery — and a small army of servants, including footmen who at dinner wore knee-breeches and powdered hair.[8] Called Knebworth House, and owned by the Earl of Lytton, it was available for a year from that September 1913 at an annual rent of £3,000 or a tenth of Michael's annual income from the imperial purse. On the lease, Michael was described as 'at present residing at Palace Anichkov in St Petersburg'.[9] The drafting lawyers in Belgravia knew, as did everyone else, that His Imperial Highness the Grand Duke Michael Aleksandrovich, 'hereinafter the tenant of the other part' ought properly to be described as 'of no fixed abode'; however that would have appeared unseemly. A palace sounded better than a hotel room.

He paid the first six-month rental in advance. However, he found it a struggle in March 1914 to pay the next six months. After almost two years his cash was running out. Suddenly, having to find £1,500 from his monthly income of £2,500 was both a problem and a cause for bitter complaint. In his absence his personal estate had generated some two million roubles of profit — and not a penny of that had come his way. Mordvinov was deaf to pleas. He and his department were 'unfair and discourteous' he complained to Nicholas. 'Life in England is very expensive…this month I have had to pay a six-month rent for the estate in which I am living, which is why I have been left without any money.'[10] The only concession was to agree that his monthly income could increase to 30,000 roubles, or £3,300.

Yet in all other respects he was more content than he had been for the past five years. At least in England he and his wife Natasha were left in peace and that had never been the case in their lives together in Russia. Looking ahead, they planned to move that September of 1914 to another but much larger estate, Paddockhurst in Sussex, owned by Lord Cowdray, with a two-year lease at a slightly higher rent of £3,460 a year.[11]

There would be time enough to decide by 1916 what next

to do. After all, who could know what might happen in the interval?

Who indeed.

THE announcement in the Court Circular published in *The Times* a few months earlier, that Grand Duke Michael Aleksandrovich was taking possession of Knebworth House, would normally have been enough for crested invitations to fall thick and fast on their doormat. Society, however, had turned a polite back on Michael and Natasha, taking its lead from Michael's cousin King George V and his aunt the Dowager Queen Alexandra that while Michael remained family, 'that woman' was not welcome in any respectable household.

One other influential and determined enemy in the British camp was Countess Torby, married to a namesake Grand Duke, Michael Mikhailovich, the 52-year-old brother-in-law of Michael's elder sister Xenia, and known in the family as Miche-Miche. On the face of it, Michael might have expected Miche-Miche and his wife to have been the first to come to his support, since they too had been banished from Russia for a very similar offence — a runaway marriage which had caused almost as much uproar as had Michael's.

In 1891, Miche-Miche had secretly married the well-born but not royal Sophie von Merenberg — a grand-daughter of the celebrated Russian poet Aleksandr Pushkin. The news came as such a shock that when Miche-Miche's mother Grand Duchess Olga received his telegram while standing on a station platform she collapsed with a heart attack and died.[12]

Alexander III banished the couple from Russia, and like Michael and Natasha 22 years later, they moved to England. Sophie was re-invented as Countess Torby, and they settled down happily in British society, eventually taking a long lease on Kenwood, a magnificent house overlooking London's Hampstead Heath. The British took a much more relaxed view about 'morganatic marriage' — between a royal and a non-royal — which was why

London was seen as a sanctuary for those who had blotted their copybook in the other courts.* Knowing that in St. Petersburg they would never be accepted as they were in London, Miche-Miche and his wife had no interest in returning to Russia and never would.

At the same time, they closed their own doors on Michael and Natasha. Miche-Miche was pressing George V for a British title[13] and that being so — though she would never get one — the much grander Countess Torby did not want the arrival of Natasha to remind anyone of her own runaway marriage. Natasha was too close for comfort, and therefore was on her black-list. She discouraged her friends from having anything to do with her, making clear that she disapproved — a double divorcée was enough for that.

Yet the British did not ignore her altogether. Since she was accepted in Britain as the lawful wife of Grand Duke Michael Aleksandrovich, her name was included whenever he was mentioned in the Court Circular, published in *The Times* and *Morning Post*; however, on the three occasions when her name was listed, confused Buckingham Palace officials changed the spelling each time.

She was listed as the 'Comtesse de Brassow' when she stayed with Michael at the Ritz Hotel on London's Piccadilly in December 1913, 'Mme de Brasov' when she went to a luncheon two weeks later, and 'Countess' when she came back with Michael from Cannes in May.[14] It did not help that at Knebworth she had personal notepaper designed with her initials NB under a coronet.[15] That in itself did not encourage invitations: no one really knew what to call her.

Michael did not mind about that. He had never cared greatly for fashionable society in St. Petersburg and never would; he took

*King George V's marriage was itself 'morganatic' — his wife Queen Mary was the daughter of the 'half-royal' and penniless Duke of Teck; in Germany or Russia she would never have been considered eligible to marry a royal, and if George had been heir to any other throne than that of Britain he would have had to find someone else as wife.

the same view in London. What mattered to him was that after the long and bitter family battles over Natasha they were at last able to live openly and peacefully together, as man and wife, and with the two children — his baby son George and her ten-year-old daughter Tata.

Nonetheless, they were by no means cold-shouldered everywhere. The luncheon at which in January 1914 the Court Circular recorded Natasha as 'Mme de Brassow' was at the home of Sir Frederick Pollock and the guests included Walter Hines Page, the US ambassador, and his wife, and the Russian actress Princess Baryatinskaya, whose stage name was Lydia Yavorska.[16] She was playing the title role in an English adaptation of Tolstoy's *Anna Karenina*, a love story with some uncomfortable reminders of Natasha's own life; Michael and she had gone to the opening night with the Russian *chargé d'affaires* and the consul-general[17]— both carefully arranging themselves so that they were dutifully beside the Grand Duke, but not next to his wife.

His Russian connections apart, Michael's principal interest that evening was a business one: he had joined with Sir Frederick in a theatrical enterprise, the New International Theatre, which had backed the play. It was a world in which both Michael and Natasha felt very much at home, and Michael took a five per cent stake in the company[18] — with his assets frozen he needed to make some money — though after some 'unlucky' investments it was to prove ultimately a total loss.[19]

There were also small victories which could bring no pleasure to Tsarskoe Selo. Grand Duke Andrew, for example, showed what he thought of it all by turning up at Knebworth House in January as he had done at Cannes after the marriage, and two months later Michael and Natasha went off to St. Moritz to join his cousin and his long-time mistress Kschessinska. Michael and Andrew skied; Natasha and Kschessinska ice-skated.[20]

They made an interesting foursome: two Grand Dukes and two of the best-known women in Europe — both the mothers of illegitimate children, with the dainty but dazzling Kschessinska admired as the celebrated prima ballerina *assoluta*, the younger and beautiful Natasha known as the most notorious woman in high society; each was outrageous and what made them more so was that each was clearly adored by the two proud Grand Dukes hovering around them. Society, pretending to look the other way, could only stare in wonderment.

They were back in England in time to offer 'open house' at Knebworth to the stars of Diaghilev's famed *Ballets Russes,* then taking London by storm. They had already conquered Paris, Berlin, Rome, Vienna and Budapest and had done much the same when they came to London in 1911. Their return in 1914 was eagerly awaited, and Natasha invited the dancers *en bloc* to Knebworth, along with the stars of the Russian opera who also were appearing as part of the 'Russian season' at Drury Lane.

Her old friend Chaliapin, who had visited them in Cannes after their marriage, was among them. Another guest was the celebrated Russian sculptor and stage designer Sudeikin, whose 'thank you' was a bust of Michael, George and Tata.[21]

Natasha was in her element in those days at Knebworth, when the house rang with laughter and music and no one went to bed until the early hours. 'On the morning after the parties, the gardeners were not allowed to start work near the house, so as to leave undisturbed the slumber of the guests, who would eventually arise, yawning, just in time for lunch'.[22]

The 'Russian season' in London that summer also included a good number of St Petersburg royals, including the Dowager Empress. Michael's sister Xenia also came with her husband Sandro to stay at the Piccadilly Hotel, and they were followed by Xenia's daughter Irina and her new young husband Prince Felix Yusupov, who owned an apartment at 15 Parkside, Belgravia. As summer wore on, the Russian imperial contingent increased when Grand Duchess George Mikhailovich, Sandro's sister-in-law arrived at Claridge's with her two daughters, bringing to nine the number of Romanovs in London, in addition to Michael and Miche-Miche.

Michael met them all, including his mother at Marlborough House where, as usual on her many visits to England, she was staying with her widowed sister Alexandra, now the Dowager Queen. Among the other Romanovs there was nothing but sympathy and concern for Michael, and sighs at the venom of Alexandra's court at Tsarskoe Selo.

No, of course he should not have married her, but yes, he had been put in an impossible position. At least that was all over, and he could make a new life for himself. Unfortunately, they would not be able to meet her. They were sure Michael understood that: no point in stirring up a family row. Not in London, and not with the Dowager Empress in town.

Michael could not complain about that, and nor could Natasha. The 'season' was not a place for a divorcée at the best of times — barred from the Royal Enclosure at Ascot races, barred from balls at Buckingham Palace, and effectively barred from any grand table likely to be dined at by a royal. With their days in top hats and designer dresses, their evenings in white-tie and ballgowns, the only outside event that anyone noticed was that on June 29 the London newspapers were reporting the assassination in Sarajevo of the heir to the Austrian throne, Archduke Franz-Ferdinand.

It was a brief sensation before society got back to the serious business of parties and balls, not least the great State Ball at Buckingham Palace, fixed for July 16, when the grandest people, including Miche-Miche and Countess Torby, but predictably not Michael and Natasha, would be present.[23]

This would be followed by racing at Goodwood and by the regatta at Cowes, which Prince Henry of Prussia, brother of the Kaiser and brother-in-law of Empress Alexandra, would be attending in his steam yacht *Carmen*.

German royals were as prominent as the Russian royals in London in the last summer of old Europe. At the State Ball the most distinguished guests included the Tecks, Battenbergs, Saxe-Coburg-Gothas, and Schleswig-Holsteins, all closely related to the British royal family, as were the Russian imperial family. That ball in Buckingham Palace would be the last time old Europe danced the quadrille. Three weeks later, the world exploded.

THE news that Germany had declared war on Russia came to Knebworth on Saturday August 1, 1914 — July 19 in Russia. Michael, determined to return to the army, cabled Nicholas at once asking permission for both he and Natasha to return. Alexandra was opposed to 'that woman' ever setting foot in Russia again, but there were larger problems to worry about now, and just as promptly Nicholas cabled back his agreement. At Knebworth, Michael's private war would now have to be set aside for the greater duty of serving his country. For both Michael and Natasha their brief peace was over.

There was much to do in the next frantic days. With some Moscow friends who had joined them in Knebworth there were twenty people seeking to get back to Russia, including secretaries, governesses, valets and servants. The best route home was across the North Sea to Norway, thence through Sweden and Finland to St. Petersburg. A ship was found, the *S.S. Venus*, which could accommodate the whole party, and it was leaving from Newcastle, 200 miles north on the River Tyne.[26]

The lease on Knebworth was to end in September, when they were due to move to Lord Cowdray's Paddockhurst estate in Sussex. Although he would not now be moving there himself, Michael still needed a property in England to house his possessions from Knebworth— furniture, paintings, books, linen, cars and horses. Besides, no one expected the war — which Britain joined on August 4 — to last very long. A year perhaps, or maybe less? Certainly it would be no longer than their two-year lease, so Paddockhurst would be home when they came back. In the meantime, he would entrust the care of that estate to Mr Bennett, the head groom he had hired at Knebworth. The only Russian who would stay behind was Mme Johnson, mother of Michael's new secretary. Having been terrified by the stormy crossing of the English Channel in her journey to Britain, she could not face the prospect of another and much longer sea journey; she would stay behind and help to manage the house. After all, they would all be back soon.[27]

On Thursday, August 13, Michael went up to Buckingham Palace to say goodbye to his cousin King George. Just over two weeks earlier the king had met another cousin, Prince Henry of Prussia, hurrying home from the yachting regatta at Cowes as the Balkans crisis deepened. It was a gloomy meeting, with the king grimly predicting that if war came it was almost certain that Britain would be 'dragged into it.'[28] Now it was Michael's turn, and a more cheerful handshake, for at least they were on the same side. But as with Henry, the farewell would also prove to be goodbye. King George would never see either cousin again.

With that, Michael and his party prepared to depart Knebworth the following day. All the servants, together with the local villagers, gathered together to wave them farewell as they began the first leg of their journey home. That Friday evening they boarded the *S.S. Venus* and escorted by British destroyers sailed off to Norway. Once there, the party crossed over to Sweden then travelled on to Finland. A week after leaving Knebworth they were back in St. Petersburg — now renamed Petrograd, patriotic sentiment having deemed that Petersburg sounded too German.

Michael's mother the Dowager Empress had also returned to Russia, but after a more eventful journey.

She had left London hurriedly, travelling with daughter Xenia through Germany; by the time the train reached Berlin the war had already started. Hostile crowds broke the windows of her carriage and tore down the blinds, until police intervened. On orders from the Kaiser, her train was allowed to continue on to neutral Denmark, and from there she got back via Sweden and Finland.[29]

Returning home to the Anichkov Palace she was naturally anxious to see Michael, albeit without Natasha, but accepted that this time he would set up home with her. There would be no further demands that they lived separately, or were not to be seen in public together. She would still be Madame Brasova, but she was also his wife, and that was a fact which it was pointless now to deny. There was also a war on. Nonetheless, there could be no question of her ever living in an imperial palace — that would be a step too far. Given that, Michael would never again live in one either.

On arriving back in the capital, Michael and Natasha had booked into the *Hotel de l'Europe*,[30] near the Anichkov Palace but on the other side of the Nevsky Prospekt. That was something they could never have done two years earlier, but the real question now was where should they make their home?

Michael was in doubt about that: it had to be his beloved Gatchina. The Blue Cuirassiers were on their way to the front line; there would be no more insults from them, and local society would have to learn that Natasha was no longer to be reviled as before.

The decision made, he and Natasha waited until her 'hideaway house' at 24 Nikolaevskaya Street, securely locked up when the children had left to join them in Cannes two years earlier, was re-opened and made a home again, though it was so run-down that Natasha was ashamed of it. She would get it right eventually, but as it stood it was the last place anyone would expect to find a Grand Duke. Nonetheless, Michael liked it so much he also bought the property next door, to house guests as well as some of his staff.[31]

With that, he was ready to go to war.

24 Nikolaevskya Street, Gatchina, the tumbledown villa which Michael would make his home after returning to Russia in 1914. The man at the window loved it... He would never live in a palace again

Sitting at their doorstep, Michael, wife Natasha, and pet dog Jack

At Nicholaevskaya Street there were no guards, and when Michael came home on leave he just parked his car in the drive, and walked through the front door, like the rest of his neighbours. No other Grand Duke lived as he did, but it was the home he wanted

PART II
War and Revolution

4. WAR HERO

WHEN Michael came back to Russia he was 36, with some 16 years of soldiering behind him; he had been colonel of two cavalry regiments, the Chernigov Hussars and the elite Chevalier Gardes, and he had proved his leadership. It was remembered, after the 1911 manoeuvres, that 'he had displayed such excellent qualities as a regimental commander that the Chernigov Hussars were unanimously found to be the smartest cavalry regiment reviewed by the Tsar'.[1] That was not evidence of competence on the battlefield, but it went to his credit when, as with other peacetime commanders, there was nothing else to go on. Ten years earlier, in the war against Japan, the Russian army had proved a disaster. There had been much-needed reforms, and new men promoted to command, but it was still an army untested on the battlefield. Confidence was high, but it always was at the start of a war.

Although his brother had approved his return, the Tsar made clear that he was anything but forgiven. He would be given a high command, but it would be far removed from the world of the Guards or even the professional cavalry. His role would be to lead a newly-formed division of Muslim horsemen from the Caucasus and who had never been in the army before. Michael's actual appointment therefore came as a surprise to the army itself. It was a public snub and intended as such. Having walked out on the Guards cavalry, he was not to think that he could walk back in, or be given a regular command.

There were two main fronts: the northern, in East Prussia, facing the Germans, and the southern, in Galicia, facing the

Austro-Hungarians. On the outbreak of war, the German plan was to defeat France first, in just six weeks, leaving their eastern border manned only by a defensive 'holding army' until the German armies in the west could turn and attack Russia, a plan hubristically summarised by the Kaiser as 'lunch in Paris, dinner in St Petersburg'. The counter to this, as the French were pressed back to Paris, was that the Russians should draw off the German army by launching an offensive on the eastern front, even before they were fully ready to do so. The Russians gallantly obliged, but a month after the war began they were heavily defeated at Tannenberg in East Prussia and then suffered humiliation at the Masurian Lakes. In the first thirty days they lost some quarter-of-a-million men in East Prussia alone. One of the dead was the beaten commander of the Russian Second Army, General Aleksandr Samsonov, who walked into a wood and shot himself.[2] Berlin, only 150 miles away, was not going to be the cavalry canter some had boasted it would be.

Tannenberg could be explained away as a necessary sacrifice made for France and a month later there was better news on the southern front, where the Russians won important successes. Their losses were no less appalling, but they had more to show for them, advancing 100 miles across the frontier, capturing 100,000 prisoners and inflicting battle casualties of some 300,000 on the Austrians.[3]

Michael's division, assigned to the Galician front in the South, facing the Austro-Hungarians, was called the Caucasian Native Cavalry; it comprised six regiments, each known by the name of the tribe or place from which it was recruited: Daghestan, Kabardin, Chechen, Tartar, Circassian, and Ingush.[4] Each horseman — or rider as they were termed in the division — was a volunteer, because conscription laws did not apply to the Caucasus under the terms agreed when it became part of the empire.[5]

The men, natural brigands, were difficult to discipline, for they would fight each other as readily as they would come to fight the Austro-Hungarians. But they were superb horsemen, fearless in a charge and terrifying to face in battle. On a training exercise, one regiment ordered to carry out a sham attack, switched to real ammunition when they ran out of blanks. As bullets whizzed past Michael's head, their urbane colonel murmured, 'I can only congratulate you on being for the first time under real fire'. The brigade commander standing beside them was furious, but 'the Grand Duke laughed'.[6] Under Michael the division would prove itself to be among the very best of the fighting units in Russia, and earn such a reputation that it would be known simply as the 'Savage Division.'[7] So absolute was its loyalty to Michael that in time it would also become known as 'the Grand Duke's private army'.

Michael's parade uniform was the picturesque *cherkeska,* the long Circassian coat which fits tightly at the waist and folds down below the knees and over the top of polished soft leather high boots. His fur cap was of grey astrakhan from a new-born lamb, and he carried a sword and a razor-sharp dagger.[8] It was a far cry from the ceremonial dress of the Blue Cuirassiers and Chevalier Gardes, and when Natasha first saw it she hated it.

The officers were all Russian, mostly professionals, and many of them volunteers from the Guards, attracted by the idea of serving under the Tsar's brother. Among them was the young Prince Vyazemsky, whose wife had become a friend of Natasha. After he was appointed one of Michael's aides-de-camp he wrote to a nephew: 'You cannot imagine how colourful the whole outfit is — the customs, the whole spirit of the thing. The officers are mostly adventurous souls with a devil-may-care attitude. Some of them have had a "tumultuous past", but they are far from dull…' As for the men, 'they seem to think that the war is a great holiday and their Muslim fatalism precludes all fear of death. They adore the Grand Duke.'[9]

As headquarters chaplain, Michael recruited Natasha's family friend, Father Popsolov, who had christened baby George in 1910. However, his most personal appointment was that of an American boxing coach; boxing was one of his enthusiasms and he saw no reason why the war should interrupt it. The commander of his Tartar regiment, Colonel Peter Polovtsov — later a senior general — remembered Michael as 'tall, very slim, a perfect sportsman, an excellent horseman, a very good shot, and his American boxing teacher always told me that it was a pity that he was a Grand Duke, because he would have done very well as a prizefighter in the ring.'[10]

Michael was well pleased with the way his division had come together in its first weeks and towards the end of October 1914 he went north to the supreme headquarters, called *Stavka*, to meet his brother who was there on a visit from Tsarskoe Selo. The headquarters were set in a clearing inside a forest of pines and birches, just outside Baranovichi, 'a miserable little country town,'[11] but which was an important railway junction and roughly at the centre of the 500-mile Russian line.

It was the first time the two brothers had seen each other in over two years, but it was not the occasion or place for a family discussion, so there was no mention of issues which were likely only to end up in a row. Nicholas simply found Michael enthusiastic about his new command. Three days later, on October 27, Nicholas wrote to Alexandra: 'I had the pleasure of spending the whole of Saturday with Misha who has become quite his old self and is again charming.' A little wooden church had been built beside the railway tracks and Michael and Nicholas went there for evening service, 'and parted after dinner'.[12]

Michael went on briefly to Gatchina to finalise his affairs there and, before returning to the front and the risks of the battlefield, to write to his brother about a matter which he had not raised when they met but which continued to trouble him: the fact that four years after his birth, his son George was still illegitimate. Whilst a divisional commander's life expectancy was considerably better than that of a junior office, rank was no protection against artillery shells, snipers, or a random bullet. Michael was also not a man to hang back in the rear; as one of his commanders would say of him later, 'the only trouble he gave us was through his constant wish to be in the fighting-line; we sometimes had great difficulty in keeping him out of danger'.[13]

Were he to be killed in the war, as might happen, Natasha would not inherit anything. The 1912 manifesto, by which Michael's assets had been placed in administration, remained in force; he was still in the same position as 'a minor or a lunatic'[14] and technically without rights to the management of his estates or monies. But to leave innocent little George as a bastard was surely to take punishment beyond anything which was reasonable. He said as much to Nicholas: 'It is very hard for me to go away, leaving my family in such an ambiguous position. I wish for my only beloved son to be accepted by society as my son and not as the son of an unknown father, as he is registered on his birth certificate…Remove from me the burden of the worry that, should something happen to me, that my son would have to grow up with the stigma of illegitimacy… You alone can do this, as it is your right… And after all, he is not to blame!'[15]

There was no reply, and Michael set off to rejoin the Savage Division with even more reason to hope that he would come back alive. Now judged ready for action, his regiments had moved by train to the Austrian border where the wide-gauge Russian railway ended. The Russian frontline was far forward into the Carpathian Mountains, and the division rode the rest of the way to the positions selected for it as part of the Second Cavalry Corps.[16]

The Austrians would have good reason to fear Michael's Muslims in the future, but the first to do so were the unfortunate inhabitants they met as they advanced over the frontier. Finding themselves on conquered territory, the men of one regiment, quartered in an Austrian village, decided to take the spoils of war, and that first night there was chaos as excited Tartars raced around the village, chasing dishevelled girls. It was only at dawn that order was restored and the most serious offenders lined up to be flogged, twenty-five lashes being considered the usual punishment, though rapists convicted at court martial could be shot. Later, two men in that regiment would be and when they were condemned the staff at Michael's headquarters offered to provide a firing squad from another regiment. However, the Tartars insisted on carrying out the execution themselves, the two men preferring, it was said, to die facing friendly faces.[17] The Savage Division was difficult to handle behind the lines, but when it reached the enemy it behaved with the courage expected of men who relished battle, whether on foot or on horseback. They would find themselves involved in very heavy fighting over the next months, and earn considerable distinction on that bloody battlefield. So would Michael. He would find himself coming out of it a national hero.

ALTHOUGH Michael was more than a thousand miles (1,600km) from Gatchina, the journey south to meet him was one which never daunted Natasha. It took two days to get there, over tracks made the slower by the amount of war traffic they were carrying. The first trip came at the beginning of December 1914, when she could only hope that he would be there when she arrived, and knowing that at best he could snatch no more than a few days from the front. Her destination was the former Polish city of Lvov, fifty miles inside Austro-Hungary and known there as Lemberg. The Russians had captured it in September; Michael's headquarters were in a village 100 miles to the southwest and he could be in Lvov in a car in a few hours. Fortunately he was able to snatch a few days from the frontline, which for Natasha more than justified the laborious journey there and back to Gatchina. Indeed, she would return the following month, and then again two months later.

Apart from her natural fears for Michael's life, what troubled Natasha particularly was her belief that he had been posted to the Savage Division in retaliation for his marriage. On her return to Gatchina she wrote to say: 'You are naturally talked about more than the division and what pains me most of all is that they say you did not go to war of your own accord, but were sent to atone for your guilt towards Russia — so your heroism, with which you wished to surprise the world, has been totally wasted...[18] In fact, it had not been wasted, but she could not know that at the time.

Nevertheless she had good reason to believe, as she would continue to do, that Michael had been sent to the most distant part of the Russian line as punishment for having married her, though Michael never seemed to care one way or another. He had come back to fight, and if that meant commanding an irregular division of Muslim horsemen, so be it. As it happened, they were very good at what they did, and that was its own cause for pride in his command.

In the New Year, he was in a sector of the front line which was quiet enough to allow him to take two weeks' leave — effectively ten days since four days of that were spent in travelling. He arrived home on January 2, 1915 — 'what a joy to be back with my family in lovely Gatchina', he scribbled in his diary[19] — and next day went to 'the detestable Petrograd' to inspect the new hospital which Natasha had organised for him in his unused palace on the English Embankment. Then, after shopping with Natasha, and calling on his mother, he went to Tsarskoe Selo to see his brother, and press him again about legitimising little George.

Nothing had been done about that in the two months since he had written to him about it, and nothing would happen this time. Nicholas avoided the subject, for it was a sore point at Tsarskoe Selo. Alexandra opposed any concessions suggesting acceptance of the marriage, and legalising George would in her mind have gone some way towards that. Michael returned home no further forward than before. It was a bitter failure. Three years later Nicholas would plead 'a father's feelings' in justifying a decision about his son Alexis, but that applied only to himself. Michael's worries were dismissed out of hand.

All too soon the leave was over and he set off back to his divisional headquarters, now at Lomna, sixty miles south-west of Lvov. 'It is so sad to leave', he wrote in his diary for January 11, though Natasha insisted on travelling with him as far as Lvov, which gave them almost two days extra together. On arrival they parted hurriedly, for the Austrians had launched an offensive, and the Russian line was being pushed back. 'The fighting is unceasing', he told Natasha in his first letter home.[20] One of his colonels had been killed, and three staff officers seriously wounded, one of whom would die two days later. Sixty of his horsemen were casualties.

Michael's headquarters had been pulled back in the fighting and in the confusion of the move all his belongings were mislaid, 'so I do not have even a bar of soap'.[21] But by January 20 he was able to report that 'the crisis is over and the enemy is in retreat along our entire frontline. We are now dealing mainly with the Hungarian troops, who fight with great persistence. Yesterday our infantry (on our right flank) lost 1,000 men, but in my division the losses were quite small.'[22]

The Carpathians are a thick belt of mountains, with one rising above another, often with a slope of one-in-six and covered in trees. These heights dominate the passes, which were deep in snow, and each had to be fought for at the point of a bayonet. It was a savage business and no one who was there could think that war was glory. Temperatures fell to minus 17 degrees and 'the poor soldiers, especially at night, freeze terribly and many have frostbitten feet and hands. The losses in the infantry attached to us have been very great,' wrote Michael.[23] The enemy suffered as greatly and sometimes more so. One Austrian regiment of some 1,800 men froze to death as it lay waiting to advance the following morning. Rifles locked solid by ice had to be heated over fires before infantrymen could be sent into battle. Trenches were so difficult to dig that men could often do no more than bury themselves in the snow.

The casualty figures in all armies were horrific and beyond anything known to history before. After six months of fighting the Russians had lost a million men, dead, wounded or captured. 'Corps have become divisions, brigades have shrunk into regiments', Nicholas confessed to Alexandra.[24] The slaughter appalled Michael, who unlike his brother, could see it at first hand. He believed the war itself to be a catastrophe, entered into blindly by men who little knew what they were doing. As he told Natasha on February 16, 1915, in a letter which said much about his own political instincts:

The war and all the great horror it involves cannot help inspiring sadness in every sensible person; for example, I feel greatly embittered... and most of all towards those who are at the top, who hold power and allow all that horror to happen,. If the question of war were decided by the people at large, I would not be so passionately averse to that great calamity; but...nobody ever asks the nation, the country at large, what course of action they would choose.

I even sometimes feel ashamed to face the people, i.e. the soldiers and officers, particularly when visiting field hospitals, where so much suffering is to be seen, for they might think one is also responsible, for one is placed so high and yet has failed to prevent all that from happening and to protect one's country from this disaster... '[25]

Two weeks earlier he had written to tell her to postpone her next proposed trip to Lvov because 'the situation is such that it is difficult to say when we might have a few free days.'[26] The fighting had not stopped since his return to the division after the New Year. It was a brutal business; on going forward to one captured position 'we saw such horrors as I am not going to describe'.[27] Yet at the same time, hoping to reassure her that he was in no personal danger, he had written that 'most of the time I sit at home and feel miserably bored. To be at war and not even take advantage of the fresh air seems so stupid.' [28]

What he did not tell her was that the day before, as his diary noted, he had been climbing on foot through freezing snow up a mountain, identified on his map as Height 673, inspecting positions which within hours would be under heavy enemy assault, 'with intense shooting from the front and both flanks, causing great losses.' One regiment 'lost 300 soldiers'.[29]

Despite the bitterness of the fighting, and Michael's request on February 4 that she postpone her next visit, Natasha insisted

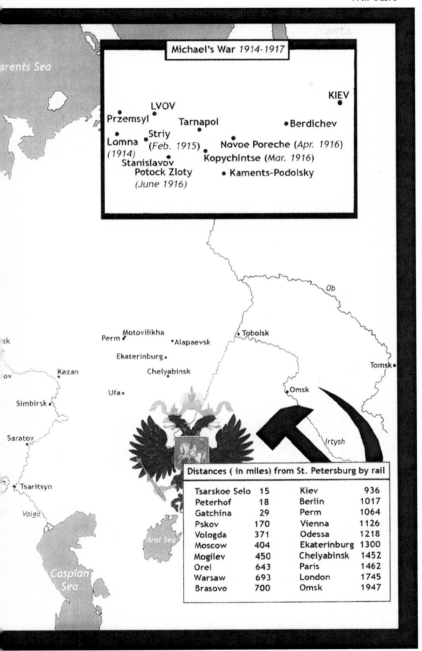

Michael's War *1914-1917*

KIEV

LVOV
Przemsyl   Tarnapol
                                    •Berdichev
            Striy
Lomna *(Feb. 1915)*   Novoe Poreche *(Apr. 1916)*
(1914)   Kopychintse *(Mar. 1916)*
      Stanislavov
      Potock Zloty   • Kaments-Podolsky
        (June 1916)

Barents Sea

Ob

                Motovilikha   • Tobolsk
        Perm•   •Alapaevsk
        Ekaterinburg•   Tomsk•
sk
    Kazan   Chelyabinsk
ov
            Ufa•   •Omsk
    Simbirsk•
                                        Irtysh
    Saratov

    • Tsaritsyn

    Volga

        Aral Sea

Caspian
  Sea

Distances (in miles) from St. Petersburg by rail			
Tsarskoe Selo	15	Kiev	936
Peterhof	18	Berlin	1017
Gatchina	29	Perm	1064
Pskov	170	Vienna	1126
Vologda	371	Odessa	1218
Moscow	404	Ekaterinburg	1300
Mogilev	450	Chelyabinsk	1452
Orel	643	Paris	1462
Warsaw	693	London	1745
Brasovo	700	Omsk	1947

on taking the chance of seeing him, setting off again on February 10. On this occasion she was lucky to see him at all, as he had warned. The Austrians had just regained two towns, Chernovitsy and Stanislavov, and the Russian Eighth Army commander General Aleksei Brusilov had ordered Michael 'to straighten out the situation'.[30] It involved a long cross-country move and the establishment of new headquarters in the town of Striy, forty miles from Lvov. Michael drove to Lvov to meet Natasha at the station, but it was the briefest of reunions. He wiped away her tears and left her in the Governor's house. Shortly afterwards he sent her a note to say that 'fighting is on and it is impossible to say how long it will last, maybe five, maybe more than ten days. Therefore I cannot ask you to stay on in Lvov and I suggest you leave at once…Yesterday there were heavy losses in the 2nd Brigade'. Then, thinking that this sounded alarmist, he added, 'there is no need to worry about my safety, for I am far from the battle area'.[31]

That was not true. He was with the frontline troops, moving from village to village, finding lodgings where he could, and 'walking with the main forces' as they came up to the Austrians, led by their famous and rightly respected Tyrolese riflemen. Outnumbered two to one, Michael's Tartars and Chechens,, fighting on foot, met the Austrians in a forest. There was a bloody hand-to-hand battle, but the bayonets of the 'stalwart Tyrolese' wavered in the face of the swords and daggers of 'the active little Tartars', their commander proudly reported.[32]

Half his men lay dead among the trees, and as Michael rode up 'he was very much impressed' by the fight the regiment had put up, but also clearly saddened as he rode through the woods full of corpses. 'A battlefield after a fight is not a beautiful picture,' noted the Tartar colonel, 'and I think that the kind heart of the Grand Duke suffered from the sight.' [33]

With that, Michael wrote to Natasha that his division had been pulled back for a rest and that they could meet again in Lvov. She arrived on March 1, and when she and Michael awoke next morning it was to find that he was being honoured with Russia's highest gallantry award, the Order of St George, on the recommendation of his tough-minded army commander Brusilov. In contrast to the Cross of St George — which could be and was awarded in the field in its thousands by battlefield generals, the Order had to be approved by no less than fifteen Knights of the Order. No honour in Russia was so highly prized.

The award, made independently of the Tsar, was made in recognition of his conduct on the battlefield 'during which he exposed his life to great danger, inspiring and encouraging the troops under constant enemy fire by the example of his personal bravery and courage and when resisting attacks by superior enemy forces…and later, when moving onto the offensive, he contributed to the successful development of our manoeuvres by his energetic actions…'[34]

The honour impressed even the cynical back-biting circles in the capital, Petrograd. Newspapers across the country published the announcement and the laudatory comments which accompanied it. Michael, wrote one war correspondent, 'always wanted to be wherever there was danger…seeing the Grand Duke at their forward positions the ranks were ready to follow him to a loyal death'.[35] He was 'the idol of his men', wrote another, 'sleeping in the open with them, and living the same life as they did, without the least indulgence…'[36]

Brother-in-law Sandro was also highly approving, noting that Michael's division, 'led by him through innumerable battles, being recognised by GHQ as our best fighting unit'[37] — and that after only six months with horsemen who had known nothing of soldiering when he took command.

'We were all devoted to him', said a colonel.[38] Ordinary soldiers simply called him *Dzhigit Misha* — meaning 'Our Caucasian horseman Michael', a compliment they gave to no other Russian officer, and because they did not distinguish rank as carefully as they should have done, they also addressed him as 'Your Majesty' rather than 'Your Royal Highness'.[39]

The men trusted him implicitly, believing that whatever their grievance they could go to him for justice. One such dispute involved an Ingush Cossack rider who had captured two officers. Taking an officer prisoner earned a medal, and the simple Ingush reasoned therefore that he was entitled to two medals. Stubbornly refusing to accept what he was told by his own officers, he argued his way into divisional headquarters and was brought before Michael. Having heard him, Michael burst out laughing: 'Lord, what am I to do with him?'

His staff had no doubt. 'You must tell him he is wrong, Your Highness.'

'I know perfectly well he is wrong, but he is offended. He places his hopes on me, and it is not within my power to help him'.

With that, the Ingush bowed. 'Do not help me', he said. 'I thought that they were lying, but if you say it, that means it is true. Do not be angry'. Michael gave him the medal he was due, and settled the matter of the second officer by handing the grateful rider twenty roubles.[40]

Some matters ended badly. Later, three men condemned to death by a court martial for looting, were taken out for execution. In the process they broke free and were shot dead, with one guard killed and another wounded in the confusion. Michael was horrified, noting that 'it all turned out to very horrible and tragic, and such a shame, as a telegram with their pardon had been received and was to be read to them at the place of execution for greater effect — and it all failed!'[41]

Michael's abiding concern for his men was its own testimony to his leadership in fashioning a formidable division from Muslim tribesmen who had never before known military discipline, and whose differences with each other hampered rather than helped the forging of a coherent unit. That in itself earned him distinction.

But with the Council of St George's approval of his high award, an Order founded by Catherine the Great but rarely given for gallantry on the battlefield, Nicholas's reaction was a curious mixture of pleasure, pride, and yet begrudging condescension. Writing to Alexandra, he told her about 'the splendid behaviour of Misha's division in the February fighting, when they were attacked in the Carpathians by two Austrian divisions...while Misha was the whole time in the line of fire.' He then added patronisingly, 'I am very glad for his sake, as I think this time that he has really earned this military distinction and it will show him that he is, after all, treated exactly as all the others, and by doing his duty well he also gets his reward'.[42]

Alexandra's response was almost breathtaking in its priggishness. 'I am sure this war will make more of a man of him — could one but get her out of his reach, her dictating influence is so bad for him.' [43]

She was too blind to her own faults to know it, but many people were beginning to think that the charge of 'dictating influence' was more true about her and Nicholas than it was about Natasha and Michael. But at least there was one private gain for Michael in all this. Ten days later he wrote to his brother, raising again the question of his son.

'Something that upsets me very much is that neither when we saw each other in January, nor in your letter afterwards, have you said anything in response to my personal request which means so much to me...please remember about it during Easter.'[44] With the Order of St George on his chest, Michael felt more entitled than ever before to demand the legitimisation of little George — and Nicholas less able to refuse him, whatever Alexandra's protests. This time the Tsar gave in, and four-year-old George had at last a named father and a title of his own — he was now to be styled Count Brasov.[45]

But that was as far as Nicholas would go. He would still not release Michael's assets; war hero he might be, but legally he was to remain in the role of madman. If he was killed, there might be some discretionary bequest now to his son, but Natasha would still be left penniless. The first three months of 1915 had seen the private tragedy of the death of her two sisters in Moscow: Olga of appendicitis in January, Vera of pneumonia in March.* If anything, it heightened her fears for Michael. If he were killed, what would she have left? She could expect nothing from a Tsarskoe Selo which still thought of her as a villainess, and would never pardon her as they had yet to pardon Michael.

As if to underline the point that he was not forgiven, the Tsar snubbed his brother when he paid a visit to the southern front in early April on 'a victory tour' and to see the newly-captured fortress of Przemysl, 70 miles east of Lvov. Although he was joined in Lvov by his two sisters, Xenia and Olga — who was nursing in Kiev — there was no invitation to any family reunion for Michael, and indeed he would not know that Nicholas had been to nearby Lvov until he read about it later in a local newspaper on April 10.[46] That raised eyebrows in the Savage Division —'the best in the Russian army' with its commander awarded the Order of St George. And the Tsar had not bothered to tell them he was coming? Odd.

Natasha, however, was in no doubt of the reason. Alexandra was not going to have Michael seen to be back in the family.

*After the death of Natasha's sister Olga in January 1915 Michael appointed the widowed Aleksei Matveev as his 'executive secretary'. Matveev moved to Petrograd, taking an apartment on the Fontanka. He would play an important role there in Michael's future and the political drama ahead.

5. ALEXANDRA THE GREAT

TWO weeks after the Tsar departed Lvov to return home, with heady talk of an advance to Vienna in prospect, Michael also went home. His sector of the front had been quiet, with relatively little action. On April 19, 1915, a German plane dropped five bombs on his headquarters 'without causing any damage', there was sporadic firing from the enemy outposts, and 'we buried a soldier, Veris, killed the day before yesterday'.[1] One dead soldier in two days; given what had gone before that was almost peace. Five days later he was back in Gatchina, his division, after six months in the frontline, being withdrawn for rest and refitting, and that would take at least a month.

That month passed so quickly that afterwards it seemed the briefest of interludes. Michael saw his brother twice at Tsarskoe Selo, and had tea with his mother at the Anichkov Palace. Otherwise he spent his whole time with Natasha. They drove out in his American Packard to have picnics with friends, went to the theatre in the capital, rode in the Gatchina palace park — and then, on May 23, Michael went back to the war. Natasha this time went with him only so far as Brest-Litovsk, a large town and railway junction some 200 miles north of Lvov, now too close to the frontline to be safe.

In the month Michael had been away the war had started to go badly for Russia. Ground won on the south-west front was now ground lost. The Tsar's victory tour of early April had been followed with a new offensive, master-minded by the Germans, and launched with an overwhelming artillery barrage which tore apart the Russian divisions facing them. Trenches collapsed and reinforcements brought up melted away as the shellfire fell on them.

Many soldiers hastily marched into the battle zone were unarmed and dependent on picking up the weapons of soldiers who had fallen. A month after the offensive began, Przemysl was recaptured and three weeks later, on June 9, 1915, Lvov fell. Caught up in the retreat, Michael's division withdrew behind the River Dniester, but held its ground thereafter. 'Oh, how I wish this atrocious slaughter could be over soon', he wrote home. In two days there were 1,000 casualties.

In the midst of this, on June 6, 1915, Grand Duke Konstantin Konstantinovich, who had died at the age of fifty-seven, was buried with great pomp in the fortress of St Peter and St Paul. The only member of the imperial family absent that day was Michael.

There was critical comment about that which upset Natasha. She wrote to him in bewilderment. 'Darling Misha, why do you always harm yourself and why didn't you come for K.K's funeral. Literally all your relatives came *en masse,* only you didn't appear…your absence was conspicuous. Even assuming that you did not feel like showing your face at a family gathering, you could have still taken that opportunity just to come home! Boris (*Grand Duke Boris Vladimirovich*) had only just left and he came back again till June 20.'[2]

That brought a stinging response from an outraged Michael. *I did not come to the funeral of Konstantin K because I had only returned from a long leave a short while before that and did not think I had a right to leave here again; there is a war on, not children's games with soldiers…while I am in command of a division, it is impossible for me to leave it so often; and if any of my relations do just that, they are wrong and they are not an example for me to follow.*[3]

The desperate fighting apart, there was another reason for his remaining at the frontline, and he tried to explain that, too. 'Our division is not a regular army unit, and it's not too easy to command it; there are a lot of different things to sort out — jealousy and rivalry between the regiments, their mutual complaints, etc. When I am here, everything gets into a more peaceful vein, but without me...it is more than difficult to control.'[4]

Natasha, having complained about his absence from the state funeral, was plainly in a bad mood that day, for she added more personal criticism in the same letter. All the officers she saw in the capital, and when her train from the front stopped at *Stavka*, were smartly dressed, in crisp uniforms, polished boots and with an elegance that fitted well in the Winter Garden Room of the popular Astoria Hotel, which had become her favoured lunching place.

In contrast, Michael, a fighting general, looked shabby, ill-dressed and muddy in almost all the photographs he sent her. 'Look how awfully you now dress,' she chided him. 'Your boots are horrible, you've done away with your aiguillettes and instead of the St George you wear a piece of some narrow ribbon...I regret to see you so changed.'[5]

Natasha had sent Michael a St George, made up for her at Fabergé, the imperial jewellers, not understanding that the only person likely to admire the gleam of a Fabergé was an enemy sniper. Personal appearance was not the uppermost consideration in the frontline, or at least in the Savage Division. As if to underline that point, Michael recorded a visit by the Ninth Army general Lechitsky to an artillery position with a large entourage of braided staff officers; it was a target too good to miss and in consequence the general and his staff 'had to spend two hours crouching in an empty trench'. It was their own fault, said Michael, for he often went to the same position 'without all that pomp and retinue' and nothing ever happened.[6]

Someone who was certainly impressed by Michael's appearance was the American war correspondent Stanley Washburn. When he visited Michael's headquarters he was surprised to find the brother of the Tsar in 'a simple uniform with nothing to indicate his rank but shoulder straps of the same material as his uniform, and, barring the St George (won by personal valour on the battlefield) without a decoration…'

What also struck him about Michael was he should find him 'living so simply in a dirty village in this far fringe of the Russian empire'. He rated Michael highly. 'He evinced the same stubborn optimism that one finds everywhere in the Russian army', he commented, 'while appearing as unaffected and democratic a person as one can well imagine.[7]

Washburn was right — Michael was optimistic, despite everything. 'I feel so distressed because of Lvov', he had written to Natasha, but adding that 'to lose heart and think that we won't win is just sinful. The morale of the army at the front is good, what I am concerned about is the attitude of the Russian people at large…'[8]

When he wrote that he had good reason to be concerned about the 'home front'. Serious rioting had broken out in Moscow. The defeats in Galicia resulted in revenge attacks on Germans living in Moscow. Many had been there for generations, owning important businesses, and thinking themselves German only in name.

Natasha went there at the end of June, 1915, and saw for herself what had happened. 'All that's left of the shops and houses with German names are just bare walls, with the insides looted and burnt…It was real pillage, just organised and made possible by the indifference and inaction of the authorities and the police…' One business friend whose home was ransacked 'told me that members of the intelligentsia were among the rioters — obvious connoisseurs came to his house and chose the best pictures to destroy. So many wonderful paintings lost, such a shame!'[9]

Michael felt 'very sorry for the unfortunate victims' and wrote that the pogrom 'clearly demonstrates the hatred that the Russian people have long felt for foreigners living in Russia…

The government ought to be ashamed that it can't prevent such things, with many victims as a consequence. How I wish for a 'wise government' for my dear Russia, so that we could boast of it to all

The fighting general with the Order of St George on his chest

Michael with members of his staff, and one of his pilots, in the Savage Division, May 1915.

The general who did not bother with the braid

Michael, as American war correspondent Stanley Washburn saw him in 1915, in 'a simple uniform with nothing to indicate his rank but shoulder straps of the same material as his uniform, and, barring the St George (won by personal valour on the battlefield) without a decoration...'

European states, but who knows if that will ever come, and if it does, I'm afraid it won't be soon! I know you will understand what I mean, and will read between the lines...

He added that 'many people now feel that I was right to have married a Russian and not a German...'[10] It was not difficult for Natasha 'to read between the lines'. His barbs were aimed at Alexandra and her circle.

Although the Savage Division suffered as much as any other as the retreat continued, by mid-July it had been pulled back to a sector which was relatively quiet, and which would remain so over the next few weeks, although on the rest of the front the fighting continued to be intense, as the Russians were pushed further and further back, with horrendous casualties. Michael took the opportunity of going back home for a brief leave — or so he thought.

In fact, having got there he went down immediately with diphtheria, dreaded as one of the great killer diseases of the age, and which he had contracted at the front just before his departure. There were no antibiotics and many sufferers died from asphyxiation as their throats closed up. The minority who survived it took a long time to recover.

Michael proved one of the lucky ones. A week after the first symptoms appeared he began to feel better and by July 30, 1915 he was well enough to have 'played the guitar a little'.[11] Six days later he was strong enough to have got up and gone downstairs for breakfast. That was encouraging, but there was little else to be cheerful about. On August 7 he grimly noted that 'the war is so bad that I don't want to write about it.' Next day he tersely recorded, 'Kovno and Novo-Georgievsk have been captured!' Then it was to write that 'Brest-Litovsk has surrendered. We've been in a bad mood for the past few days.'[12]

One reason for these failures, Michael believed, was that Russian strategy was wrong, as events would prove. The war was not about holding or taking territory, he told Natasha, but about destroying the enemy's army.

*What's happening is that they are trying to achieve the opposite.
All high commanders panic over every inch of land captured by the
enemy instead of taking a huge fist and punching the enemy where
it hurts. This simple and, one would think, reasonable tactic has
not so far been used. They want to be strong everywhere, along the
entire frontline, which of course is impossible and as a result, we are
everywhere equally weak.*[13]

Over the past three weeks the advancing Germans had
captured Warsaw, then the string of Russian fortresses which
in theory should have barred an enemy advance into Russia
proper. Millions of shells had been locked up in them, along with
hundreds of guns and tens of thousands of men. Now they had
all gone with nothing to show for them.

In the first year of the war the Russian army had lost one and
a half million men, the equivalent of the whole of its peacetime
army; whereas it had been fighting until the spring beyond its
own borders, now, for the first time since Napoleon, an enemy
was advancing deep inside Russia's homeland, driving back not
only the army but hundreds of thousands of refugees flooding
west in flight from homes and crops burned behind them.

Something had to be done and that something was firstly the
dismissal of the disastrous war minister Sukhomlinov; he was not
only incompetent but corrupt, supporting his high-spending and
pretty young wife — at thirty, half his age — with bribes taken
from army contracts.

For very different reasons the Supreme Commander, Grand
Duke Nicholas Nikolaevich — 'Uncle Nikolasha' — was to be
brought down. The Grand Duke was well regarded by both the
British and the French, and by the Germans no less, and his great
height and soldierly bearing had impressed foreign correspondents.
He was also more victim than villain in the scandal of an army
without enough shells, rifles, and boots. Neither the public nor the
army sought him as scapegoat. Nevertheless he was removed.

But what shocked Russia, and its allies, was the name of
his successor. The new Supreme Commander was to be a man

who had never been on the battlefield, and whose last military command had been almost a quarter of a century earlier and then only as an officer in a squadron of the Hussar Life Guards.

The Tsar appointed himself.

Few approved. Michael's cousin and friend Grand Duke Andrew observed that 'thoughtful people believe that this step will cause general ill-feeling and discontent and have serious consequences'.[14] The British military observer, Colonel Alfred Knox, who saw the army reaction at first hand, concluded that the misgivings 'were almost universal'.[15] The French ambassador Paléologue wrote that 'the news has produced a deplorable impression.'[16] Michael's commander-in-chief Brusilov judged that Nicholas has 'struck the last blow against himself'.[17]

But if Nicholas was to take himself off to *Stavka,* then who would represent him in the capital and handle the day-to-day affairs of state? The man who knew nothing about war answered that by appointing someone who knew nothing about politics. He gave the job to his wife.

The move was made almost casually within days of his arrival at headquarters and after a letter from her in which she wrote: 'Do not fear for what remains behind...don't laugh at silly old Wify but she has "trousers" on unseen...'[18] His reply was as she had hoped. 'Think my Wify, will you not come to the assistance of your hubby now that he is absent? What a pity that you have not been fulfilling this duty for a long time, or at least during the war!'[19]

The invitation was eagerly accepted. 'Oh, Sweetheart, I am so touched you want my help. I am always ready to do anything for you, only never liked mixing up without being asked...'[20] Since there was no formal announcement that Alexandra was now effectively Regent on the home front, it took some time before the public realised that henceforth Russia was to be ruled by a domineering, neurotic and hysterical Empress and behind her, hiding in her shadow, by the scandalous and hated figure of her hypnotic 'holy man', Grigory Rasputin.

THE power of Rasputin had grown massively over the past ten years as again and again he appeared to demonstrate that only he could save Alexandra's son from the 'bleeding disease'. When Alexis lay at the point of death in 1912, after injuring himself while jumping into a boat, an anguished Alexandra sent Rasputin a telegram begging his help, and received back a cable to say that 'the Little One will not die. Do not allow the doctors to bother him too much.'[21] Shortly afterwards the crisis passed. A man who could save her son even by telegram was surely a man sent by God and she would ever after be utterly dependent on him.

A distracted and desperate mother vulnerable to a charlatan? Rasputin was not, in fact, the first mystical figure to influence affairs at Tsarskoe Selo. His most notorious predecessor was a hypnotic French quack, a former butcher's assistant from Lyons and a man well known to the French police. Calling himself Dr Philippe — his real name was Philippe Nizier-Vachod — he appeared on the scene in 1901, long before the birth of Alexis. As with Rasputin he was known as 'our Friend' by both Nicholas and Alexandra.

Indeed, Alexandra's references to Dr Philippe could easily be confused with her later references to Rasputin: 'how rich life is since we know him and everything seems easier to bear', she would write that year. Grand Duke Konstantin would note disturbingly that, after sessions with Dr Philippe in the nearby villa of Alexandra's long-time companion Anna Vyrubova, Tsar and Empress would return 'in an exalted state, as if in an ecstasy with radiant faces and shining eyes'.[22]

It was Dr Philippe who convinced Alexandra that she was at last, after four daughters, going to give Nicholas the son and heir she so obsessively sought. In August, 1902, as St Petersburg eagerly waited for the bells to ring and the cannon to roar, there was an unexpected disappointment. It was a phantom pregnancy,[23] although Russia could not of course be told that. Even so, 'our Friend' survived that embarrassing setback; it was another eighteen months before Nicholas, with regret, felt it would be wiser to dismiss him. He died shortly afterwards, in 1905, in France.

Someone was bound to step into his shoes and so it was with the arrival of a new 'Friend' with hypnotic eyes — Rasputin. By 1915, Paléologue concluded that Alexandra 'lives in a kind of hypnosis'; whatever Rasputin's opinion or desire 'she acquiesces and obeys at once. The ideas he suggests to her are implanted in her brain without provoking the slightest opposition.'[24]

Because few people outside court circles knew about the carefully guarded secret of Alexis's haemophilia, wider society did not understand why Rasputin — a notorious womaniser and drunkard — was tolerated at all by Tsarskoe Selo. In the spring of 1915, British diplomat Robert Bruce Lockhart witnessed a disgraceful scene in an exclusive Moscow restaurant. From one of the 'cabinets' came wild shrieks, a man's curses, the sound of broken glass and the banging of doors. 'The cause of the disturbance was Rasputin — drunk and lecherous and neither police nor management dared evict him'.

It was only after a direct order from the assistant minister of the interior, General Dzhunkovsky, that Rasputin was arrested and taken away, 'snarling and vowing vengeance'. Although released next day on 'instructions from the highest quarter',[25] the public clamour was so great that Nicholas felt impelled to send him back to his Siberian village. Two weeks later Alexandra prevailed over her husband, and Rasputin was back as before. Three weeks later the general who had dared to arrest him was sacked.

The Supreme Commander 'Uncle Nikolasha' was also to pay the price of offending Alexandra's 'Friend'. When Rasputin offered to come and bless his troops, the ramrod Grand Duke had said in reply: 'Yes, do come. I'll hang you.'[26] With that, the jealous Empress and the vengeful Rasputin had worked together to ensure his downfall, as they did.

Alexandra had suspected that 'Nikolasha' had ambitions to usurp the throne — an idea unsupported by any evidence whatsoever — because of his popularity in the army. During the

Tsar's victory tour it was noted that in contrast, as the French ambassador commented, 'everybody has been struck by the indifference, or rather coldness, with which the Emperor was received by the army'. One reason for that, he went on to say, was that 'the legend which has grown up around the Empress and Rasputin has been a serious blow to the prestige of the Emperor both with the men and their officers'.[27]

Michael, shaking his head in disbelief as he convalesced in Gatchina, was as appalled as everyone else by his brother's decision to take over the Supreme Command, but like the others he was helpless to do anything about it. Russia's new warrior Tsar, a man who had never heard a shot fired in anger, took over the war without any idea about how that war might now be best fought, save that he would be in charge.

His cousin Andrew, visiting a 'terribly worried' Dowager Empress, reported that she feared that the removal of Nikolasha 'will be the ruin' of the Tsar and 'laid all the blame' on Alexandra. 'It is all her work… she alone is responsible for all that is happening now. It is too awful.' Her elder son Nicholas was 'lovable, honest, good,' but with Alexandra behind him the Dowager Empress could only wring her hands and cry, 'What are we coming to, what are we coming to?'[28] Duke Alexander of Oldenburg, known in the family as 'Uncle Alex', was in equal despair when he saw the Dowager Empress. As she would tell Andrew afterwards, 'he rolled on the floor'.[29]

The young Grand Duke Dimitri — who had won the Cross of St George in 1914 after dismounting from his horse under heavy fire to carry a wounded corporal to safety — was as shocked as anyone by the news. When the French ambassador told him that he doubted that the Tsar would change his mind, Dimitri angrily threw away his cigarette and cried: 'Then we're lost. Henceforth it will be the Empress and her *camarilla* who command at *Stavka!* It's maddening.'[30]

Alexandra was quite frank, and startlingly so, in showing her dominance over her husband. When the British ambassador,

Sir George Buchanan, met her at Tsarskoe Selo and told her of his worries about Nicholas assuming the Supreme Command, she told him: 'The situation requires firmness. The Emperor, unfortunately, is weak; but I am not and I intend to be firm.'[31] However true, to say that to the ambassador of an allied country, duty bound to report it to his government, was wholly unforgivable.

None the less, on August 25, 1915, the Tsar ended his first day as Supreme Commander on a confident note. 'We had only just finished playing dominoes,' he wrote to Alexandra, when news came that the southern army had captured 'over 150 officers, over 7,000 men, thirty guns and many machine-guns. And this happened immediately after our troops learnt that I have taken upon myself the Supreme Command. This is truly God's blessing...'[32] To underline this sign from Heaven, he sent the same news by telegram next day, so that she could be doubly assured about 'our glorious success' and that 'this happened immediately after the declaration of my appointment'.[33]

MICHAEL was soon to find out for himself what life was like at *Stavka* with his brother as Supreme Commander, for two weeks after Nicholas took over the armies he summoned Michael to join him. With the Russian armies in retreat, general headquarters had been earlier forced to withdraw from Baranovichi and find somewhere safer.

The place chosen was the provincial capital of Mogilev, 180 miles (290km) further east and it was there, eight weeks earlier on his way back from the front, that Michael had breakfasted with Nikolasha in the tent set up beside the commander-in-chief's train, never thinking that the next time he was at *Stavka* it would be with his brother in charge.

The first and most obvious change he would find was that the new Supreme Commander no longer lived in a train. 'In view of the dampness of the wood, where the train was standing', Nicholas took comfortable quarters in the Governor's mansion.[34]

The suggestion that Michael should be called to Mogilev came from Alexandra. While he had been at the front he had been ignored, but recovering from illness and back at Gatchina with 'that wife' of his to tell him what was being said in the capital, there was now no knowing what might happen. Alexandra wished to avoid a rival court and to make sure of that she wanted Michael with his brother, not with Natasha.

Thus, as Nicholas arrived in Mogilev, Alexandra wrote to him: 'Won't you send for Misha to stay a bit with you…would be so nice and homely for you, & good to get him away from her & yr. brother is the one to be with you.'[35] Six days later she was anxiously enquiring: Have you news from Misha? I have no idea where he is. Do get him to stop a bit with you — get him quite to yourself.'[36]

Four days later, on Thursday, September 10, 1915, a still groggy Michael set off on the 500-mile (800km) journey southward to Mogilev. He got there next day and Nicholas immediately cabled Alexandra to say so, adding surprisingly that 'he looks well'.[37] Two days later Nicholas wrote home again: 'The weather continues to be lovely. I go out every day in a car with Misha and we spend a great deal of my leisure together, as in former years. He is so calm and charming…'[38]

It was encouraging news for Alexandra, who replied by continuing to impress on Nicholas the importance of having his brother at his side — 'your very own brother, it's just his place and the longer he stops with you, away from her bad influence the better it is and you will get him to see things with your own eyes'.[39] She meant her eyes. Her only warning was that 'I fear Misha will ask for his wife to get a title — she can't — she left two husbands already & he is your only brother'.[40]

In response, Nicholas's letters did not encourage Alexandra in her hopes of a repentant Michael eager to admit the errors of his ways and ready to dump 'that wife'. Nor was there anything to show him a stalwart champion of Nicholas against the dark forces of the Duma. Despite their long hours together, all that

Alexandra would learn was that 'Misha often sits with me.'[41] Yet, alone together, there was plenty to say that week, and Michael did his best to say it even though, as he would later reveal, it was sadly to no avail.

Nevertheless, that week at Mogilev gave Michael, as nothing else would do, a clear insight into how his brother was conducting affairs in the midst of the greatest military, parliamentary and governmental crisis since 1905. With the enemy fast advancing, the Duma had been in such uproar that Nicholas had ordered it to be adjourned. Ministers were openly quarrelling among themselves. And every day Michael saw Nicholas sit down, cigarette in hand, and read what Alexandra believed he should be doing.

A letter might be fifteen pages long, Alexandra's pen leaping from one thought to another, and from one demand to another. She always wrote in English, and at such speed that she often seemed to be rambling incoherently, with words frequently misspelt. In that week she wrote six letters to Nicholas, each containing an average of 2,000 words. Pausing only to stub out one cigarette and light another, Nicholas read through her letters impassively as she urged him to do this and do that.

'I long to put my nose into everything — to wake up people, put order into all & unite all', she had written just before Michael's arrival.[42] Order and unity, in fact, meant a Russia in which everyone did exactly what she told them to do.

In the event, Michael's visit was dominated not by the terrible defeats of war but by home-front politics — a crisis meeting of ministers called to *Stavka* shortly after his arrival, and after they had signed a letter to the Tsar demanding the removal of the aged prime minister Ivan Goremykin, appointed in 1914. At seventy-six he was exhausted and broken: 'the candles have already been lit round my coffin', he said, 'and the only thing required to complete the ceremony is myself.'[43]

The Duma, which had not met in the first six months of 1914, was largely composed of conservative and liberal members

— landowners, industrialists, lawyers, academics, and well-off businessmen. What they wanted was a greater voice in government, a share in policy-making, and ministers who were more accountable to them. The current Duma was the fourth since the now side-lined Sergei Witte had become the first prime minister in 1906. The first two had swiftly come and gone; the third had run its full course of five years and the fourth, elected in 1912, still had two years to run.

The session which had opened on July 19, 1915, had seen the emergence of a new 'Progressive Bloc', a liberal-conservative alliance which represented 250 of the 402 Duma deputies. Because of the military disasters at the front, this majority group demanded the creation of a 'government of public confidence'. Alexandra had vehemently opposed the Duma being called at all — 'it's not their business...they speak too much...Russia, thank God, is not a constitutional country'[44] — and by the end of August 1915 she was urging Nicholas 'only quickly shut the Duma'.[45] He did, four days later.

The closure was immediately followed by strikes at the giant Putilov munitions factory in Petrograd and did nothing to solve a growing crisis in the government itself. Most ministers favoured working more closely with the Duma and believed that what was needed was co-operation not confrontation, but their efforts were frustrated by the doddering Goremykin, whose sole policy seemed to be that of 'for me, an imperial command is law'.[46] He seemed not to have grasped that imperial commands now came from Alexandra.

In turn, Alexandra was in no doubt about the right response to the ministerial rebellion. 'Clean out all, give Goremykin new ministers & God will bless you...Show your fist, chastisen (*sic*), be the master & lord, you are the Autocrat & they dare not forget it, when they do, as now, woe unto them.'[47] Competence was no longer the determining factor in government. 'The ministers are rotten, be decided, repremand (*sic*) them very severely for their behaviour.'[48]

She offered Nicholas mystical support in his forthcoming confrontation with a comb blessed by Rasputin. Having told him it 'would bring its little help', she urged him 'to comb your hair with His comb before the sitting of the ministers'.[49] Divinely groomed, Nicholas dealt briskly with them and proudly cabled Alexandra to say afterwards that 'the conference passed off well. I told them my opinion sternly to their faces...[50] Michael, in witnessing this political drama, was given little encouragement that his brother would make the kind of changes which he believed were now essential. Believing in constitutional government as he did, and which he had seen to be the norm in Britain, he could not understand why his brother was so opposed to it — until he realised that it was not Nicholas but his wife who ruled the roost.

But nothing that Michael said made any difference. Nicholas listened to him, thanked him, but then went back to his desk and to his orders piling up on his desk from his wife.

The day after the ministers left, Michael left also, knowing that there was nothing more he could say that would be of any use. Afterwards, Alexandra, blind to anything but her own conviction, wrote to Nicholas to say that 'you must miss Misha now — how nice that you had him staying with you — I am sure that it must have done him good in every sense.'[51]

She was to be disappointed. Seeing things through his brother's eyes had done Michael no good whatsoever.

6. RIVAL COURTS

MICHAEL, kept out of the frontline as he recovered from diphtheria, had settled very happily back into the domestic routine of Gatchina. Although his assets were still frozen, he had managed to extract enough money from his reluctant administrators to have the house at 24 Nikolaevskaya Street, renovated and improved. It was no longer the tumbledown it had been, with a rickety fence which the local police had complained about as a danger to passers-by. The courtyard had been covered with gravel, the summerhouse painted white, the garden filled with flowers, and a new tennis court built at the rear. Michael loved it and wanted nothing more.

He had, by imperial standards, only a handful of servants, some of whom lived in the house, and others with quarters in the one next door. They included his valet and chauffeur, Natasha's long-serving personal maid Ayuna, a cook, the maids who cleaned and helped in the kitchen, and a washerwoman living above the washhouse in the back courtyard. There was also a new English governess, the redoubtable Margaret Neame — her predecessor, hired at Knebworth, having gone home. There were also two ADCs and an adjutant on his military staff, though they lived elsewhere in the town, as did his secretary Nikolai Johnson, who had taken an apartment on Baggout Street, near the Warsaw railway station, and close to the apartment where Natasha had lived with Wulfert.

But his household had no butler to wait at table, or liveried servants in attendance at formal dinner parties, and in that respect he did not live as grandly as at Knebworth, or could have done at Gatchina palace, where an army of retainers continued to preserve state rooms which in the main only they walked through. Michael made full use of the park, and he took advantage of the gymnasium sited in one of the quadrangles adjoining the main palace, but otherwise he was not seen there at all.

He took no precautions for his personal safety. There were no guards and apart from the low wooden picket fence, the house lay open to the front. When Michael returned home he simply parked his car on the short drive to the side of his house, walked through his front door and stepped into the living room — like every other owner of the villas and his neighbours in that suburban road.

In town, he was a familiar figure in the street and shops; he took his family to the palace church on Sundays. He spoke to the townspeople as freely as they would speak to each other, and regularly attended social gatherings and other like activities of a small community. Evening after evening was spent in committee work on various charities, and when he was convalescing stepdaughter Tata would 'often remember him coming in dead tired' after an exhausting round of lengthy meetings.[1] He was a keen handyman, and when he got up in the morning he would often go first into the garden, to his workshop, and there 'with his sleeves rolled up to the elbow, he would plane, chisel and saw. He loved working on a lathe'.[2] In the evenings his favourite pastime was music, and often he noted in his diary that he had 'played the guitar', sometimes with his aide and fellow enthusiast Prince Vyazemsky, or with Johnson as accompanist on the piano.

One official posted to the garrison was 'astonished by the Grand Duke's approachability and simplicity'. He first encountered him when he went one evening to the local cinema — 'a filthy hovel... a stuffy shed', crowded with ordinary soldiers and townspeople. In the semi-darkness he asked one of the audience if the place in front of him was free; the man said it was. As the official settled down, he realised that the man behind him seemed to be in the uniform of a general. Astonished, he whispered to his neighbour, asking the general's name. The man glanced round. 'What, behind us? Why that's Grand Duke Michael Aleksandrovich', was the reply.[3]

Unusually good-natured, he surprised everyone when he lost his temper. On one occasion, his neighbours were startled to hear him yelling from his windows, and then to see him leaping into the roadway, half-shaved and still in his nightshirt, wielding a whip and bellowing as he broke up a dog fight in front of his house. 'There were blows and curses…in his temper he was quite oblivious to his appearance or dignity.'[4]

In the best sense of the term, Michael was a simple man; sometimes he was too trusting of others. When beggars approached in the street, he would give them money; when asked to provide job references, 'he never refused'. Inevitably his open trust was abused, as when he recommended a man who had been sacked three times for bad conduct.[5] His own shrugging answer to that kind of thing was to say that 'it was impossible to live if one could not trust anybody'.[6]

Other than on official business, Michael went to 'detestable' Petrograd primarily for the theatre, ballet or a concert. In the last three months of 1915, he visited the capital six times,[7] but never to parties there, or to mingle with the bankers, diplomats, politicians, and businessmen who thronged Petrograd; he kept himself within a small circle of close friends. Natasha would go there regularly, for lunch and shopping, but invariably she went on her own.

In the year since her return, Natasha had established an ever-widening circle of friends as she had never been able to do when she had arrived there in 1911 as mistress. Marriage, and having a husband who was a war hero, opened doors that had never opened before. And, to the fury of Tsarskoe Selo, her circle now included three young Grand Dukes who had become regulars at her home in Gatchina. One was Dimitri, eleven years her junior, who had fallen in love with her at first sight in exactly the same way as had Michael. He had seen her on the platform at Baranovichi as she was returning from Lvov in December 1914, and he was returning from *Stavka,* where he now served as a staff officer. Despite his own gallantry award won in the first weeks of the war, Dimitri was cursed with tuberculosis, and was never allowed a battlefield posting again.

Next day, having found out that she was his cousin's wife, and discovering that she lunched regularly in the Astoria Winter Garden, he turned up there, and introduced himself.[8] After that he became a regular visitor to Gatchina. A surprising new friend? In March 1915 the handsome Dimitri had followed her to Moscow, knocked on the door of her suite at the National Hotel, and then confessed that he was in love with her.[9]

It was very flattering to have a second Grand Duke in love with her — more than flattering, extraordinary — but also very awkward. She had come to be very fond of Dimitri, he 24 and she 35, but there could only be one man in her life, and that was, and always would be ever after, Michael. In accepting that, Dimitri told her that he 'had decided to run away from me', she wrote to Michael.[10] Nonetheless, he kept in touch, writing to her regularly as 'your devoted friend' and coming to the Gatchina house frequently, though without saying anything again that might embarrass her.

Grand Duke Boris had also become a member of what a bitter Alexandra called her 'bad set'. Meeting her for the first time when he came to Sunday lunch with his brother Andrew — an established friend of Natasha — in August 1915, he told Michael she was *charmante*.[11] With three Grand Dukes driving out to Gatchina, and with Dimitri's sister Grand Duchess Marie also becoming a regular guest, it was beginning to look as if Gatchina was becoming a rival court. Certainly that is how it appeared to the resentful eyes at Tsarskoe Selo.

Petrograd society was also left in no doubt that Madame Brasova, as she still was, seemed to be rising high. On October 18, 1915, it would have its first sight of Michael and Natasha together in public when they went to a ballet at the imperial Maryinski. The last time Natasha had been there, three years earlier, was when she had been humiliated by a Blue Cuirassier officer, shouting at her for having 'compromised the Grand Duke'; another officer who had dared to go into her box in 1911 had been thrown out of the regiment in disgrace. Now she would have sweet revenge.

The chandelier-lit Maryinski, packed with uniformed officers, men in white tie and tails, and bejewelled ladies, had seen Michael and Boris go into the ornate imperial family box at the rear of the theatre, and Natasha, barred from sitting there, go into a nearby box. But at the interval, the imperial box emptied, and moments later the two Grand Dukes were in her box on the first tier, sipping champagne, and making clear to all those staring up at them that wherever Natasha sat was where they preferred to be. A month later, she was back and the same thing happened, except that Andrew was there also, so that there were now three Grand Dukes joining her in the interval in row 11 of her first tier box.[12]

But Natasha's circle had widened far beyond Petrograd society. At her regular table in the Astoria Winter Garden, she was often to be seen lunching there with Duma deputies. The gossipy French ambassador had already heard enough in his round of the salons and at his own table to know that 'she has been parading very strong liberal opinions for some time. Her circle is frequently open to deputies of the Left. In court quarters she has already been accused of betraying Tsarism — a fact which pleases her enormously, as it makes her views notorious and lays the foundations of her popularity. She becomes more independent every day and says the most audacious things — things which in the mouth of any other would mean twenty years in Siberia!'[13]

In so saying, Paléologue was reflecting the prejudiced views of the dinner tables he frequented, and one persistent source of his intelligence was Princess Paley, who also denigrated Michael no less than she did Natasha. Paléologue had never met either, and never would, so when he said of Michael that he 'had fought bravely' he also dismissed him as 'the feeblest of men',[14] a description almost certainly borrowed from Princess Paley since she would so describe Michael herself. In her cultivation of salon hostesses, she saw her role as promoting the views of her patroness Alexandra, who took no part in the Petrograd social round, and Michael and Natasha were therefore constant targets for her sniping tongue. It won her plaudits in Tsarskoe Selo, and served to confirm her absolute loyalty to the court.

Dimitri Abrikosov, who as a young man in Moscow had been an early admirer of Natasha, and was now in the diplomatic service in Petrograd, became one of her regular lunch guests at Gatchina, and was at the table there one Sunday, with Grand Dukes Boris and Andrew, when the discussion turned to the defeats suffered by the Russian armies and the scandal over the shortage of munitions. Natasha suddenly exploded. 'It was you Romanovs who brought Russia to such a state!' The room hushed 'and the Grand Dukes looked down at their plates'. Afterwards Abrikosov took Natasha aside and told her that 'it was no wonder she was regarded at court as a revolutionist'.[15]

She was anything but, and while she had become friends with a number of Duma deputies they were by no means 'deputies of the left'. Her first Duma friend and regular lunch companion was Count Kapnist, a monarchist albeit one who like most wanted constitutional government, not autocracy — a view which Natasha strongly supported, however distorted that view became when embellished for the benefit of Tsarskoe Selo. But not everything said about her was gossip.

One of the most remarkable statements with which the names of Michael and Natasha were linked politically came at a conference of the majority Progressive Bloc on October 25, 1915, when relations between crown and Duma were at rock bottom. The conference, with the Duma suspended by Nicholas, was in effect the Duma by another name.

The first speaker, a non-party liberal, M. M. Fedorov, was quoted as saying: 'Grand Duke Michael has been told about the situation by a person close to his wife. He has spoken to the Tsar, and says that the Tsarita, Goremykin, and Rasputin are prepared to go as far as closing the Duma.' That was true: Alexandra did not want it suspended, as it was; she wanted it to be shut down permanently, never to be heard of again.

Fedorov then went on to say: 'To the question of whether or not he would be prepared to succeed to the throne, the Grand Duke replied "May this cup pass me by. Of course, if this were, unfortunately to come about, I sympathise with the British system. I can't understand why the Tsar won't take it calmly."'[16]

Aleksandr Kerensky, a leading socialist destined to play a decisive role in the drama to come, was also to recount an incident so astonishing and so unlike Michael that at face value it cannot seem true. 'In the autumn of 1915' he would recall in his memoirs, 'I was visited by an old friend, Count Pavel Tolstoy, the son of one of the Tsar's equerries. He was a close friend of the Tsar's brother, Grand Duke Michael, whom he had known since childhood.' So far, so good. He then went on: 'He told me that he had come at the request of the Grand Duke, who knew that I had connections with the working class and left-wing parties and who wanted to know how the workers would react if he took over from his brother, the Tsar.'[17]

Michael would never have authorised nor suggested such an approach to Kerensky. At the same time, Kerensky had no reason to invent it. The question is therefore whether Count Tolstoy went to see him on his own initiative, or was sent there by someone else — and the only person who was likely to have done that was Natasha. Since Kerensky dodged the answer, nothing of this encounter reached Michael's ears and so it never went any further. However, the probable truth is that Natasha was behind this, and that when Tolstoy reported that he had drawn a blank, the question was buried.

Although Michael never sought nor desired his brother's downfall, he feared for his future if Nicholas did not bring about change, curb the power of Alexandra and dismiss Rasputin.

Shortly after returning from his week at Mogilev, Michael sat on the verandah at Nikolaevskaya Street one Sunday evening and talked to Dimitri Abrikosov about the future. Everyone else had gone for a drive.

'He told me that he often thought how difficult it was for his brother, who sincerely wanted to do only what was good for the people, but who was hindered by his wife. Several times he had tried to convey to his brother what people were saying about him, and about the dangerous influence of the Empress...' Michael thought that 'Nicholas was indifferent to his fate, leaving everything in the hands of God, but under the influence of Rasputin, God had assumed a strange shape.' As dusk came, Abrikosov turned on the light. 'I was shocked by the utter despair on the pale face before me...'[18] Abrikosov, in the weeks he had come to know Michael, came to think of him as far superior to Natasha, despite the greater force of her personality. 'I have never met another man so uncorrupted and noble in nature', was his final judgement.[19]

Whatever he told Abrikosov in confidence, Michael never said anything critical of his brother in public. When the British consul Bruce Lockhart met him in Moscow, at a conference about improving the railway system — critical to the war effort — he observed that Michael 'talked quite freely about the war' but made only one comment which could be thought to have political overtones.

'Thank God', he said, 'the atmosphere at the front is so much better than the atmosphere of St Petersburg'. The diplomat left Michael thinking that here 'was a prince who would have made an excellent constitutional monarch'.[20]

This was also the image which Natasha indirectly projected among her contacts in the Duma by her own support of the reforms the 'constitutionalists' sought. If Michael were Regent, in place of Alexandra, all would be accomplished. Much was inferred, but what could not be ignored was the stark contrast between the wife of the Tsar and the wife of the Tsar's brother.

Both were strong-minded and opinionated; one hated the Duma and wanted unrestricted autocratic power; both were thought of as having a decisive influence over their husbands. Inevitably Natasha was seen as an ally by those who saw Alexandra as an enemy.

Public recognition of the difference between the two — and indeed the difference between the brothers — came in February, 1916, at the re-opening of the Duma at the Tauride Palace. Abrikosov escorted Natasha there and into the box reserved for distinguished guests, though several members of the Duma were also seated there. Abrikosov noted that 'from the respect they showed her it was obvious she was becoming known in Duma circles'.[21]

That day was an historic occasion, for the Tsar had agreed to be present. On the few times he had addressed the Duma over the past ten years he had always done so at the Winter Palace — now, for the first time he was not demanding that they went to him, but instead he was going to them. Although it was widely hoped that this was to be signal for a new relationship between crown and Duma it would prove, in fact, no more than a ploy to smooth over the introduction of his newly-appointed prime minister, Boris Stürmer, pushed forward by Alexandra and blessed by Rasputin.

The old prime minister Goremykin had finally been retired in January; Stürmer, at sixty-eight, was only ten years younger, but Alexandra has pressed his appointment on Nicholas because he 'very much values Grigory wh. is a great thing'.[22] In the real world he was damningly seen as 'worse than a mediocrity' with a 'third-rate intellect, mean spirit, low character, doubtful honesty, no experience and no idea of State business'.[23]

To give himself moral support at the Duma, Nicholas took along Michael; it was their first State appearance together in the capital since Michael's marriage and exile. Michael, pushed to the sidelines since his return to Russia, was now being brought centre-stage for the convenience of the moment. In the eight years in which she had known Michael, this was the first time that Natasha, sitting in her box, had ever seen the two brothers together. It would be the only day she — or any of the Duma members present — would do so.

That morning Michael and Natasha had breakfasted with Duma deputy Count Kapnist, who had then escorted Natasha to the Duma and the waiting Abrikosov while Michael went off to the Pavilion at the Tauride Palace to join his brother at the ceremonial entrance into the adjacent Catherine Hall. Nicholas was 'deadly pale and his hands were trembling with agitation'.[24] He was not looking forward to the ceremony.

The Catherine Hall was packed, with diplomats as well as Duma members, the mood hopeful that the Tsar's visit would prove the beginning of change for the better, an expectation encouraged by the presence of Michael, whose support for the Duma was taken as fact by those lobbied by Natasha over the past year. Duma members wanted the Tsar to be no less supportive. As the influential Kadet leader Pavel Milyukov put it to Paléologue, what Nicholas had never understood was that his party was not 'the opposition *against* His Majesty but His Majesty's Opposition'.[25] Perhaps today he would alter that view. Most hoped so.

After a *Te Deum*, throughout which Nicholas stood pale, his mouth tightened and his discomfort obvious, he made a short welcoming speech, 'stopping and stumbling over every word'. To Paléologue it was 'painful to watch'.[26] It was also disappointing for those members who hoped that he was going to announce some important reform. There was nothing of that; what he had offered was a gesture, but no more.

When Nicholas left, Michael stayed on, taking a seat in the semi-circular assembly hall for the whole of the three-hour session, which closed with the Progressive Bloc calling for a government of 'public confidence'.

Michael thought that Serge Shidlovsky, the Progressive's leader, 'spoke well', but he was unimpressed by the new prime minister Stürmer, 'who could hardly be heard'.[27] Mikhail Rodzyanko, president of the State Duma, was also dismissive of Stürmer, who left the speaker's tribune 'amid dead silence...from the very outset Stürmer revealed himself as an utter nonentity'.[28]

That evening, Michael and Natasha were also at the opening session of the 192-strong Council of State, of which half the members were appointed by the Tsar and the others by an amalgam of institutions, including the Church, universities, landowners and the nobility. Once again, Nicholas turned up briefly, was escorted into the meeting room by Michael, made another short and no more successful speech, and then departed back to Tsarskoe Selo, having been received in 'an atmosphere of cold officialdom'.[29]

Having said goodbye to his brother, Michael returned to the assembly room and joined Natasha's box where she was sitting with her friend Count Kapnist. As earlier in the day, he stayed for the full session.[30]

Merely by being there, in the company of a Duma deputy, Michael was making his own political statement and endorsing as clearly as he could his support for a new start in Russian government. But at Tsarskoe Selo that would be thought of only as confirmation that it was time for him to get back to the war. As Alexandra had already told Nicholas, 'I assure you that it is far better that he should be in his place there, than here with her bad set'.[31]

In turn, that 'bad set' was wondering how best to get rid of Alexandra.

7. WAR ON TWO FRONTS

MICHAEL went back to the war immediately after the reopening of the Duma in February 1916. Promoted to lieutenant-general, the 2nd Cavalry Corps, his new command, comprised the six regiments of his old Savage Division, as well as a Cossack division and a Don Cossack brigade. The corps was part of the Seventh Army under General Shcherbachev and its front was on the far left of the Russian line, south of Tarnopol and therefore in the same general area where Michael had been in 1915.[1]

Michael had spent Christmas with his family at Brasovo, their first time at his country estate since the spring of 1912.[2] Nicholas had at last given up his control of Michael's assets, his manifesto in October 1915 removing the 'madman' order imposed after his marriage. In the three years in which Brasovo had been subject to the guardianship order it had been sadly neglected, as Michael discovered. His former ADC Mordvinov, appointed by the Tsar, had proved a bad manager and he was dilatory in rendering his accounts, in handing over estate papers, and jeopardising urgent repair work.[3]

Natasha complained endlessly about inefficiencies in his personal office in Petrograd, based in rooms set aside in his embankment hospital, and about the way in which, in his absence, his various retainers, servants, and appointees were either incompetent, greedy, or light-fingered. Every month Michael had money transferred to England to pay the rent and bills on his Paddockhurst estate — the lease would not end until September 1916 — but 'they never send it on time, there is always a delay of about two weeks.' [4] When their hospital in Gatchina was temporarily closed for repairs, Natasha reported that the supply manager continued ordering provisions for it, selling them to local shopkeepers and keeping the cash. He succeeded in stealing a whole 'railway car full of meat, cereals and flour'.[5]

Petitions to his office from wounded soldiers were also causing difficulties. A month after Michael returned to the front they were running at some sixty per day and rising. Michael was generous but, as Natasha warned, the word had got round, so that every soldier satisfied brought in other soldiers eager to claim the same. 'You can't support the entire wounded army on your own money', Natasha pointed out. There had to be a budget 'otherwise there will never be enough'.[6]

Michael had arranged that Natasha had her own money, so that she was financially independent, with enough funds to do charitable works of her own choosing. One of her interests was a hospital in Kiev, funded by her but bearing Michael's name. A large portrait of her had been hung in the entrance hall, but in June 1916, arriving there unannounced, she found it had been taken down and hidden in a back room. The hospital was expecting a visit by the Dowager Empress, who had moved to Kiev to be near to her daughter Olga and her hospital*, and the management had decided that sight of Natasha's picture was likely to cause offence to her disapproving mother-on-law.

Natasha was incensed. Not only was it maintained entirely at her cost, but she was constantly sending gifts there both for wounded soldiers, and staff. 'It was extremely disrespectful...for my own part I will complete detach myself from this hospital and if they want more money they can ask the people whose pictures do cover their walls.'[7]

Two weeks later she was complaining bitterly to Michael that

*Michael and his disapproving sister Olga had not spoken since his marriage four years earlier to Natasha. However, they met briefly in Kiev on May 22, 1916, kissed and made up — Olga then having herself been divorced, and about to marry her longstanding lover Captain Kulikovsky, abandoning the high moral ground she had taken until then. Michael would not go to her wedding, nor see her again.

even his own hospital in Petrograd was the subject of official slights, with attempts to remove his name from it. Natasha blamed Alexandra. 'She hates you and does all she can to prevent your name even being mentioned. Petrograd is full of hospitals bearing the names of the Heir, Olga, Nikolasha and others — and in your name there is only one, which they are trying to get rid of. And that's a hospital where the officers' ward exists entirely on your money, so it is virtually your hospital...'[8]

Proof of just how petty and vindictive Alexandra was being came only a few days later. Just before Michael had returned to the front, he and Natasha had gone to the studios of fashionable Boissonnas & Eggler and had a series of pictures together, as well as separately. Later, a leading Petrograd society magazine opted to feature one of her photographs on its front page, together with a glowing description of her hospital work. Encouraged by that, Boissonnas & Eggler decided to mount a window exhibition devoted to Michael and Natasha, using the pictures taken in February. He was a war hero; she was beautiful and increasingly celebrated — in combination the studio thought that would be good business for them.

Natasha at thirty-five, though it was her good fortune to seem younger than her years, was looking better than ever before. She turned heads wherever she went, as the French ambassador would confirm for himself when he chanced upon her for the first time at Soloviev's, a bookshop in the Liteiny, near to the apartment in which Natasha had spent so many unhappy months four years earlier, in 1912.

Paléologue was already in the shop and glanced up as she walked in. Though he did not know who she was, he could not take his eyes off her. Leaving the bookshop he saw a 'very smart car' parked behind his. His chauffeur, noting his interest, asked him: 'Didn't your Excellency recognise the lady?' Paléologue shook his head. She is 'the wife of His Imperial Highness the Grand Duke Michael Aleksandrovich', said the chauffeur.[9] Paléologue needed to hear no more. The woman he had seen in the shop was not only extraordinarily beautiful, but from what he had been told at the dinner tables, dangerous. He would never see her again, but he would never forget her. That night he devoted his diary to her charms.

As I was examining several fine 18th-century French editions in the back of his empty shop, I saw a slender young woman of about thirty come in and take a seat at a table on which an album of prints was laid out. She was a delight to watch. Her whole style revealed a quiet, personal and refined taste...Her pure and aristocratic face is charmingly modelled and she has light velvety eyes. Round her neck a string of superb pearls sparkled in the light... There was a dignified, sinuous and soft gracefulness about her every movement... [10]

That portrait was precisely the kind that Alexandra was determined to destroy, which was why she was so enraged when told that the exhibition at Boissonnas & Eggler was drawing crowds. Her immediate response was to order Prince Obolensky, governor of the imperial palace, to have the exhibition closed down. On Friday morning, July 15, 1916, he arrived with the police, who then stood by to ensure that the studio cleared the window.

'I cannot tell you how incensed I am at such disgraceful treatment,' she wrote to Michael. It was humiliation, with 'the public driving past to witness how the shop was cleared of our pictures with the police being present and all the stir it created...' [11]

Michael was equally outraged, and also furious with the palace governor, who had served under him in the Chevalier Gardes, but who still followed the Tsarskoe Selo line that Natasha was unspeakable and a menace to the rightful order. 'I was greatly appalled' he wrote. 'That's such impudence, such disgraceful lack of tact...it's not for nothing that I have always despised Petrograd high society...there are no people more devious than they are; with a few exceptions, they are all scum.' [12]

To Natasha, his appointment to command the 2nd Cavalry Corps also served to show that Tsarskoe Selo's aim was to keep him as far away from the capital as they could. 'None of the other Grand Dukes sits in such a hole as you do, so why should you be worse off than the others?'[13] Petrograd was crowded with braided Guards officers stationed only a few hours from the capital, and even *Stavka* was only a day away. 'They shove you into the worst possible place' because, she said, 'they want to get rid of you.'[14]

Michael objected to the idea that he was only at the front because of court machinations. 'It is a matter of conscience, too. I would be ashamed to be somewhere on the home front, when the Russian people are shedding their blood for their country and for future peace'. If the war had any purpose now, he added, it was as 'a war for peace'.[15]

But even he could not close his eyes to some snubs. There had been no announcement of his appointment to command a Corps, and in July 1916 he found that his name was not included in the list of ADCs to the Tsar. As a Grand Duke it was the convention that on promotion to lieutenant-general he would simultaneously be made an ADC to the Tsar — an adjutant-general. In itself it meant little, but he would have worn different epaulettes, and aiguillettes in gold rather than silver.

Although privately Michael remained indifferent to such distinctions, he had ordered the gold insignia, because his Corps expected to see him wearing them, and that having been promoted he would then have a 'formal position in the Retinue'.[16] It was only then that he found that he was to be the exception: he had not been made an ADC. That was a public slap in the face; it was also in his mind an insult to his Corps.

An oversight? Coming as it did at the same time as the police were removing his photographs from the shop window, Natasha thought not. 'The Tsar is deliberately set against you', she said.[17]

'All I will say', replied Michael tersely, 'is that it is not a misunderstanding, but was deliberately done that way. Therefore I believe that no one should remind or ask the Sovereign about it, not even in ten years' time.'[18]

MICHAEL's corps was involved in heavy fighting all that summer. The Brusilov Offensive, so called because it was his south-western armies which launched it, promised to reverse the defeats of the last twelve months, and breakthrough the Carpathians to Vienna — a repeat of the hopes of April 1915. By the end of June, Michael noted that the 'approximate count of prisoners in the whole offensive was 5,620 officers and 266,000 men, 312 guns, 833 machine-guns'.[19] The Austrians had been mauled, but then so had the Russians.

On both the western and the eastern fronts in the First World War, casualties were horrific; indeed when Michael was recording his statistics, the British had suffered 58,000 casualties, half the men involved, and 20,000 of them dead on just the *first day* of their offensive on the Somme. In the previous year, the total casualties on the western front — French, British, German — had been two million. In the past few months the battle of Verdun had turned into a bloodbath.

Michael hated the slaughter on both sides. The sight of a dying Czech prisoner in a field dressing station could sadden him, enemy or not. 'There are so many such unfortunate heroes who are dying away from their country and worse still — away from their nearest and dearest and in strangers' hands. I was sorry for that poor Czech as much as for anyone else', he told Natasha.[20]

As the summer wore on the casualties on the Russian front continued to mount, but the prize slipped away. Elation was followed by disappointment. Brusilov was one of the best generals in any army in that war, but although the Russian line had been pushed forward, overall there was little to show for the sacrifice. The Guards Army, judged the best troops of all, were wasted by clumsy generalship — one corps ruined by incompetence on the part of its newly-appointed commander Grand Duke Paul 'whose only failing was that he knew nothing about military affairs',[21] commented Brusilov. Paul had been stricken with gallstones, and was in no condition to go to war. After the mishandling of his corps he was quietly removed from his post and returned unheroically to Tsarskoe Selo, which he would have been better never to have left.

In contrast, Michael would earn his second high gallantry award — the red enamel cross of the Order of St Vladimir with Swords 'for distinction in action against the enemy'.[22] As a corps commander he was, of course, less exposed to personal danger than before, but occasionally there were brushes on the frontline. On August 23, returning from a conference at his old Savage Division headquarters, his driver took the wrong turning and headed straight for the Austrian lines. After half a mile 'we were bombarded by an Austrian outpost…several bullets whizzed by'. To get them out of it, 'I took the wheel because I knew how to drive better'.[23] Fortunately, unlike most generals, Michael preferred to sit at the front, not in the back, so it was a matter of only a few frantic seconds before he had thrust aside his hapless corporal, and was reversing at high speed back down the road. He made no mention of that to Natasha, but he did admit that 'there has been very severe and very bloody fighting all this time'.[24]

There was then a lull in his sector. He took the opportunity to travel to Mogilev, arriving there on August 31. He had last seen his brother in March when Nicholas came south to Kamanets-Podolsky to inspect units. Michael had told his brother then that when his next appointment came along he would like a transfer to headquarters. Nicholas would have none of it. The two parted on strained terms.

Afterwards, Nicholas wrote to Alexandra, telling him about his request. 'Then I began to preach to him about our father, about the sense of duty, example to others and so forth. When I had finished and we had said goodbye to each other, he then asked me coldly and quite calmly not to forget his request, as if I had not spoken at all. I was furious!'[25]

Michael, who normally recorded every meeting with Nicholas, made no mention in his diary of seeing him at Kamenets-Podolsky. He would not speak to him for another five months, and when next in Tsarskoe Selo, during a brief trip home in May

1916, he would not trouble to visit the Tsar's Alexander Palace. However, he did bump into Alexandra. There was no enthusiasm on either side. He stopped for a moment, politely, then hurried on. Alexandra simply reported to Nicholas that 'going to church, met Misha, stopped, talked a minute, and then he went back to Gatchina'.[26]

At *Stavka*, he and Nicholas met privately in the Tsar's salon before tea. This time there were no lectures about 'remembering his duty' — awkward, given the second high gallantry award on Michael's chest — and the Tsar this time conceded what he had refused to consider in March: that with his next appointment, Michael could join *Stavka*. He was also belatedly promoted to Adjutant-General.

This was not a signal of change in the family war conducted from Tsarskoe Selo. What Michael did not tell his brother was that Natasha, whom he had not seen for three months, had also come to Mogilev and was staying in his carriage. In the four days she was there she kept well away from the headquarters proper, going for walks in the town, and having lunch in the restaurant of the *Bristol Hotel*. She also went to the cinema, while Michael was dining with his brother.

It was after Michael had left that Nicholas found out about Natasha. His source was a furious Alexandra. 'You know Misha's wife was at Mogilev!!' she exploded in a letter to him. 'Georgi (*Grand Duke George Mikhailovich*) told Paul he sat near her at the cynema (*sic*). Find out where she lived (perhaps wagon) & how long, & forbid strictly it happening again.'[27] It would not happen again. Michael never took up an appointment at headquarters and the next time he saw Nicholas it would be in circumstances so desperate that both had more important matters to worry about.

WITH the summer offensive having ground to a halt, and stalemate on the south-western front, Michael's corps would spend that autumn of 1916 refitting and preparing itself for what looked like a long winter. So leaving Mogilev with Natasha, he took her to Brasovo for the start of an extended leave, his first that year. They arrived on September 4, 1916, delighted to be in a place into which the outside world could never intrude. Natasha had worked wonders in the house, decorating it and refurnishing so that it was now better than it had ever been. Michael went fishing on the mill pond, catching 150 fish in one morning in a big sweep-net, and then with his aide Vyazemsky he chopped down thirty-six trees near the house.[28] The two children joined them, and leaving Brasovo they went on to Moscow, staying at the National Hotel. After six weeks they were back in Gatchina, with Michael preparing himself to go back to the front.

It was not to be. Suddenly he succumbed to a fever and no sooner had he recovered than he went down again with a new attack of his 'damned stomach pains'; a week later he was still ill. After being examined by a team of specialists in Petrograd he was advised to go to the warm Crimea and rest. A month of sitting doing nothing and he would feel a different man; if he ignored their advice and returned to the army, he would not be doing either the army or himself a favour.

Given that, he had little choice. But before he departed there was one thing he had to do, and that was to write to Nicholas. His weeks back from the front had exposed him to the reality of public opinion in Russia and what he had heard and seen had alarmed him greatly. In the months he had been at the front, the mood had darkened much more than he had realised. He had known enough to have warned his brother face to face about the political risks he was taking; now, having heard so much more in these past weeks on the home-front, for the first time he did so in writing. On November 11, 1916, he went into his study at Nikolaevskaya Street, to tell his brother that time was running out.

'A year ago…you invited me to share my thoughts with you candidly whenever I felt it called for. The time has come…I am deeply concerned and worried by what is happening around us.

There has been a shocking alteration in the mood of the most loyal people; on all sides I observe a way of thinking which fills me with the most serious apprehension not only for you and for the fate of our family, but even for the integrity of the state order.

'The public hatred for certain people who allegedly are close to you and who are forming part of the present government has, to my amazement, brought together the right, the left, and the moderate; and this hatred, along with the demands for changes are already openly expressed at every opportunity. Please don't think that I am writing this under someone's influence (*he meant Natasha*): these impressions I have tried to verify in conversations with people of various circles — level-headed people whose loyalty and devotion are beyond any doubt and, alas, my apprehensions have been confirmed.'

Having underlined the fact that he was speaking from his own experience, not merely repeating what Natasha and her 'bad set' had told him — though he could have no doubt that Alexandra would blame her anyway — he did not mince his words thereafter:

'I have come to the conviction that we are standing on a volcano, and that the least spark, the least incorrect step could provoke a catastrophe for you, for us all and for Russia…it seems to me that, by removing the most hated persons and replacing them with unblemished people, towards whom there is no evident mistrust on the part of society (which now means Russia as a whole), you will find a good way out of the situation in which we now are; and for such a decision you will certainly find support both in the Council of State and the Duma…It seems to me that the people who are urging you to follow an opposite course are concerned far more with keeping their own posts than with protecting you and Russia. Half-measures in this case are only prolonging the crisis and thus making it more acute.

'I am deeply confident that everything that is said in this letter will be confirmed by all those among our relatives who are at least slightly familiar with the moods pervading the country and society.

I am afraid these moods are not so strongly felt and perceived at *Stavka*…the majority of those who come with reports will never tell you the unpleasant truth, for they are protecting their own interests…I cannot help feeling that if anything happens inside Russia, it will be echoed with a catastrophe as regards the war. That is why, painful as it is for me to do it, my love for you has urged me to share all my worries with you without keeping anything back.'[29]

He could hardly be clearer; and it was not necessary to mention Alexandra. He had done that often enough before. Would Nicholas pay any heed? Everything Michael had written was true, his advice sound, and his forecast of the catastrophe which awaited if nothing was done was to prove tragically accurate. In the event, Nicholas never replied.

Six days later, on November 17, Michael and Natasha set off to stay at his sister Xenia's house on the shores of the Black Sea, twelve miles from Yalta. They would be there a month, before returning to Brasovo for Christmas and a houseful of guests invited to join them. They arrived in Brasovo on December 20, shortly before the children, staff and their house party arrived from Petrograd.

Of their guests, only one — Grand Duke Dimitri — failed to turn up. As they would discover, he had been arrested.

8. MURDER MOST FAIR

MICHAEL'S warning letter to his brother came at what proved to be the beginning of the end for Nicholas and Alexandra. On the battlefield the summer offensive had produced only stalemate at the cost of horrific casualty figures. Industrial and politically-motivated strikes had been almost unknown in the first months of the war, but by the end of 1916 the number of strikes would reach a million, double the number in the previous year. Facing their third winter of war, Russians now looked inwards and not outwards. Talk of betrayal was commonplace, with many convinced that the source of that treachery lay in the boudoir of the German-born Empress in the government she had largely created, and which did her will.

Alexandra was no traitor, but what was true was that she and Rasputin now dictated political affairs almost without hinder from the Tsar at Stavka. Two of the best ministers who had survived her original purge were now dismissed. The first to go was the effective war minister Polivanov, ludicrously described by Alexandra as 'simply a revolutionist.'[1] The shrewd British military observer, Colonel Alfred Knox, judged him to be the 'ablest military organiser in Russia' and his departure 'a disaster'.[2]

The second to be shown the door was the long-serving and respected foreign minister Sergei Sazanov. He had long been in her sights — why is he 'such a pancake?' she had asked Nicholas — after he complained to the Tsar about 'the dangerous part that the Empress had begun to play since Rasputin gained possession of her will and intellect.'[3] There was no replacement; the obsequious prime minister Boris Stürmer now became his own foreign minister in a government which had fallen into the hands of men who, in the majority, were appointed simply because they had been approved by 'our Friend'.

On the front-line, Michael was appalled. 'We were all greatly surprised here', he wrote to Natasha. 'I did not know Sazanov well but it was apparent that he was trusted and now with Stürmer, I am afraid we are in for some rotten business...such unsuitable people are chosen for such responsible posts, it's too awful for words.'[4]

One such appointee he had in mind was the new 50-year-old interior minister Aleksandr Protopopov, who had been a vice-president in the Duma, and who overnight became a convert to Alexandra's mystical autocracy; increasingly deranged, he was destined to become as hated as his mentor Rasputin.

Michael was not the only one in the Romanov family to despair at Alexandra's disastrous conduct of government. His warning letter of November 11 was echoed by others two weeks later, to no greater effect. Grand Duke George Mikhailovich and his brother Nicholas —known as 'Bimbo'— both wrote to the Tsar supporting Michael's views in similar terms.

George, reporting that the 'hatred for Stürmer is extraordinary', begged the Tsar to 'form a responsible ministry', for only that 'can avert a general catastrophe'.[5] Bimbo was even more outspoken about the empress. 'You trust her', he wrote, 'but what she tells you is not the truth; she is only repeating what has been cleverly suggested to her...You are on the eve of new troubles...Believe me, if I insist so much on your freeing yourself from the chains that have been forged, I do so...only in the hope of saving you and saving the throne of our dear country from the most serious and irreparable consequences.[6]

By chance, this letter fell into the hands of Alexandra, unread by the Tsar. Her response was a furious attack on Bimbo — 'am utterly disgusted...He has always hated & spoken badly of me... he is the incarnation of all that's evil. Sweety mine, you must back me up for your and Baby's sake…We must show that we have no fear & are firm. Wify is your staunch One & stands as a rock behind you.'[7]

Unfortunately, Alexandra was not a rock but a millstone. Her elder sister Ella was among those who knew it. After the assassination of her husband Serge in 1905 she had retreated from the world and had set up her own order of nuns. Alarmed by the mounting public outcry against the empress, she had gone to Tsarskoe Selo from her convent in Moscow intent on making Alexandra see reason. However, as soon as she mentioned Rasputin, Alexandra coldly cut her short. Rising, the empress called a servant and ordered her sister to leave.

On reaching Petrograd a shaken Ella went to the Yusupov palace on the Moika; Prince Felix Yusupov, son-in-law of Michael's sister Xenia, was waiting for her with his wife Irina, eager to hear how her meeting had gone. She came into their private drawing room trembling and in tears. 'She drove me away like a dog!' she cried. 'Poor Nicky. Poor Russia!' [8] The two sisters would never see each other again.

Yet none of this served to penetrate the calm of Nicholas, who ignored it all, and who appeared helpless against the tirades of his wife. Dimitri told Felix Yusupov that while at the Stavka he had become convinced that 'the drugs administered to the Tsar were paralysing his will power and were given with this intention.'[9]

Rasputin seemed to confirm this, telling Yusupov that 'the Emperor is given a tea which causes Divine grace to descend on him. His heart was filled with peace, everything looked good and cheerful to him.' The 'tea' was provided by a quack doctor called Badmaev, using 'herbs provided by nature herself…God makes them grow, that's why they have Divine properties.'[10]

Paléologue, the worldly French ambassador in Petrograd, who knew Badmaev as 'an ingenious disciple of the Mongol sorcerers', concluded that judging by its effects, the 'tea' must be a mixture of henbane and hashish for 'every time that the Tsar has used this drug…he has not only recovered sleep and appetite, but experienced a general feeling of well-being, a delightful sense of increased vigour and a curious euphoria.'[11]

Given that, it was clear that whatever the protests to him, the Tsar would never assert himself against his wife, and would never get rid of Rasputin — 'the principal scoundrel', as Michael put it. In which case, he would have to be removed by others. He would have to be killed.

FOR most of Russia's élite, the death of Rasputin was the best news of the year. He was murdered in the early hours of Saturday, December 17, at the Yusupov's magnificent palace on the Moika, which among other things boasted a theatre which could seat 1,000, as was to be expected in a family which was richer than any of the Romanovs. Apart from Prince Felix Yusupov and his co-conspirator Grand Duke Dimitri, three others were involved — Vladimir Purishkevich, a right-wing member of the Duma, Dr Lazovert, an army doctor, and Captain Serge Sukhotin, a friend of Yusupov.

As a preliminary to the murder, Yusupov cultivated Rasputin's friendship, and in so doing found him boastfully frank. Alexandra 'has a wise, strong mind, and I can get anything and everything from her'. Nicholas was 'a simple soul...he is made for family life, to admire nature and flowers, but not to reign'. As for the ministers, 'all owe their positions to me...they know very well that if they don't obey me, they'll come to a bad end...All I have to do to enforce my will is to bang my hand on the table.'[12]

He also told Yusupov about the future. 'We'll make Alexandra regent during her son's minority. As for him, we'll send him to Livadia for a rest. He'll be glad to go, he's worn out and needs a rest...The Tsarina is a very wise woman, a second Catherine the Great. Anyway, she's been running everything lately and, you'll see, the more she does, the better things will be. She's promised to begin by sending away all those chatterboxes at the Duma.'[13]

Rasputin condemned himself. The plan was to poison him, lacing cakes and drink with cyanide potassium provided by Dr.

Lazovert. The bait they offered Rasputin was Yusupov's wife Irina — she was eager to meet him, he was told; in truth, she had gone off to the Crimea for Christmas.

A basement was hurriedly converted into a dining room. Yusupov collected Rasputin from his apartment on Gorokhovaya Street on Friday evening, December 16, and drove him to the Moika. Taking him into the basement dining room he told Rasputin that Irina would join him as soon as she could get rid of her last guests upstairs; to keep up the pretence of a party, the other plotters were talking noisily in the room above and playing 'Yankee Doodle' on a gramophone.[14]

Yusupov handed out cakes, which Rasputin devoured with obvious relish, while drinking glass after glass of poisoned wine, firstly Crimean then Madeira. To Yusupov's horrified amazement, neither the cakes nor the wine had any apparent effect. Two hours after his arrival, Rasputin appeared no worse than before. Making an excuse that he wanted Irina to come down, Yusupov hurried frantically upstairs to report that the poison had failed entirely. Aghast, the plotters swiftly decided that the only alternative now was to shoot him. Dimitri offered to do it, but when Yusupov insisted that this was his task, he handed him his revolver.[15]

Yusupov went back downstairs, gave Rasputin another glass of Madeira and, after suggesting that they look closely at a crucifix on a cabinet, shot him through the chest. Rasputin gave 'a wild scream' and crumpled onto the bearskin rug. When the others rushed down at the sound of the shot, they found Rasputin lying on his back, his blouse bloodstained, and his face twitching. In a moment he was motionless; the doctor examined him and pronounced him dead.

The plotters went back upstairs, leaving the body in the basement. Dimitri, the doctor and the captain then drove off to Gorokhovaya Street, the captain in Rasputin's overcoat and cap, so as to pretend that Rasputin had returned home safely. Dimitri then went to collect his closed car in which the body was to be taken away to be dumped in the frozen Neva. It was reasoned that the corpse, weighted down with chains, would stay hidden under the ice until the spring thaw. It would be at least three months before he could possibly be found.

While Yusupov and Purishkevich were waiting for Dimitri to return, Yusupov went back to the basement to check on the body. As he bent over him he was horrified to see an eye open, and then with a violent effort the 'dead man' leapt to his feet and grabbed at Yusupov, his hands reaching out to strangle him. Yusupov desperately struggled to free himself, then rushed upstairs to Purishkevich.

The two men came back just in time to see Rasputin, 'gasping and roaring like a wounded animal',[16] stumbling out through a side door in the basement to the courtyard outside. Running after him, Purishkevich fired two shots, and then two more. The fleeing Rasputin collapsed into the snow. This time he must be dead. Although he had clearly survived the first bullet, he could not survive four more.

However, the shots had been heard, and a curious policeman arrived to find out the cause. Yusupov stood so that he could not see the body and told the policeman that there had been some 'horseplay' and a dog had been shot. The man went away, but returned after his superiors queried his explanation. This time, Purishkevich confronted him and boldly told him what had actually happened, but adding that 'if you love your country and your Tsar, you will keep your mouth shut'.[17]

The man nodded, as if in promise, turned and went away. After he had gone, Dimitri and the others returned. Desperate to get rid of the body, they bundled it into Dimitri's car, and raced off through the dark, early-morning streets to Petrovsky Island where they realised that in their haste they had forgotten the chains intended to weigh down the body. It was too late to do anything about that. At a bridge they took the body and threw it into the icy Neva below.

Two days later, on Monday December 19, searching police found the corpse, visible just below the ice, with one arm outstretched. A post-mortem examination found there was water in his lungs, suggesting that he was still alive when he was thrown into the river.[18] Nevertheless, poisoned, shot or drowned, it came to the same thing. The hated Rasputin was no more.

THERE was never any chance that the identity of those involved in the murder would remain unknown. The policeman who had spoken to Purishkevich filed a full report; two servants had seen the body in the courtyard; and at Tsarskoe Selo they knew that Rasputin was going to the Yusupov palace that Friday evening, because he had announced it. By early Saturday evening, hardly more than twelve hours after his body was dumped in the Neva, Petrograd was alive with rumours of his death — at seven p.m. the French ambassador Paléologue was noting the details of it all.[19]

It was about that time that Dimitri went to the Michael Theatre, taking his place in a box as if nothing had happened. He would not be there long, fleeing to 'escape the ovation of the audience.' And when he got back to his palace on the Nevsky Prospekt it was to find 'people kneeling in prayer'; he had become so much a hero that in churches across the country candles were being lit in his honour before icons of St. Dimitri.

This was not what he and Yusupov had intended. The murder planned to be kept secret for months had become public knowledge even before the discovery of the body. Yusupov, who had intended to go off to the Crimea to the house just vacated by Michael and Natasha, was ordered to stay in the capital; next day at lunchtime, Dimitri, who was about to leave to spend Christmas with Michael and Natasha at Brasova, found himself 'under house arrest'. In both instances the order came from the Empress — as ever, assuming powers she did not properly have. Yusupov later claimed that Alexandra's first instinct was to have Dimitri shot.[20]

Dimitri, in fact, was at risk of being killed in a revenge attack at his palace on the Nevsky Prospekt. At the beginning of the war he had given it over and it was now the Anglo-Russian hospital, staffed by British doctors and nurses; however he maintained an apartment on an upstairs floor. While he was there, a gang of armed men, probably sent by the interior minister Protopopov, arrived to hunt him down — but went away after the British staff convinced them that Dimitri was not in the building. Troops were then sent to guard the palace from any further threats.[21]

Rasputin was buried in near-secrecy at Tsarskoe Selo on Friday, December 23, on a plot of land owned by Alexandra's devoted companion Anna Vyrubova, four days after his corpse was pulled from the Neva, and with a grief-stricken Alexandra pinning a farewell note to his body. [22]

Afterwards the punishment Nicholas decreed for Dimitri was his immediate exile to Kasvin, on the Persian front. Yusupov was banished to his estate in Kursk. However, Purishkevich was deemed too powerful and escaped punishment entirely, as did the others in consequence.[23]

WAITING for Dimitri at Brasova, Michael and Natasha did not know that he had been arrested until the arrival from Petrograd of other guests joining them for Christmas. Michael had written in his diary on the day Rasputin's body was found that 'we read in the papers that Grigory Rasputin was assassinated in Petrograd',[24] though there were no details, and thereafter the newspapers were banned from reporting more. However, when their guests and staff arrived, they brought them all the rumours from the capital.

Natasha's 13-year-old daughter Tata, whose schoolgirl crush on the handsome Dimitri remained as strong as the day he had first walked through the door of the Gatchina villa two years earlier, 'was thrilled to the core' on learning that 'my darling Dimitri' was among the plotters, though downcast when she realised that not only would he miss Christmas but that it might be years before any of them would see him again.[25]

Although Natasha had often talked to Dimitri about the need

to get rid of Rasputin — as had Michael — neither were privy to the plot to murder him. But had Natasha, in particular, influenced his decision? Alexandra certainly thought so, believing that she and her 'bad set' bore some responsibility, hardly surprisingly since she included Dimitri among them. Five months earlier she had written to Nicholas about Dimitri: 'Don't let him go to that lady so often — such society is his ruin — nothing but flattery and he likes it...and don't let him be too free with his tongue either.'[26]

What would have confirmed her suspicions about Natasha's role was that as soon as he arrived in faraway Persia, to begin his exile, Dimitri wrote to her in Gatchina. 'Natasha, dearest, how often I remember now our charming conversations, how much I miss them, be happy and do not forget me...'[27] A second letter arrived a month later in the same terms. 'We are so far apart, 2,500 miles separate us, my lot is a miserable one...please don't forget your sincerely devoted and truly loving friend.'[28]

Both letters were opened and read by the *Okhrana* before delivery, as Dimitri knew they would be. But neither contained any clue to her prior knowledge of the murder or anything said by either Michael or Natasha about Rasputin. Dimitri was too careful to compromise them in that way; in any event, by then all the talk in Petrograd was no longer about the dead and gone Rasputin, but what now should be done about Nicholas and Alexandra.

9. PALACE PLOTTERS

WHEN Michael and Natasha returned to Gatchina at the New Year of 1917 it was to find that the death of Rasputin had done nothing to ease tension, for it had provided drama but no other tangible improvement in political conditions. The government had not fallen, the hated Protopopov was still interior minister, claiming that he was now guided by Rasputin's ghost,[1] and Alexandra was still effectively Regent, grieving but otherwise unchanged in her purpose. The only desperate action had come from an officer who attempted to assassinate her on December 28 *en route* between the palace and her hospital in Tsarskoe Selo. Caught, he was hanged next morning, although his arrest and execution were kept 'absolutely secret'.[2]

Nevertheless, there was still hopes of a palace coup, as there had been before Christmas when there had been hot-headed talk by the three Vladimirovich brothers — Grand Dukes Kirill, Boris and Andrew — of a night march on Tsarskoe Selo by four Guards regiments. This excited plot, aimed at the seizure of Alexandra and her despatch to some faraway convent, came to nothing since only the three brothers believed it to be possible. Even so, they continued to press the case for it.

At one champagne supper party, Boris was reported to have been discussing the timing and the regiments which could be used, seemingly indifferent to the fact that the whole conversation could be overheard by servants, gypsy singers and with 'harlots looking on and listening', noted Paléologue in his diary for January 9.[3]

Nicholas made clear that he was prepared to face any family challenge head on. After Dimitri's departure, a letter from his father Grand Duke Paul, asking the Tsar to revoke his order, was returned to him with a note scribbled in the margin: 'No one has the right to kill...'[4] Bimbo, who had added his name to the letter, was banished to his remote estate on New Year's Day and it was enough to stop any family rebellion in its tracks.

By January 15, Paléologue judged that Nicholas 'obviously intended to frighten the imperial family. He has succeeded. They are terror-stricken.'[5]

A week later, the Tsar told Grand Duchess Marie Pavlovna that 'in their own interests' it would be best if her sons Kirill and Andrew should depart the capital for a few weeks.[6] They went quietly, leaving their mother to scurry around for other allies, in vain.

Grand Duke Paul recognised that they had failed when he admitted to Paléologue that 'the Emperor is more under the Empress's thumb than ever. She has persuaded him that the hostile movement against her is...nothing more than a conspiracy of the Grand Dukes and a drawing room revolt'.[7]

She was deluding herself. There were more serious plots afoot. All were intended to bring about the abdication of the Tsar and thereby Alexandra's removal from the political scene, and the substitution of twelve-year-old Alexis as Emperor, under the Regency of Grand Duke Michael Aleksandrovich. The question in January 1917 was no longer whether this should be done, but when and by whom.

MICHAEL had returned to Gatchina too late to be consulted about the family petition on behalf of Dimitri, but there was never any doubt about where his sympathy lay. Alexandra had to be removed from any further influence on affairs. Early in the New Year he drove to Tsarskoe Selo to meet his brother, and to press the case for a change of course — as indeed he had pressed him in his warning letter to Nicholas eight weeks earlier

RUSSIAN LINE OF SUCCESSION
January 1917

1. Tsarsevich ALEXIS Nikolaeovich *(aged 12)**
2. Grand Duke MICHAEL Aleksandrovich (38)*
    m.1912 (*divorcée*) Mme Natasha Wulfert
3. Grand Duke KIRILL Vladimirovich (40)
    m. 1905 (*divorcée*) Princess Victoria Melita of Saxe-Coburg
    ('Ducky')
4. Grand Duke BORIS Vladimirovich (39) *unm.*
5. Grand Duke ANDREW Vladimirovich *(37) unm.*
6. Grand Duke PAUL Alexandrovich (56)*
    m(2) (*divorcée*) Olga Pistolkors (later Princess Paley)
7. Grand Duke DIMITRI Pavlovich (25)*unm. banished Dec. 1916*
8. Grand Duke NICHOLAS Konstantinovich (66)
    m. 1882 Mme Nadejda Dreyer (*banished*)
9. Prince IOANN Konstantinovich (30)*
    m.1913 Helen of Serbia
Followed by *son* Vsevolode, b. 1914
and then by Ioann's *brothers* Gabriel, Konstantin*, Igor, George
15. Grand Duke Dimitri Konstantinovich (56) *unm.*
16. Grand Duke NICHOLAS Nikolaeovich (60)
    m. 1907 (*divorcée*) Anastasia of Montenegro
17. Grand Duke PETER Nikolaeovich (49)
    m. 1889 Militsa of Montenegro
18. *(son)* Prince Roman Petrovich (20) *unm.*
19. Grand Duke NICHOLAS Mikhailovich ('Bimbo') (58)* *unm.*
20. Grand Duke MICHAEL Mikhailovich ('Miche-Miche') (55)
    m.1891 Sophia, (later Countess Torby) *banished*
21. Grand Duke GEORGE Mikhailovich (49)*
    m. Princess Maria of Greece
22. Grand Duke Alexander Mikhailovich ('Sandro')
    m. 1894 Xenia, elder dau. Tsar Alexander III, sister of Nicholas
    and Michael.
Followed by six sons
29. Grand Duke Serge Mikhailovich (47) *unm**

* murdered 1918

and before the crisis which now engulfed him. Nicholas did not attempt to browbeat him, as he had done in dealing with the other members of the family. Instead, he was clearly rattled, not least by the intervention a few days earlier of the British ambassador Sir George Buchanan, speaking informally on behalf of the British government which had given him permission to talk personally to the Tsar, albeit not officially on behalf of London or King George V. Even so, Nicholas was well aware that what Buchanan was saying was what London believed to be the truth. It did not make for a happy interview, as he now confessed to Michael.

Alarmed by the open talk in the capital of an impending palace coup, Buchanan told him that interior minister Protopopov 'is bringing Russia to the verge of ruin', that in the event of a revolution, 'only a small part of the army can be counted on to defend the dynasty', and that the only safe course now was for the Tsar to 'break down the barrier that separates you from your people and to regain their confidence.'

Nicholas's face hardened at that. 'You tell me that I must regain the confidence of the people. Isn't it rather for my people to regain my confidence?'[8]

Buchanan departed in despair. However, the meeting had shaken Nicholas, despite his outward show of disdain. A government minister who met him immediately afterwards found him 'trembling and distrait'.[9] He was still clearly troubled by it all when Michael arrived, for he recounted to him everything that Buchanan had said to him — its own admission that he was not as confident as he pretended to be, though too proud to admit that to anyone other than his brother.

How could Michael help? The answer to that came when he unexpectedly turned up shortly afterwards at the apartment of Mikhail Rodzyanko, the president of the state Duma, on Furshtadtskaya, near the Tauride Palace, home of the Duma.

Rodzyanko was surprised to see him. When they sat down, Michael came straight to the point. 'I should like to talk to you about what is going on, and to consult you as to what should be done. We understand the situation perfectly.' In saying 'we' he made clear that he meant the Tsar, who did not understand at all, but that in talking to Rodzyanko he was not going behind his back.

Rodzyanko's response was as frank as the question invited him to be. 'The entire policy of the government must undergo a radical change. Ministers must be appointed whom the country trusts, not men whose very presence in the government is an insult to public feeling. I am sorry to tell you that this can only be done on condition that the Empress is removed. She exercises a deplorable influence on all appointments, even those in the army. Alexandra Fedorovna is fiercely and universally hated and all circles are clamouring for her removal. While she remains in power, we shall continue on the road to ruin.'

'Buchanan said the same thing to my brother,' replied Michael 'The whole family is aware of her evil influence. She and my brother are surrounded by traitors. All decent people have gone. But things being so, what is to be done?'

'Your Highness, you, as his only brother, must tell him the whole truth — point out the pernicious results of the Empress's influence...'

'Do you think there must be a responsible ministry?'

'The general demand is only for a strong government...the country's desire is to see at the head of the Cabinet a man enjoying the confidence of the nation. Such a man would form a ministry responsible to the Tsar...for God's sake, Your Highness, use your influence to get the Duma summoned, and Alexandra Fedorovna and her set put out of the way.'

According to Rodzyanko this interview lasted for more than an hour. 'The Grand Duke agreed with everything and promised to help...'[10] Rodzyanko's wife thought Michael was there 'on some mysterious mission, I think he was sent secretly by his brother'. But she reported to a relative that 'he knows and understands everything, and listened attentively to all that was said and promised to prevail upon the Emperor to see [my husband]'.

When Nicholas then did agree to meet Rodzyanko, she wrote that 'it is more than likely that the audience was granted after Michael Aleksandrovich's expositions.'[11]

That meeting between the Tsar and the Duma president came on Saturday January 7 in Nicholas's study at Tsarskoe Selo. Rodzyanko spoke frankly about the mood of the country, the disastrous influence of the Empress, and the mistakes which now threatened to plunge Russia into anarchy. His message was blunt: unless he agreed to grant concessions and to remove Alexandra from politics, he faced disaster. 'Your Majesty, do not compel the people to choose between you and the good of the country.'

The Tsar pressed his head with his hands and said, 'Is it possible that for 22 years I tried to act for the best, and that for 22 years it was all a mistake?' Rodzyanko did not flinch from his answer. 'Yes, Your Majesty, for 22 years you have followed the wrong course.'[12]

But if Rodzyanko hoped for a new start he was to be disappointed. Once he had bowed and set off to return to the capital, Nicholas went on as before. Nothing was to be done, nothing would change. The Tsar would retreat to his army headquarters in distant Mogilev leaving Alexandra in their Tsarskoe Selo palace to deal with ministers who did whatever she demanded.

There was little more immediately that Michael could do, for on January 19 he departed back to the front line. Three days later he was in Kiev, and on his way to the south-western headquarters of his 2nd Cavalry Corps. His new appointment, effective as of January 29, was that of Inspector General of Cavalry, but before taking up the post he needed to hand over his Corps formally and to make his farewells to the divisions, brigades and regiments. Over the next days he travelled the front line by sleigh, inspecting trenches and outposts. He thanked 'the riflemen for their service, tasted the food, inspected the wooden barracks of the lower-ranking men, and then went to a hut for a bite to eat.'[13] After the atmosphere in Petrograd it was almost a relief to him to be at the front line and he enjoyed his tour. He found nothing in his Corps to suggest that morale was low, or that the ferment in the capital had affected his troops. As before, when he had left the Savage Division ten months earlier, they cheered him, played trumpet farewells, sang songs, gave him tea and looked sorry to see him go, he noted in his diary.[14] What he also noted was that he had been spared making a speech, as he did when departing the Savage Division. Doing so, he lamented, 'must have taken at least three years of my life. I am always so frightfully nervous, but I pulled myself together and spoke loudly, slowly, and clearly.'

Yet politics could not be kept at bay. Before returning to Gatchina he went to say goodbye to his commander-in-chief Brusilov at his headquarters in Kamenets-Podolsky, arriving there on Wednesday, February 1.

'I was very fond of him'. Brusilov recalled, 'for he was an absolutely honourable and upright man, taking no sides and lending himself to no intrigues...he shunned every kind of gossip, whether connected with the services or with family matters. As a soldier he was an excellent leader and an unassuming and conscientious worker.'[15]

As the two men said farewell on February 1, Brusilov thought the situation too serious for just polite talk. 'I expounded most earnestly...the need for immediate and drastic reforms...begging him to explain all this to the Tsar and to lend my views his personal support.' Michael promised to do so, but cautioned that 'my brother has time and time again had warnings and entreaties of this kind from every quarter, but he is the slave of influence and pressure that no one is in a position to overcome.'[16] He meant the Empress.

The two men shook hands, and Michael set off home next day. It was a slow journey. 'We are moving with a delay of 3 hours, probably because of snowdrifts. I say "probably", as you can never know the real cause of happenings. But the truth is that everything is in complete disorder everywhere.'[17]

It was going to get worse.

THE serious plotters were now well advanced in their plans for a palace coup. Discounting the near-hysterical 'champagne plot' at the Vladimir palace, which served only to extinguish any hopes that the Romanovs could put their own house in order, there were a number of conspiracies, none knowing much if anything of the others. All necessarily were shadowy and perhaps only two were credible.

The Progressive Bloc of conservatives and liberals in the Duma had prepared a list of ministers who would form the government after a coup, with Michael as Regent, though they were vague as to how this was to be accomplished.

Demands that something should be done could be heard on all sides. Vladimir Stankevich, a henchman of the radical left-wing Duma deputy Aleksandr Kerensky, saw 'a general determination to have done with the outrages perpetrated by court circles and to overthrow Nicholas. Several names were suggested as candidates for the throne, but there was unanimous agreement that Michael Aleksandrovich was the only one who could guarantee the constitutional legitimacy of government.'[18]

But talk was not action. Among those determined to act were Aleksandr Guchkov, the 55-year-old leader of the Octobrists, a right-wing party in the Duma, but one which favoured 'constitutional government'; among his supporters were the liberal Nikolai Nekrasov, and industrialist Mikhail Tereshchenko, all destined to play a leading part in the events to come. Nekrasov and Tereshchenko were young men, the former 36 and the other only 29.

Guchkov, a former President of the Duma, had been hated by the Empress since 1912 when he had bitterly denounced Rasputin — 'Oh, could not one hang Guchkov?" was her response.[19] The gossipy French ambassador Paléologue called him 'the personal enemy of Their Majesties',[20] so it was no surprise that he should now want to be rid of them.

Guchkov's reasoning was that without change a revolution was inevitable and if it was left to extremists and the street mob then it would be they who would rule afterwards. 'I fear that those who make the revolution will be at the head of that revolution'. The alternative was to be a bloodless palace coup, for none wanted that Michael should become Regent for Alexis 'surrounded by lakes of blood'.[21] The plan which they slowly pieced together was to capture the Tsar's train while it was travelling between the capital at the army headquarters at Mogilev, and thus present the country next morning with a *fait accompli.* To make this feasible Prince Dimitri Vyazemsky, a brother of Michael's ADC Vladimir, had been charged with the task of recruiting 'like-minded' army officers.[22]

But would Michael agree to be Regent? The plotters took that for granted, though they made no approach to him in advance. Certainly Guchkov seemed entirely confident. After all, he argued, faced with the reality of Nicholas compelled to abdicate, he would have no choice but to accept, willingly or otherwise. 'The only illegality would be the moral pressure exerted. After that, the law would come into effect.'[23]

A second and unrelated plot went to the heart of the *Stavka* itself where General Alekseev, the chief of staff, supported it. One of the principals was Prince Lvov, the popular leader of the civic and volunteer organisations across Russia. Their intention was to arrest Alexandra on one of her regular visits to *Stavka*, and compel the Tsar to remove her to Livadia; if he refused, as they knew he would, then he would be compelled to abdicate — with the same result as in the Guchkov plot: Michael as Regent.[24] This plan had not been developed because Alekseev had been ill for several weeks, but it remained in being.

However, the arrival in the capital in early January of General Aleksandr Krymov, a 46-year-old cavalryman from Brusilov's army in the south, gave the Guchkov plot the better chance of success. In Krymov they had the military leader they needed. In the wider picture, it also helped that Krymov knew Michael and they respected each other.

At a meeting in Rodzyanko's apartment, attended by a number

of senior Duma representatives, Krymov made clear his intent. 'The feeling in the army is such that news of a *coup d'etat* would be welcomed with joy. A revolution is imminent and we at the front feel it is to be so. If you decide on such an extreme step, we will support you. Clearly, there is no other way...the Emperor attaches more weight to his wife's nefarious influence than to all honest words of warning. There is no time to lose.'[25]

The meeting lasted far into the night. Although Rodzyanko declined to have any part in it — 'I have taken the oath of allegiance' — the others were less squeamish, one quoting Brusilov's remark that 'if it comes to a choice between the Tsar and Russia, I will take Russia'.[26]

The plot, though lacking detail and with more questions than answers, was now a commitment. With the general in their ranks they were confident of recruiting enough officers for the task in prospect.

Michael was not made privy to any of this, for it was well understood that he could never allow himself to have any hand in bringing down his brother. He would become Regent, but that would be the direct result of the Tsar's abdication, not because of any act on his part. He would take over with clean hands.

That said, they had first to capture and arrest the Tsar, and they were still weeks away from being ready to do that. But ready they would be, they were confident of that, as they were confident that the Tsar, once in their hands, would have no choice but to do as they commanded. Failure was not an option. They would strike in the middle of March.

In the event, that would be too late. What would be known as the February Revolution would render all that planning of no account. The end for Nicholas would be very different to the one which they had designed. Yes, he would sign his abdication as a result, and in a train as it turned out, but Michael would not be Regent, he would be Tsar.

10. 'MAKE YOURSELF REGENT'

BACK home in Gatchina on Saturday, February 4, Michael telephoned his brother-in-law Sandro in Petrograd. Had there been any sign that Nicholas was ready to make concessions—anything hopeful at all—while he had been away at the front? The answer was depressingly No.[1] Michael arranged to meet Sandro in the capital, and then proposed that the two of them should go together to Tsarskoe Selo in yet another desperate attempt to persuade him to see sense, appoint a responsible government, and take his wife out of politics altogether.[1] Sandro agreed, but suggested that he first went there and confronted Alexandra privately. What had to be said to her in front of Nicholas would come better from him alone than with Michael. At least his wife Xenia, as the Tsar's sister, could not be accused of being in 'a bad set'.

Arriving in Tsarskoe Selo, Alexandra reluctantly agreed to meet Sandro. Nicholas led him into her mauve bedroom. 'Alix lay in bed, dressed in a white negligée embroidered with lace...I kissed her hand and her lips just skimmed my cheek, the coldest greeting given me by her since the first day we met in 1893. I took a chair and moved it close to her bed, facing a wall covered with innumerable icons lit by two blue-and-pink church lamps.'

With Nicholas standing silently, puffing away on his cigarettes, Sandro told her bluntly that she had to remove herself from politics. Their exchange became heated, until all pretence at politeness vanished. 'Remember Alix, I remained silent for thirty months!' he shouted at her in a wild rage. 'For thirty months I never said as much as a word to you about the disgraceful goings-on in our government — better to say in your government! I realise that you are willing to perish and that your husband feels the same way, but what about us? Must we all suffer for your blind stubbornness? No, Alix, you have no right to drag your relatives with you into a precipice. You are incredibly selfish!'

Alexandra stared at him coldly. 'I refuse to continue this dispute', she replied tersely. 'You are exaggerating the danger. Some day, when you are less excited, you will admit that I knew better.'

He got up, kissed her, received no kiss in reply, and strode out in anger. He would never see Alexandra again.

Passing through the mauve salon he went straight to the library, ordered a pen and paper and sat down to write a report on his meeting for Michael. As he did so, he looked up and saw the Tsar's ADC watching him, as if on guard. The aide refused to leave, and 'in a fury' Sandro stood up and stormed out of the palace.[2]

The next day he returned with Michael. Meeting them in his study, Nicholas smoked, listened impassively, but seemed deaf to anything that Michael said as he tried in vain to impress upon his brother that without change he faced disaster. Sandro judged that they were 'wasting his time and ours' and when it came his turn to support Michael's arguments he found by the end that 'I was hardly able to speak...emotion choking me'.[3]

With that, Sandro gave up in despair. However, Michael told him he would try yet again, hopeless though it seemed, and on Friday February 10 — six days after coming back from the front — he drove once more to Tsarskoe Selo.[4] The meeting in Nicholas's study was as pointless as the earlier one, though it was interrupted by the arrival of Rodzyanko. Nicholas agreed to see him, and went out into the audience chamber.

Rodzyanko was standing with a report from the Duma which simply underlined the points which Michael and Sandro had been making, but 'the Emperor listened not only with indifference but with a kind of ill-will', recounted Rodzyanko. 'He finally interrupted me with the request that I hurry a bit, as Grand Duke Michael Aleksandrovich was waiting for him to have a cup of tea.'[5]

Four days later Sandro wrote to his brother Nicholas about his depressing meetings at Tsarskoe Selo, and added that Michael 'can also see no way out, except sending her to Livadia'[6] — the imperial estate in the Crimea. Yet suddenly a week later there was a moment of hope that in fact Nicholas had been listening and had finally yielded to the arguments put to him that change was imperative. He told his prime minister Prince Golitsin that he was prepared to go to the Duma next day, Tuesday, February 22, and concede to the demands for a responsible ministry. But just as suddenly he changed his mind, and instead of going to the Tauride Palace he ordered his train and went off in the opposite direction — disappearing back to *Stavka*.

Next day Alexandra dashed off a letter to him, urging him as she had always urged him — 'Be firm...'[7]

His reply showed a touch of irritation but also the extent of his own self-deception. 'What you write about being firm — the master — is perfectly true. I do not forget it — be sure of that, but I need not bellow at the people right & left every moment. A quiet sharp remark or answer is enough very often to put the one or other in his place...'[8]

That would never be enough ever again.

THE revolution intended to come from above came instead from below and without any real warning. It was a spontaneous rising, with no master-plan or even a decisive leader who could be identified afterwards. Unrest become disturbance, disturbance grew into rebellion, and then in turn into revolution. And yet all this was in large part confined to the capital, with the rest of the country unaffected, at least in the beginning, and with some regions unaware of events until they were all over. The ostensible cause was fear of a bread shortage; although supplies were adequate the fear was self-fulfilling in that housewives hoarded, creating the shortage. But that was only one of many factors. There had been large-scales strikes, following a lock-out of workers at the giant Putilov factories, with an estimated 158,000 men idle by late February. Petrograd itself was a vast military camp, with 170,000 armed troops in barracks, many of them susceptible to agitators — among them German agents actively fermenting resentment in the hope of bringing about a revolution that would remove Russia from the war.

In Gatchina on Saturday February 25 — just three weeks after returning from the front — Michael noted that 'there were disorders on Nevsky Prospekt today. Workmen were going about with red flags and throwing grenades and bottles at the police, so that troops had to open fire. The main cause of disorders is — lack of flour in the shops.'[9] The day left six dead and some 100 injured.

But what was most alarming was that one of the dead was a police inspector who, intent upon seizing a red flag, was killed by a Cossack trooper as he rode into a crowd of demonstrators gathered around a statue of Alexander III in a square beside the Nicholas station, the main terminus for Moscow.[10] The Cossacks were the traditional scourge of rioters and demonstrators — and if they were no longer reliable, no one was.

Next day, Sunday, there were placards all around the city, forbidding meetings or gatherings, with notices that troops were authorised to fire to maintain order. The crowds took no notice of these warnings and that evening Michael noted in his diary that 'the disorders in Petrograd have gathered momentum. On the Suvorov Prospekt and Znamenskaya Street there were 200 killed.'[11]

More ominously, a company of the élite Pavlovsk Guards had mutinied in their barracks, and when their colonel came into confront them he was attacked and his hand cut off.[12] With that, the mutineers had no way back: it was revolution or the hangman's noose.

A desperate Rodzyanko telegraphed the Tsar. 'The capital is in a state of anarchy. The government is paralysed...General discontent is growing. There is wild shooting in the street. In places troops are firing at each other.' There must be a new government, under someone trusted by the country', he urged as he had so often urged before, except that this time he warned that 'any procrastination is tantamount to death...'[13]

Reading that, Nicholas dismissed it as panic. 'Some more rubbish from that fat Rodzyanko'.[14] However he did decide to put together a loyal force and despatch it to the capital, and to return to Tsarskoe Selo himself. That should settle matters. The rebel soldiers were no more than an armed rabble. They would never stand against proper frontline troops.

That complacent view was easier held in Mogilev than in the streets of Petrograd. The rebels indeed were not frontline soldiers but depot reservists, many of them new recruits, the scrapings of the military barrel. Their officers were mainly men convalescing after being wounded at the front, or young inexperienced subalterns fresh from the military academies. It was certain, observed the British military observer Colonel Alfred Knox, that 'if the men went wrong, the officers were without the influence to control them'.[15]

Military discipline was a thin veneer which was easily stripped away, turning such troops into a uniformed mob. Nevertheless, they had guns and were as well-armed as any soldiers being sent to face them. By noon on Sunday, only some 24 hours into the disorders, 25,000 troops had gone over to the side of the demonstrators; however among the rest there were few willing to march out either for them or against them. The bulk of the available forces simply stayed in their barracks as the rebels and the mob took command of the streets.

The Arsenal on the Liteiny was captured, putting into the hands of the rebels thousands of rifles and pistols, and hundreds of machine-guns. The headquarters of the *Okhrana*, across the Neva and opposite the Winter Palace, as well as a score of police stations, were overrun and set on fire. The prisons were opened and their inmates freed, criminals as well as political detainees. By the evening of that second day, only the very centre of the city, around the Winter Palace, could be said still to be in government control.[16]

Michael would begin his diary entry for Monday, February 27, by writing that it was 'the beginning of anarchy'.[17]

AS Michael was composing his diary, Nicholas was puffing on a cigarette in his quarters at *Stavka*, reading a letter newly arrived from Alexandra. Having told him that three of the children had gone down with measles, she was otherwise cheerful and confident about the events in the capital, for all around her agreed that it was nothing like as serious as the revolution of 1905, which had begun with a massacre of demonstrators in front of the Winter Palace on what history remembered as 'Bloody Sunday'. The difference was 'because all adore you & only want bread...it seems to me it will be alright — the sun shines so brightly.' There was also the consolation of her prayers at the grave of Rasputin. 'I felt such peace & calm on His dear grave — He died to save us.'[18]

Nicholas was also striving to be calm. The day before, in church, he had felt 'an excruciating pain in the middle of my chest, which lasted for quarter of an hour. I cannot understand what it was, as I had no heart beating, but it came & left me at once when I knelt before the Virgin's image.'[19] Writing to say 'how happy I am at the thought of meeting you in two days' he then reported that 'after the news of yesterday from town — I saw many faces here with frightened expressions.' Not knowing that his chief of staff had been involved in a plot with Prince Lvov to get rid of him, he added: 'Luckily Alekseev is calm...'[20]

There was also reassuring news from the capital. Early that afternoon the war minister General Mikhail Belyaev cabled Mogilev to tell Nicholas that while 'it has not yet been possible to crush the rebellion...I am firmly convinced that calm will soon arrive. Ruthless measures are being adopted to achieve this.

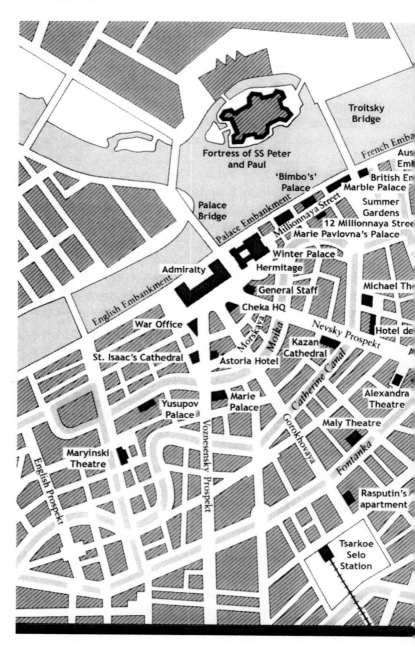

Troitsky
Bridge

French Emba

Fortress of SS Peter
and Paul

Aus
Emb

'Bimbo's'
Palace

British En
Marble Palace

Palace
Bridge

Summer
Gardens

Palace Embankment

Millionnaya Street

12 Millionnaya Stree
Marie Pavlovna's Palace

Winter Palace

Admiralty

Hermitage

General Staff

Michael Th

English Embankment

Cheka HQ

War Office

Morskaya

Moika

Nevsky Prospekt

Hotel de

St. Isaac's Cathedral

Astoria Hotel

Kazan
Cathedral

Catherine Canal

Yusupov
Palace

Marie
Palace

Alexandra
Theatre

Gorokhovaya

Maly Theatre

Maryinski
Theatre

English Prospekt

Voznesensky Prospekt

Fontanka

Rasputin's
apartment

Tsarkoe
Selo
Station

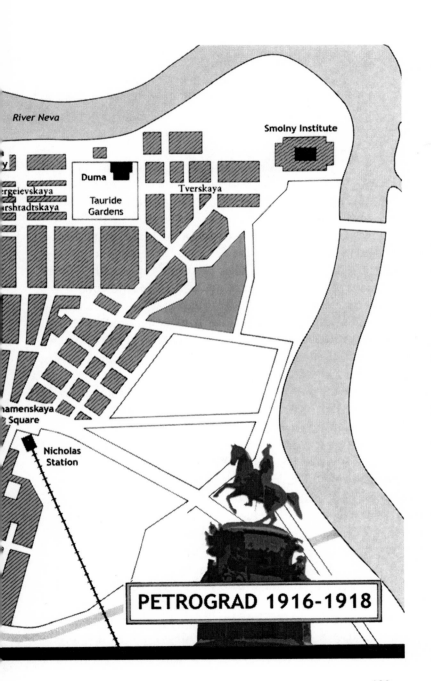

River Neva

Smolny Institute

Duma

rgeievskaya
rshtadtskaya

Tauride
Gardens

Tverskaya

amenskaya
Square

Nicholas
Station

PETROGRAD 1916-1918

The authorities remain totally calm.'[21] If he had written 'totally panic-stricken' it would have been nearer the mark, but Belyaev, appointed only seven weeks earlier, could not bring himself to admit that he had already lost control of the army in Petrograd.

At the Tauride Palace the Duma was in uproar. Just 13 days after its new session had begun, deputies arrived to find that the Duma had been shut down again. Prince Golitsin, the third prime minister in the past year and a reluctant appointee, had used a 'blank' decree to prorogue the Duma, thinking it would defuse tension by silencing the more radical elements.[22]

However, the deputies refused to disperse, adjourned to another chamber in the building, and set up a 'temporary committee' under the chairmanship of their president Rodzyanko. Within 24 hours this would claim to be the *de facto* government.

That said, none of them had any idea of what their role could be. *'What shall I do? What shall I do?'* Rodzyanko cried out in vain hope of any answer.[23] Another Duma member recalled that 'we did not have an idea of what was happening and certainly no plan or idea of how to deal with it'.[23]

So Rodzyanko then turned to the only man he thought could rescue them. He slipped out of the chamber and telephoned Michael in Gatchina, urging him to come to the capital immediately. The call would appear to have been around 3.45 p.m. for that was when Michael telephoned his brother-in-law Matveev at his embankment law office in Petrograd, only to be told that he had left at 3.30 p.m. and was on his way home to the Fontanka. Instead, Michael spoke to his chauffeur, telling him to be with a car at the Warsaw railway station just after six p.m. By the time Matveev was home, and telephoned Gatchina to find out what was happening, Natasha told him that Michael had already left for Petrograd with his secretary Nikolai Johnson.[25] Their special train left at 5 p.m.

Just over an hour later they were at Petrograd's Warsaw station, with Michael relieved to find that 'things were comparatively quiet.'[26] Met by Matveev's chauffeur, he was whisked away to the

Marie Palace on St Isaac's Square to join an emergency conference attended by the prime minister, war minister Belyaev, Rodzyanko and other leading members of the Duma's new 'temporary committee'.

In the government there was only resigned defeatism. That evening the hated interior minister Protopopov had been persuaded to resign and as he shuffled off into the night he muttered that there was nothing now left to him 'but to shoot myself'.[27] No one cared what he did and no one bothered to say goodbye to the man so trusted by the Empress, so despised by the nation. Yet his departure was also its own signal that the government was no more. Golitsin accepted that his ministry was finished, but did not know how to write out the death certificate. He hoped Michael would do that for him.

There was not a moment to lose. As Michael would note afterwards, 'By 9 p.m. shooting in the streets began and almost all the armed forces became revolutionary and the old rule ceased to exist.'[28]

So what was to be the new rule? In the conference which followed Rodzyanko would later claim that he urged Michael 'to assume on his own initiative the dictatorship of the city...compel the personnel of the government to tender their resignations and demand by telegram, by direct wire from His Majesty, a manifesto regarding the formation of a responsible cabinet.'[29] These were dramatic proposals: the Duma president— who had prided himself on refusing to be a rebel — was proposing that Michael should seize power, effectively proclaim himself Regent and present his brother with a *fait accompli*.

Rodzyanko would later claim to be dismayed that Michael refused to follow his advice, complaining that the 'irresoluteness of Grand Duke Michael Aleksandrovich contributed to a favourable moment being lost. Instead of taking active measures and gathering around himself the units of the Petrograd garrison whose discipline had not yet been shattered, the Grand Duke started to negotiate by direct wire with Emperor Nicholas II.'[30]

However, this picture of an 'irresolute' Michael and a decisive, ruthless and clear-headed Duma president depends on Rodzyanko's own self-serving account, written long afterwards and published in 1922, when many of his contemporaries were revising their roles in the revolution of 1917. Rodzyanko was then anxious to rebut criticism that it was he who had proved irresolute and it is that which more easily explains his improbable scenario of February 27; it helped to excuse all that followed. In fact, as others would remark over these critical days, Rodzyanko was in 'a blue funk' with no idea of what to do.

What further coloured his account was that when it came to the choice of a new prime minister that evening, Michael nominated someone else for the post Rodzyanko believed was his by right. At Gatchina Michael had been more in touch with political opinion than Rodzyanko might have expected, and knew that the majority Progressive Bloc in the Duma had already opted for Prince Georgy Lvov. It was therefore his name which Michael put forward, and which the conference endorsed.

Lvov was not at the conference but he knew of the proposal to make him prime minister and had agreed to take the post if offered to him. Michael already knew that; Rodzyanko did not. Lvov was not a member of the Duma, though as long-time head of the powerful union of local authorities, the *Zemstovs,* he was the best known civic leader in the country and more popular and more trusted among the radical elements than the authoritarian bull-voiced Rodzyanko.

Pavel Milyukov, leader of the Kadet party, and a powerful voice in the Duma, believed that the choice of Lvov was 'made easier by his reputation everywhere in Russia; at the time he was irreplaceable. I cannot say, however, that Rodzyanko was reconciled to the decision.'[31] Rodzyanko would still behave as if he were leader, but his real power died that night.

Nevertheless, the two-hour conference in the Marie Palace did adopt in a broad sense the measures of which Rodzyanko would later boast himself author. Michael would telegraph his brother and convey the proposals, supported as they were by his present prime minister, that he should act as Regent in the capital, with the power to appoint a new prime minister but one competent to choose his own Cabinet, unlike those which had gone before. With his high reputation in the army, Michael as lawful Regent was well-placed to win over the vast number of troops who had stayed in their barracks; a new 'responsible ministry' under a respected man at its rudder, would isolate the extremists behind the disorder. The real question, however, was whether the Tsar would accept any of this.

Michael had, of course, repeatedly pressed on his brother privately the necessity for a new responsible ministry, but this was the first time he would be saying so not only openly but as spokesman for the political leadership in Petrograd. He would wrap it up in the politest of language but his message to the Tsar would be clear: the days of autocracy were over.

The next four hours would be decisive. If Nicholas accepted the reality of the disaster confronting them all, there could be a new government by the next morning, with every chance that by the end of the day, with the majority of troops who had not left their barracks rallying to Michael, the revolutionaries would have slunk off into the night. Otherwise the revolution unchecked might prove impossible to contain.

Leaving the Marie Palace, Michael crossed the square to the nearby residence of the war minister on the Moika and there at 10.30 p.m. he began his despatch to his brother.[32] He was using the Hughes apparatus, a kind of primitive telex, with a keyboard, in which one party typed out a tape and then waited for a reply tape. It was slow but it was all they had for communication over such a long distance. At the receiving end in Mogilev was the sympathetic chief-of-staff Alekseev and Michael 'talked' to his brother through him.

Grand Duke Michael Aleksandrovich on the apparatus. I beg to report the following to His Majesty the Emperor on my behalf. I am firmly convinced that in order to pacify this movement, which has

143

assumed huge proportion, it is essential to dismiss the whole Council of Ministers, a course urged on me by Prince Golitsin.

That in itself already said much. Michael, using a war ministry machine, quoting the support of the prime minister, was not in fact acting on his own behalf, but as representative voice of those the Tsar believed to be acting for him. It was a slap in the face. Michael went on: *If the Cabinet is dismissed, it will be essential to appoint replacements at the same time. All I can suggest in current conditions is to settle your choice on someone who has earned Your Imperial Majesty's trust and enjoys respect among wide sections of the population, entrusting him with the duties of the Chairman of the Council of Ministers and making him solely accountable to Your Imperial Majesty.*

It is essential that he be empowered to appoint a Cabinet at his own discretion. In view of the extraordinarily serious situation, Your Imperial Majesty may wish to authorise me to announce this on behalf of Your Imperial Majesty as a matter of urgency. For my part, I would suggest that the only possible candidate at this moment is Prince Lvov. ADC General Michael.

Stripped of its apparent deference, the message could not be clearer; Michael was publicly promoting a new and responsible ministry under Prince Lvov, with a Cabinet picked by him not by Nicholas or Alexandra. For the first time, Michael was openly telling his brother that he had to sack his government, and that the days of autocracy were over.

Alekseev's reply came back on the tape. 'I will report Your Imperial Highness's telegram to his Imperial Majesty immediately. His Majesty the Emperor is leaving for Tsarskoe Selo tomorrow.'

Leaving *Stavka* tomorrow in the middle of a crisis and out of touch while he travelled 450 miles in a train? Every hour was vital, every hour lost potentially fatal. Michael replied immediately. 'I am convinced that it may be advisable to delay His Majesty the Emperor's journey to Tsarskoe Selo for several days.'[33]

Forty minutes later General Alekseev passed on Nicholas's reply. It was uncompromising, almost dismissive.

Firstly. In view of the extraordinary circumstances His Majesty the Emperor does not consider it possible to delay his departure and will leave tomorrow at half past two p.m. Secondly. His Imperial Majesty will not deal with any measures touching on changes to his personal staff until his arrival in Tsarskoe Selo. Thirdly. ADC General Ivanov is leaving for Petrograd as Commander-in-Chief of the Petrograd Area and has a reliable battalion with him. Fourthly. As of tomorrow four infantry regiments and four cavalry regiments from amongst our most reliable units will begin moving from the Northern and Western Fronts to Petrograd.

Reading that, Michael knew that his brother had ignored everything he had said, and that his wire had been a waste of time, as had the discussion at the conference in the Marie Palace. Michael had been told to mind his own business.

Alekseev was clearly unhappy for he added a message of his own, directly supporting Michael's original proposals. *Allow me to conclude with a personal request that, when making personal reports to His Imperial Majesty, Your Imperial Highness will be so kind as to give firm support to the ideas which you expressed in your preceding message, both as regards to the replacement of the present members of the Council of Ministers and as regards the method by which a new Council is to be selected and may the Lord God aid Your Imperial Highness in this important matter.*

Michael in reply repeated his concern that Nicholas was leaving Mogilev 'since under the present conditions literally every hour counts...' Alekseev agreed and promised to raise the matter at the morning conference because 'I realise perfectly well...that time lost cannot be compensated for'.[34]

It was a dispiriting end to a long night, in which Michael had achieved precisely nothing. He summarised his efforts in his diary, concluding with one word: *Alas.*[35]

And alas indeed, for by refusing to empower his brother the Tsar now had no government at all. When the lights failed at around midnight in the Marie Palace the last of the ministers there simply drifted away into the night and they never met again.

Thus, when at 11.35 that evening in Mogilev the Tsar sent off a telegram to his prime minister saying that 'I personally bestow upon you all the necessary powers for civil rule',[36] there was no prime minister, no power and no rule. Prince Golitsin had gone home. Over the next 24 hours he and most of the Tsar's other ministers would be arrested by the revolutionary mob and for some their ultimate fate would be a firing squad.

THE immediate question for Michael was where he went now. It was impossible to return to Gatchina immediately 'because of heavy machine-gun fire and grenade explosions'. His secretary Johnson had hidden their car in the courtyard of the Moika building but at 3 a.m. when 'things had quietened down somewhat', he decided to make an attempt to reach the station, still hoping to get home if he could. However, as his car and a military escort drove through unlit streets a revolutionary patrol tried to stop them. Michael accelerated and got away, but his military escort was arrested. 'We could not proceed further and decided to make for the Winter Palace.'[37]

He arrived to find the war minister Belyaev with the dejected garrison commander Khabalov 'and a force of 1,000 troops'. With only a few machine-guns and little artillery they had been defending the Admiralty but were marched out when their commander General Zankevich decided that it would be more symbolic 'to die in defence of the palace'.

Michael recognised a different kind of symbolism — that it had been from the Winter Palace that troops had fired on the crowds marching into the palace square in January 1905, killing men, women and children. Michael had been with his brother at Tsarskoe Selo that day and twelve years later the memory, and the lesson of the revolution which followed, remained with him. Whatever the events of the next hours and days, if there was to be any chance of restoring order, he was not prepared to allow another 'Bloody Sunday', and hand the revolutionaries a propaganda victory that could only add fuel to the flames. Moreover, the

Winter Palace was indefensible. Across the Neva were the rebel guns of the Fortress of St Peter and St. Paul. They could reduce the Winter Palace to rubble if they chose to open fire.

Tersely, the garrison commander was told to remove his troops back to the stronger and less politically sensitive Admiralty, 'the poor General Khabalov' being 'very grateful' to avoid a battle he could only lose.[38]

That done, where was he to go? It was 5 a.m. and he needed refuge close by and quickly. The best idea seemed the apartment of his old friend Princess Putyatina at 12 Millionnaya Street, just 500 yards away, and opposite the palace of Bimbo, banished by the Tsar for defending Dimitri.

He and his weary secretary Johnson slipped out of the Winter Palace into the courtyard of the adjacent Hermitage then, watching out for revolutionary patrols, waited until their path was clear before running across the snow-covered road and knocking on the door of No 12.[39]

The concierge heard their banging and recognising Michael's voice opened up before leading them up two flights of stairs to the apartment of Princess Putyatina, using her pass-key to admit them inside. The princess, whose husband Pavel was away at the front, was alone with her young daughter. 'I woke with a start hearing violent knocking on my bedroom door. At this noise, seized with fright, I could only imagine that armed soldiers had burst into my apartment.' She was relieved when she recognised the voice of Johnson. Dressing hurriedly she went into the study where Michael was waiting. He was 'very tired and seemed very upset', but apologised with his 'usual good grace' for having disturbed her, adding: 'Are you not afraid, Princess, of putting yourself at such risk by having such a dangerous guest?'[40]

Her maid produced coffee and they were gratefully sipping it when they heard boots on the stairs and the sounds of shouting from the apartment above. A revolutionary squad, forcing their way through the service entrance at the rear of the building, had come to arrest the Tsar's chamberlain, Nicholas Stolypin, a brother of the former prime minister Peter Stolypin, assassinated in a Kiev theatre six years earlier. He was dragged away, but as they held their breath there was no knock on their door — or not yet.

Break-ins of suspected homes would be commonplace over the next days as mutineers went around the city looking for officials and ministers associated with the Tsar's government, or who were simply people judged to be enemies of the revolution. Princess Putyatina had so far been lucky, her concierge telling rampaging mobs that in her apartment was only a soldier's wife and child. She was not likely to remain so, however, if the mutineers learned that the Tsar's brother was there, in an unguarded building they could enter with one blow of a rifle butt.

For the moment that was a problem for the morrow. Silently, but gratefully, Michael and Johnson collapsed exhausted on settees and went to sleep.

11. ADDRESS UNKNOWN

AS Michael was slipping out of the Winter Palace and making his way to Millionnaya Street in the pre-dawn of Tuesday, February 28, the train carrying his brother back to Tsarskoe Selo was leaving Mogilev, its windows darkened, its passengers asleep. Another train, carrying members of his suite, had set off an hour earlier, at 4 a.m.[1] After the telegraph exchange with Michael, the start-time had been moved forward from 2.30 p.m. because it had been decided to take a roundabout route back, so as to leave the direct line to Petrograd clear for the relief force ordered to the capital. The change would mean adding nine hours and 200 miles to the normal journey. With luck he would arrive home at around eight o' clock the following morning, Wednesday.

'Every hour is precious,' Michael had told his brother on the wire from the war ministry on Monday night, and he had urged him not to leave Mogilev at all, so that he could be in direct communication throughout the crisis. On his train, Nicholas would be virtually *incommunicado*. Russia no longer had a government and over the next crucial twenty-seven hours or more it would, for all practical purposes, be without an emperor. If, that is, all went to plan.

Nicholas had gone to bed in the train at 3.15 a.m. having talked late with General Nikolai Ivanov,[2] the former commander on the south-western front and the man now charged with restoring order in the capital and beyond. What Nicholas hoped was that when he reached Tsarskoe Selo next morning he would hear that Ivanov had crushed the rebellion.

Ivanov had been given a crack battalion comprising 800 men who had each won the Cross of St George,[3] and from Mogilev Alekseev had commanded the despatch of reliable battle-hardened formations to be sent on the direct rail route to the capital, giving Ivanov another four infantry and four cavalry regiments, plus artillery.[4]

Late that Tuesday afternoon, Alexandra received at Tsarskoe Selo a confident telegram: 'Left this morning at 5. Thoughts always together. Glorious weather. Hope you are feeling well and quiet. Many troops sent from front. Fondest love. Nicky. The telegram, sent from Vyazma at 3 p.m. arrived at Tsarskoe Selo less than two hours later, at 4.49 p.m.[5] Some things still seemed to be working.

It was certainly reassuring news. Vyazma was 420 miles away, and if the trains kept to schedule, Nicholas would be home as planned, for breakfast on Wednesday. Darkness had fallen when the telegram arrived, but Alexandra knew that all around the palace were well-armed and reliable troops who would stand guard throughout the night.

The men protecting the imperial palace were hand-picked and their personal loyalty to the Tsar was beyond question. There were Guardsmen, Cossacks of the Emperor's Escort, artillerymen, riflemen, and the tall marines of the *Garde Equipage*, whose proud commander was Grand Duke Kirill.[6] They were not just crack troops — as Alexandra said to her loyal confidante, Lili Dehn, they were 'our personal friends'.[7]

Rodzyanko doubted that, given the tumult in the capital. He sent a message urging Alexandra to evacuate the palace and put herself and her family on a train[8] — which made no sense at all at Tsarskoe Selo, given that the Tsar was heading towards the palace in his train, and Ivanov and his battalion of heroes were hastening towards them, followed by eight regiments of frontline troops.

Yet there were grounds for concern. Truckloads of mutineers had arrived in the town itself, but their revolutionary fervour had been diverted into looting the wine shops.[9] There was the sound of shooting beyond the palace gates, but as darkness fell, within the ring of troops, the palace itself seemed entirely secure. In the late evening, with a black fur-coat thrown over her nurse's uniform, Alexandra and her 17-year-old daughter Marie walked among the troops, praising them for their loyalty.[10]

When she came back, Alexandra seemed 'possessed by some inward exaltation. She was radiant. They are all our friends... so devoted to us, ' she told Lili Dehn.[11] By morning, Nicholas would be back, and Ivanov marching into town. All was well.

Nicholas still expected to be back on schedule. At around 4 a.m. on Wednesday morning he was less than 100 miles away, having covered 540 miles since leaving Mogilev. It was then that the train stopped, at the town of Malaya Vishera, an alarmed aide hurrying into his carriage to tell him that revolutionaries had blocked the line ahead.[12] It was the bitterest of moments for Nicholas; no more than five hours from home, and he could go no further.

Since he had no troops save for a few train guards, there was no hope of fighting their way forward. That being so, there was only one choice for them: the two trains would have to go back to Bologoe, halfway between Petrograd and Moscow, and then head west for Pskov, headquarters of General Nikolai Ruzsky's Northern Army. It was the nearest safe haven, though it would still leave Nicholas 170 miles from home and worse off than if he had stayed in Mogilev where he could command the whole of his armies. His journey had been entirely wasted.

'To Pskov, then,' he said curtly and retired back to his sleeping car.[13] But once there he put his real feelings into his diary. 'Shame and dishonour,' he wrote despairingly.[14]

The return to Bologoe would take around five hours, and from there it was 221 miles on the branch line to the ancient town of Pskov. For the next and decisive 15 hours the Emperor of All the Russias would once again vanish into the empty snow-covered countryside, a second day lost.

At Tsarskoe Selo, an increasingly worried Alexandra would

wait for a man who was not coming, and when she dashed off a telegram to him to find out where he was, ordering it to be sent immediately to 'His Imperial Majesty', it was returned, with the stark message, scrawled across it in blue pencil: '*Address of person mentioned unknown*'.[15]

WITH no government and a nomadic Tsar lost in a railway train going nowhere, power in Petrograd passed on Tuesday February 28 to the revolution, with competing powers in the Tauride Palace trying to establish their own agendas for the reshaping of Russia. Home of a Duma that was no more, the parliamentary building now housed a noisy mass of workers, soldiers and students, joined together in a new organisation, a Soviet on the lines which had emerged in the 1905 revolution. The few hundred respectable deputies who backed the Temporary Committee of the Duma now jostled for places in rooms and hallways packed with a thousand excited street orators, mutineers and strike leaders. It was chaos and would remain so for days to come.

When Vladimir Nabokov, a lawyer destined to play a leading part in the events of that week, arrived at the smoke-filled Tauride Palace it looked to him like an improvised camp: 'rubbish, straw; the air was thick like some kind of a dense fog; there was a smell of soldiers' boots, cloth, sweat; from somewhere we could hear the hysterical voices of orators, addressing a meeting...everywhere crowding and bustling confusion...'[16]

In that crush of people, the young man who was beginning to stand out as the dominant figure was Aleksandr Kerensky aged 36. As both a member of the Temporary Committee and as vice-chairman of the new 'Petrograd Soviet of Workers' and Soldiers' Deputies', he bestrode both camps. He was also the finger of justice.

When the mutineers dragged in their first important prisoner, the chairman of the State Council Ivan Shcheglovitov, Kerensky strode up to him and shouted dramatically: 'Your life is not in danger. The Imperial Duma does not shed blood'.[17] The arrested

TRAIN JOURNEY OF NICHOLAS II
FEBRUARY 28th - MARCH 3rd 1917

Distances (miles)
from Petrograd

Bologoe	199
Dno	153
Dvinsk	329
Malaya Vishera	100
Mogilev	450
Pskov	170
Vitebsk	353

Bologoe to Pskov 221

FINLAND

Lake Lagoda

Gulf of Finland

PETROGRAD

Gatchina

Tsarkoe Selo

To Perm

Luga

Malaya Vishera
4 a.m. Wednesday March 1st

PSKOV
7 p.m. Wednesday March 1st
leaves 1 a.m. Friday March 3rd

Dno

Bologoe
arrives approx. midnight
returns 9 a.m. Wednesday

Direct line to Petrograd

return route to Mogilev

Dvinsk

To Moscow

Sirotino
sends telegram to
'Emperor Michael II'
2.56 p.m. Friday

Vitebsk

To Moscow →

Vilna

Smolensk

Vyazma
3 p.m. Tuesday

N
↑

Minsk

Orsha

MOGILEV *5 a.m. Tuesday Feb 28th*
returns 8.20 p.m. Friday March 3rd

153

man was led off to the Government Pavilion, a separate building with some anterooms previously reserved for ministers who had come to address the Duma. It was connected to the main hall by a glass-roofed passage and technically was not part of the parliamentary building, so that deputies avoided the stigma of 'turning the Duma into a prison'.

There would be hundreds of men like Shcheglovitov in the next hours and days — hunted down and brought to the Tauride Palace as prisoners, fearing to be shot, and it was to Kerensky's credit that he protected them from violence. Even the hated former interior minister Protopopov — the man who had so recently fallen on his knees before the Empress, calling out 'Oh Majesty, I see Christ behind you' and now the man most likely to be torn to bits — was safe once inside the Tauride Palace. Found hiding in a tailor's shop, Protopopov, 'trembling with terror' was almost unrecognisable: a shrunken, frightened figure, all posturing gone. Kerensky pushed forward and stood over him. 'Don't touch that man', he cried with a raised arm that commanded what was otherwise a rabble.

The crowd fell back silent as Kerensky pushed on, the cringing Protopopov trailing in his wake. 'It looked as if he were leading him to execution, to something dreadful...Kerensky dashed past like the flaming torch of revolutionary justice and behind him they dragged that miserable little figure in the rumpled greatcoat, surrounded by bayonets.'[18]

Goremykin, prime minister until the previous year, was another prisoner brought in, though at first he was treated with special consideration on the insistence of the 'old school' Duma deputies. It would be a brief respite.

Kerensky found him in Rodzyanko's room. 'In a corner sat a very old gentleman, with exceedingly long whiskers. He wore a fur coat, and looked like a gnome.' Kerensky, noting that he had taken the trouble to hang round his neck the Order of St Andrew, refused to be impressed. 'In the name of the revolutionary people I declare you under arrest', he shouted.[19] Rodzyanko, faced with this challenge to his own authority as leader of the Duma committee, backed down helplessly. Two soldiers led away the confused and crestfallen old Goremykin to join the others.

Kerensky was everywhere. 'I was summoned and sent for from all sides. As in a trance, regardless of day or night...I rushed about the Duma. Sometimes I almost lost consciousness for fifteen or twenty minutes until a glass of brandy was forced down my throat and I was made to drink a cup of black coffee.'[20]

Kerensky would become more and more excitable as the hours and days passed. Nabokov, seeing him for the first time, was struck by his 'loss of emotional balance'. He was also astonished when Kerensky, coming out of one meeting 'excited, agitated, hysterical,' put up his hands, grabbed the corners of his wing collar, and ripped them off,' achieving a deliberately proletarian look, instead of that of a dandy'.[21]

His power, nevertheless, was enormous for there was no doubting among the Duma deputies that the new Soviet, with a thousand members milling around the Tauride Palace, was master if it chose to be. Kerensky was the bridge between two rivals in an uneasy coalition, and for the Duma members he was a bridge they could not afford to cross. The Temporary Committee of the Duma had the better claim to government, but its members knew that in this revolution they could only lead where Kerensky was willing to follow.

TRAPPED in Millionnaya Street, Michael knew little that day of events in the world aside. After a few restless hours on a settee, he was awakened by 'the noise of heavy traffic and movement of cars and lorries filled with soldiers who were shooting mainly in the air and there were also explosions of hand-grenades. The soldiers shouted and cheered, waved red flags and had red ribbons and bows on their breasts and buttonholes'.[22]

Peering cautiously out from the apartment windows, Michael guessed from the jubilation of the troops driving by that there was no longer any resistance in the capital. There had been fierce fighting that morning around the Admiralty building until the last of the loyal troops, holed up there since the evacuation of the Winter Palace at 5 a.m., surrendered after warnings that the guns of the St Peter and St Paul Fortress would be turned on them.[23] Thereafter the streets belonged to the revolution and the head-hunting gangs seeking out policemen, and anyone deemed 'a traitor' to the revolution.

One target was Grand Duke Andrew's mistress Kschessinska. In the depths of winter, when the fuel depots were empty and people freezing in their homes, four military lorries, laden with sacks of coal, had arrived at her mansion on Kammenny-Ostrov Prospekt.[24] To the mob, she was not an admired ballet star but the pampered recipient of blatant imperial favours, and a profiteer in arms deals. A vengeful crowd therefore descended on her house and sacked it from top to bottom. Kschessinska, forewarned, fled the house just in time, dressed like a peasant and with a shawl over her head, but not before remembering to pack a small suitcase with the most valuable of her jewels.[25]

At the nearby Astoria Hotel, a mob stormed in, after claiming that shots had been fired from there, and wrecked it. British and French officers staying there — military observers attached to the Russian army — were left alone, and indeed one was astonished to find himself being saluted as rebel troops ran up the staircase in search of Russians hiding in their rooms. Many of these, women as well as men, were dragged away as 'prisoners of the revolution', their fate uncertain.[26]

For Michael it was galling to think what might have been, if his brother had given him the free hand he had requested. Now there was no authority, no rallying point for those who would have welcomed the chance to turn the tables on the lawless mob rampaging throughout the capital. Where was the relief force so confidently promised by Nicholas? There was no sign among the celebrating rebels that they feared their arrival, and since the telephones were not working Michael could not contact anyone to find out what had happened to them. There was therefore nothing to do but sit tight and wait out the day. Fortunately their luck held. The bands searching the city for prisoners, not knowing that Michael was in 12 Millionnaya Street, left the building alone. 'The day passed peacefully and no one bothered us', he wrote that evening in his diary.[27]

Next morning, Wednesday March 1, there was cause for alarm when a squad of uniformed men broke into the apartment above, the home of the Procurator of the Holy Synod, and dragged him away shouting that he was 'under arrest'. In the house next door, an old general, Baron Staekelberg, defended his home for hours against a gang of soldiers and sailors, and when they broke in they lynched his servant and killed the general, hauling his body to the Neva and throwing it in.[28]

Fortunately, local telephone lines in central Petrograd began to be restored during that morning and at last Michael was able to call out. Johnson spoke to Rodzyanko and told him where they were. An armed guard of five officers and 20 cadet officers was swiftly organised and despatched to Millionnaya Street as protection. By noon the apartment was secured, the armed sentries at the doors explaining themselves to any roving bands passing by that they were 'acting on the orders of the Temporary Committee of the Duma'.[29] The officers and cadets were housed in the study and in the empty flat below; with their arrival the building was thereafter left untouched.

With that, Michael was back in business. He had scribbled a note to Natasha that 'our brains are wide-awake and the order of the day is to find a way of contacting representatives where we are renting an estate' — a reference to their English property and thus code for the British ambassador Buchanan.[30]

As visitors now began to arrive, a courier was found to get that message to a fretting Natasha so that she would know where he was. Among those who sped to Millionnaya Street was a lawyer, Nikolai Ivanov, an aide of Rodzyanko, who brought with him an 'imperial manifesto' which he wanted Michael to sign. This promised a constitutional monarchy as soon as the war ended, and immediate recall of the Duma and the formation of a government 'that enjoys the trust of the country'.[31] The busy Ivanov had already secured the signatures of Grand Dukes Paul and Kirill, and in so doing Rodzyanko hoped that it would also prove to be to his personal advantage, with he, and not Prince Lvov, emerging as prime minister.

The manifesto, drafted by Rodzyanko and Ivanov, was to be credited to Paul; he had already shown it to Alexandra, though predictably she had greeted it with her usual scorn. 'Paul has worked out some idiotical manifesto about a constitution after the war,' she wrote to Nicholas, in a letter, which would reach him when it no longer mattered.[32] Nevertheless, to Rodzyanko it appeared to offer one last chance to seize back the initiative, as he canvassed supporting signatories. If this was endorsed by the family — a Grand Duke's manifesto — it might well persuade even Nicholas that he no option other than to sign it.

Michael agreed to add his name. It met the immediate necessity of a new start under a new style of government, and if the family were to unite behind that, then it might offer hope of some last-minute reprieve for his brother. Expecting Nicholas to be back in Tsarskoe Selo that evening, and the promised arrival of his relief force, Michael was determined to meet him and plead yet again for a new start for Russia. A Grand Duke's manifesto could only help his arguments. Looking on the bright side, he wrote to Natasha to say that if Nicholas did accept it, 'Russia's new existence will begin'.[33]

That afternoon the British ambassador Buchanan turned up at the apartment, and agreed that the new manifesto might just save Nicholas's throne. Michael told him that he had 'repeatedly urged the Emperor to grant reforms, but in vain, and that he greatly regretted that Nicholas 'had not done spontaneously what he would now have to do by force.'[34]

Buchanan, knowing that Michael was planning to see Nicholas that night in Tsarskoe Selo — but equally unaware that the Tsar was now heading in the opposite direction, to Pskov— asked him 'to beseech the Emperor, in the name of King George, to sign the manifesto, to show himself to his people and to effect a complete reconciliation with them'. Michael agreed to press his brother to do so.[35]

Yet quite how Michael was to get to Tsarskoe Selo, with the mobs in control of the streets, was another matter. However, both assumed that Rodzyanko could provide the necessary security and that the Duma men in the Tauride Palace had more control than they actually possessed. Rodzyanko had said as much, for unless Michael did hand over the manifesto to Nicholas, it was not worth the paper it was written on — as almost immediately would prove to be the case.

The blame for that would fall in large part on the ambitious Grand Duke Kirill who had signed the manifesto the day before. For at the very moment that Michael was putting his name to the document, Kirill effectively tore it up — marching into the Tauride Palace at the head of a battalion of his marines, a big red bow on his chest, to 'declare his loyalty to the Temporary Duma Committee'.[36] His marines guarding Tsarskoe Selo would also be withdrawn on his orders.

Kirill, like Michael and every other Grand Duke, had sworn an oath of loyalty to 'serve His Imperial Majesty, not sparing my life and limb, until the very last drop of my blood'; now, on Wednesday, March 1, he joined the revolution, whilst Nicholas was still Tsar. Paléologue, driving later past Kirill's palace on Glinka Street, would see a red flag flying on its roof.[37]

One of those who saw Kirill's arrival at the Tauride Palace was General Polovtsov, once commander of the Tartar regiment in Michael's Savage Division, and someone who continued to respect him. In Petrograd by chance, he had been recruited by Guchkov to serve on the Duma's 'military committee'. To his eyes, the arrival of Kirill 'made a great impression and was understood by the crowd as a sign that the imperial family refused to fight for its rights and recognised the revolution as an accomplished fact'. The monarchists in the Duma 'did not like it.' [38]

Kirill's later justification for his actions was that the Duma Committee was the only effective authority in the capital, and because it had ordered all units in the capital to report to it 'to show its allegiance', he had no alternative as a commander of one of those units but to obey.

'They were the only loyal and reliable troops left in the capital... to have deprived them of leadership would simply have added to the disaster.' His concern, he protested, 'was to do my utmost to re-establish order in the capital...so that the Emperor could safely return.'[39] Few believed that, either then or on reading his subsequent apologia, which he boldly entitled *My Life in Russia's Service.*

Kirill's hostility to Tsarskoe Selo was well known, as were his own ambitions. However much he protested his innocence, he was bound to be suspected of having gone to the Duma in the hope of ingratiating himself, and with Nicholas gone, it would be the 'loyal' Kirill who would be asked to become Regent, even Emperor. Unfortunately for Kirill, as the Duma Committee came to see Nicholas's abdication as the only hope of saving the monarchy — and as the price of a deal with the Soviet — the only man being talked about as Regent was Michael. Kirill had spent his reputation for nothing.

Understandably, he was therefore outraged, as was uncle Grand Duke Paul, that Michael should have emerged as the hope for salvation. Paul suspected that it was all the work of the scheming Natasha and her left-wing friends in the Duma. As he wrote to Kirill: 'the new intention to make Misha Regent displeases me greatly. It is inadmissible and it is possible that it may be merely the intrigues of Brasova...if Nicky agrees the manifesto which we have sanctioned...the demands of the people will have been satisfied.'[40]

Kirill replied immediately in similar cloud-cuckoo terms: 'I completely agree,' he wrote furiously. 'But despite my entreaty to work together and in conformity with the family, Misha sneaks away and communicates secretly with Rodzyanko,' he wailed. 'I have been left completely alone during these days to bear responsibility towards Nicky and to save the situation while recognising the new government.'[41]

Kirill's petulant response was understandable: his march into the Tauride Palace had gained him nothing but odium. As for Paul, his manifesto was already dead even as he was advancing its merits. It had been vetoed by the Soviet and as that became clear it ceased to matter, and was put away in a drawer.

Simply too little, too late? Ironically, Nicholas would still think it was too much, too soon. In any case, what the family wanted did not matter to him and it would not be they who would dictate what was to come. As for Alexandra, it had taken just five days, but her hated ministers were now under arrest, her despised government was no more, and her humiliated husband lost in a train. Her downfall, the prospect of which had occupied the minds of so many for so long, was already complete. What she thought and said was no longer of any consequence and never would be again.

AT about seven o' clock that Wednesday evening, after travelling 860 miles, Nicholas's train crawled into Pskov station, and he was at last back in contact with the world, albeit one very different to that he had left 38 hours earlier, at 5 a.m. the previous day. There was no one to meet him, though shortly afterwards the 63-year-old army commander, General Nikolai Ruzsky, turned up at the station, 'bent, grey and old, wearing galoshes,' his eyes behind his spectacles 'unfriendly'.[42]

Sitting in the Tsar's study aboard the train, Ruzsky was uncomfortable about discussing constitutional issues, but he was convinced of the need for concessions of the kind which Michael had argued for, and he pressed on doggedly to say so. There was a gloomy dinner, then the talks resumed.

Nicholas thought Ruzsky rude and the general would later admit that 'we had a storm brewing'.[43] As stubborn as ever and still blind to his own peril, Nicholas refused to give up his autocratic powers, though he conceded that he was willing to appoint Rodzyanko as prime minister, albeit with a Cabinet responsible to the Tsar.

Ruzsky was getting nowhere, until a telegram arrived from General Alekseev at Mogilev, urging the same concessions. Nicholas, now in an uncomfortable corner, sought compromise. He insisted that, whatever else, the ministers for war, navy and foreign affairs should continue to be accountable to him. Ruzsky would not even concede that: all ministers, he argued, should be accountable to the Duma.

Nicholas went to his sleeping car a rattled man. In refusing the demands of politicians and dismissing the pleas of his brother and others, he had assumed the absolute loyalty of his senior military commanders. Now they, too, seemed to be against him. At 2 a.m. he called Ruzsky to his carriage and told him that he had 'decided to compromise'; a manifesto granting a responsible ministry, already signed, was on the table.[44] Ruzsky was authorised to notify Rodzyanko that he could now be prime minister of a parliamentary government.

However, that proved only how little the Tsar knew of what had happened in the capital since Michael had wired him at 10.30 p.m. on Monday night, a little more 48 hours earlier. When, at 3.30 a.m. Ruzsky got through to Petrograd on the direct line, Rodzyanko's reply was shatteringly frank: 'It is obvious that neither His Majesty nor you realise what is going on here... Unfortunately the manifesto has come too late...and there is no return to the past..everywhere troops are siding with the Duma and the people, and the threatening demands for an abdication in favour of the son, with Michael Aleksandrovich as Regent, are becoming quite definite.'[45]

When Ruzsky finished his long and painfully slow discussion on the direct wire, the time was 7.30 a.m. on Thursday March 2. Before the day was out, Nicholas would abdicate not once, but twice.

12. POISONING THE CHALICE

HIS discussion on the wire with Rodzyanko was the first time that Ruzsky knew that the crisis in Petrograd had moved beyond demands for a constitutional monarchy to that of the abdication of Nicholas. He therefore sent on Rodzyanko's taped message to Alekseev at Supreme Headquarters and at 9 a.m. that Thursday morning Alekseev cabled his reply: 'my deep conviction that there is no choice and that the abdication should now take place...it is very painful for me to say so, but there is no other solution.'[1]

Having made his own views clear, at least to Ruzsky, Alekseev — less pained than he pretended — did not wait for a reply but sent out his own telegrams to his other army commanders and to the admirals commanding the Baltic and Black Sea fleets. Russia had a war to fight and Alekseev was determined that the revolution in Petrograd should not undermine the frontline armies waiting to begin their spring offensive. He summarised the discussions between Ruzsky and Rodzyanko, putting the case in black and white and more bluntly than the Duma president had done himself. 'The dynastic question has been put point-blank', he told his commanders. 'The war may be continued until its victorious end only provided the demands regarding the abdication from the throne in favour of the son and under the regency of Grand Duke Michael Aleksandrovich are satisfied. Apparently the situation does not permit another solution...'[2]

His cables went out at 10.15 am. Four hours later, at 2.15 p.m., he wired the Emperor at Pskov giving him the first three replies. They would prove decisive.

Nicholas had been given a transcript of the early-morning tapes when he arose in the late morning, and he also read the cable from Alekseev recommending abdication. There was 'a terrible moment of silence,' Ruzsky remembered, as Nicholas absorbed the shock,[3] but he gave no sign of his inner turmoil when he went for a walk along the station platform with Ruzsky at lunchtime. A few hours earlier he had assumed that in conceding a responsible ministry he had given more than enough; now he was being asked to contemplate the unthinkable: that he should give up the throne. Later it would be said by those who deplored his abdication that Ruzsky bullied him into it, shouting at him and thumping the table with his fist, saying 'Will you make up your mind to go!'[4]

No, he was not bullied and Ruzsky had no reason to do so knowing that the decision depended on the replies awaited from the commanders. There was no comfort for Nicholas there in the cable from Alekseev, which incorporated the first three responses.

The reply from Grand Duke Nicholas — 'Uncle Nikolasha', the former Supreme Commander sacked in 1915, and now commander on the Caucasus front could not be more frank:

As a loyal subject I feel it my necessary duty of allegiance in the spirit of my oath, to beg Your Imperial Majesty on my knees to save Russia and your heir, being aware of your sacred feelings of love for Russia and for him. Make the Sign of the Cross and hand over to him your heritage. There is no other way…

The second was from Brusilov, Michael's former commander-in-chief, and the most successful fighting general in the army:

At the present time the only solution…is the abdication in favour of the heir Tsarevich under the Regency of Grand Duke Michael Aleksandrovich. There is no other way out; speed is necessary, so that the popular conflagration, which has grown to large proportions, can be rapidly extinguished otherwise it will result in incalculable catastrophic consequences. By these acts the dynasty itself would be saved in the person of the lawful heir.

The third was from General Aleksei Evert, the commander on the western front: *Under the conditions which have been created and not seeing any other answer I implore Your Majesty to make a decision which would be in agreement with the declaration of the President of the State Duma…as the only measure which apparently can stop the revolution and thus save Russia from the horrors of anarchy.*[5]

Ruzsky, armed with these, and backed by two of his generals, went back to the Emperor in his railway carriage. He handed over the text, letting it speak for itself. Nicholas, smoking one cigarette and then lighting another, read it and then put it down on the table before rising and going to the window, staring out unseeingly. He could have contempt for politicians, and ignore his brother, but he could not defy his generals and they had just passed a vote of no confidence in him, both as Tsar and Supreme Commander. He could not sack them, as he could sack politicians, nor could he argue with them.

Suddenly he turned and said calmly: 'I have decided. I shall renounce the throne'. He made the sign of the Cross and the three generals, realising the enormity of what had just been said, followed suit.[6]

Two short telegrams were drafted for Nicholas — the first to Rodzyanko.

There is no sacrifice which I would not bear for the sake of the real welfare and for the salvation of our own dear Mother Russia. Therefore I am ready to abdicate the throne in favour of my son, provided that he can remain with me until he comes of age, with the Regency of my brother the Grand Duke Michael Aleksandrovich.

That was the response that was hoped for by the Duma men — Nicholas gone, a boy Emperor, Michael as Regent. His second telegram, to Alekseev, was in similar terms.[7]

Ruzsky was just about to send these off when an unexpected cable arrived from Petrograd announcing that two members of the Temporary Committee, Guchkov and Shulgin, were on their way to Pskov to meet the Tsar and were leaving at 3.35 p.m.

Not knowing the significance of this, Ruzsky held up despatch of the abdication cables and went back to Nicholas with the unexpected news of the two deputies.[8] Could they be coming with some offer that would make the abdication unnecessary? Was Nicholas II in fact to be reprieved?[9]

However, fifteen minutes later, reality returned to the imperial carriage. The frontline commanders had spoken and that being so Nicholas could not remain Emperor. His original abdication cables were handed back to Ruzsky, Nicholas telling him to send them out to Rodzyanko and Alekseev. The time was 3.45 p.m.[10]

At that moment Nicholas ceased to be Tsar, Alexis was the new emperor; and Michael was Regent. Or so it was assumed when his cables were circulated by Alekseev to the military commanders and Rodzyanko spread the word in the Duma. Indeed, his abdication was so generally known that in London his cousin King George V that night wrote in his diary: 'Heard from Buchanan that the Duma had forced Nicky to sign his abdication and Misha had been appointed Regent...' The king was in no doubt about the reason: 'I fear Alicky (*the Empress*) is the cause of it all and Nicky has been weak'.[11]

What was not taken into account was that his abdication cable contained a condition in respect of Alexis— 'provided that he can remain with me until he comes of age' — which would have been more than three years later, in August 1920.

It was disregarded firstly because no discussion or thought had yet been given to that particular question, but more significantly because it was deemed irrelevant to the fact of his abdication. To say as he did that he was 'ready to abdicate' concealed the reality that he had been forced off the throne, after being abandoned on all sides. He was in no position to 'abdicate conditionally' or dictate the terms of his going; he was finished. And that being so, his son Alexis automatically succeeded him, for that was the law.

Moreover, the question of his future over the next three years was not the issue in the crisis engulfing the capital and thus the wider nation. The sole imperative was that with an innocent boy on the throne and the constitutionally-minded Michael as Regent, the monarchy could be secured, which is what mattered to all but the socialists in the Soviet.

To say as he did in his cable that *There is no sacrifice which I would not bear for the sake of the real welfare and for the salvation of our own dear Mother Russia* meant nothing at all if immediately contradicted by his saying *except for having to part with my son*.

But that, it turned out, was precisely what he was saying. Millions of fathers had lost their sons to the war, and if order was not restored, tens of thousands of others would lose theirs in the resulting chaos. Nicholas hoped to be not among them. Their sacrifice was not to be his.

MICHAEL was keeping closely in touch with developments at the Tauride Palace and on that Thursday, March 2, there were constant comings and goings at Millionnaya Street as Duma emissaries arrived with news. Michael had known the night before that while 'all the power is now in the hands of the Temporary Committee', the Duma men 'are in difficulties because of the strong pressure by the Committee of Deputies of Workers and Soldiers'.[12]

Early that morning he knew that his brother had, belatedly, offered a responsible ministry under Rodzyanko — disregarding his own advice that it should be under Prince Lvov — but he also knew that this was no longer enough. It was frustrating sitting in Millionnaya Street, unable to do anything to help. Should he go to the Tauride Palace and declare his support for such a new government? Rodzyanko, who knew the mood there among the socialists, thought that potentially dangerous. The arrival of the red-bowed Kirill at the Tauride Palace had created more astonishment than uproar in the Soviet, for it had seemed to them a surrender of the imperial family, though it had also strengthened the standing of the Duma men who appeared now to be able to command even a Grand Duke.

There was less interest when, later that same day, Bimbo

turned up and also offered the Duma his support. Bimbo had only just arrived back at his Millionnaya Street palace having taken the revolution as signal that he could end the exile imposed upon him on New Year's Day by the Tsar. Tall, bald, fat and still a bachelor at 58, Bimbo was a gossip who had never concealed his contempt for Nicholas and Alexandra; as a young man in the Chevalier Gardes he had been known as 'Phillipe Egalité' because he insisted on calling his soldiers 'my friends'.[13] At the Tauride Palace his support for the Duma was acknowledged, but not thought of having any political significance. As for the Soviet, they hardly knew he was there.

But Michael was neither an eccentric Grand Duke nor the discredited Kirill. The Soviet might take his appearance as political interference, as an attempt to put his name behind the Duma and forestall the Soviet's demands for a 'democratic republic'. While the Duma men might earn credit for having two Grand Dukes signal their support for them, Michael was a different story: if he turned up, the revolutionaries might well be tempted to keep him there, as hostage for their own necks. In the event, by the time Rodzyanko got round to replying to Michael, to dissuade him from going to the Duma, he knew that Nicholas had abdicated, and that Michael was Regent. That being so, it was not his place to go to the Duma; it was for the Duma to come to him.

SHARING the Tauride Palace, the Duma Committee and the Soviet shared little else. Both were the product of revolution, but both hoped for different outcomes. The Duma was intent upon a constitutional monarchy, the Soviet for a republic. The question was not now whether Nicholas could remain on the throne, but whether the throne itself remained in being.

The struggle for the future of Russia began in the meeting room of the Duma Committee just after midnight and would go on for the next twenty hours of Thursday, March 2, so that it began with the expectation of Nicholas's abdication, but ended with it being known that he had.

The Soviet executive, led by their chairman, Nikolai Chkheidze, a 53-year-old Georgian schoolmaster and socialist deputy, included many radical members of the intelligentsia, as well as political prisoners just released from the Kresty prison across the Neva. With the exception of Kerensky, none of the Soviet members thought of themselves as sufficiently politically experienced to be thought of as competent ministers in any new government. Nevertheless, they were determined to fashion its agenda.

Political convictions apart, the great difference between the Duma and the Soviet was that the members of the latter had their necks at stake. If the revolution ended in failure, the gallows beckoned for its leaders as well as many of the soldiers who thronged the Catherine Hall. Kerensky would escape, for he had saved the lives of the prominent men taken into 'protective custody'. The 'gentlemen of the Duma' would also emerge unscathed for they would be needed if order was to be restored.

Even if Nicholas abdicated, and they did not know yet that he would, the monarchy with Michael as Regent would want a reckoning with those who had murdered for the revolution. Officers and mutineers who had killed policemen or their fellow soldiers could expect no mercy.

In August 1916, when mutineers in the 2nd Brigade murdered their colonel, 20 men were shot. Three months later, when two regiments, called to a strike at the Renault factory fired on police, 150 men were executed.[14]

So as part of its deal with the Duma Committee the Soviet demanded a complete amnesty for all revolutionaries, soldiers as well as any others accused of terrorism or murder. The Soviet and the rebel troops both know that if they did not hang together now, they would hang together later.

So, as part of its agenda, the Soviet sought guarantees that the garrison in Petrograd would not be dispersed into the army as a whole, to be picked off later, or disarmed. With these and other measures, the Soviet aim was to continue to hold a loaded pistol at the head of a new government, should it later be tempted to seek revenge. It had already shown that, whatever might be agreed, it knew who was boss. The day before, in its Order No 1, it had stated in its Point 4 that *The orders of the Military Commission of the State Duma shall be executed only in such cases as do not conflict with the orders and resolution of the Soviet of Workers' and Soldiers' Deputies.* The message was that the Duma Committee could have all the attributes of government, provided that it did not do anything of which the Soviet disapproved. It could bark, but it should remember that it was on a short lead.

When the Soviet delegates filed into the Duma Committee with their agenda they found Rodzyanko at a far table, drinking soda water. Facing him, at another table, was the white-haired Pavel Milyukov, sitting behind a pile of papers, notes and telegrams. Across the floor the other Committee members, including Prince Lvov, occupied a row of chairs and armchairs, with other deputies standing around them.[15] After desultory conversation, the Soviet executive read out its conditions for supporting the Duma as government. The most difficult over the next 40 hours would be their 'Point Three': in effect, the future of the monarchy.

The man who would have nothing to do with their demands for a republic was Milyukov, though he was prepared to yield on the other issues, including an amnesty. 'He spoke for the entire Duma Committee; everyone considered this a matter of course,' noted a Soviet member. 'It was clear that Milyukov here was not only a leader but the boss of the right wing.' He would not yield on the monarchy and on this the 'bourgeois leader was irreconcilable'.

Milyukov attempted to make a reformed monarchy appear utterly harmless, without power or influence, a fig leaf for those who did rule. It could not affect the kind of government which Russia would enjoy, and it could not threaten the safety of those who had joined the revolution. There was nothing the Soviet need fear, for Alexis was 'a sick child' and Michael if he became Regent was 'a thoroughly stupid man'.[16]

This ploy, judged 'naive' by one,[17] did not impress the three men staring back at him. An army general, twice decorated for gallantry in the battlefield, married to a woman known for her strong political opinions — whatever he was, he was not stupid.

By eight o' clock on Thursday evening, with all now knowing that Nicholas had abdicated that afternoon, the issue of the monarchy was still not settled. It was then that Milyukov played his trump card, by announcing that if there was no Tsar, then he would not be in government. 'Now, if I am not here, there is no government at all. And, if there is no government, then...you yourselves can understand...'[18]

An ultimatum or a bluff? The Soviet could not know which, but if it was a bluff it was one they did not dare call. Reluctantly, and unhappily, the Soviet gave way, grudgingly agreeing that the status of Russia should be decided by a future elected Constituent Assembly, leaving Russia as a monarchy until then. However, it made clear that it would 'engage without delay in a broad struggle for a democratic republic'.[19]

The monarchy had been reprieved, but only just. Russia could have its sickly boy Emperor, with Michael as figurehead Regent. And with that, surely, the revolution after six tempestuous days was now all but over. Russia was set on a new course.

That afternoon the shape of the new government had become clear. It comprised many of the same men who would have been in any government designed to have public confidence. Milyukov, perched on a table, had jotted their names down on a sheet of paper and distributed the portfolios with little discussion.

The prime minister was to be Prince Lvov, the man Michael had recommended to his brother on Monday night 'as the only possible candidate'. Rodzyanko, whom Nicholas thought he had appointed prime minister that morning, was not even in the twelve-man Cabinet, though he continued to head the Duma. Milyukov was foreign minister; Guchkov, then on his way to Pskov, was war minister. Kerensky, the only member of the Soviet included in the Cabinet, was justice minister.

As the meeting with the Soviet came to a close that evening, the name of this self-appointed government was chosen almost casually. Milyukov suggested 'The Provisional Committee of the Duma'; the Soviet member Nikolai Sukhanov suggested instead that it be called more simply 'The Provisional Government'. Milyukov nodded, and scratched that name down.[20]

By 10 p.m., with everything seemingly settled, The Provisional Government was born. However, almost at that same moment, Nicholas in Pskov was to throw everything into turmoil again. There was to be no boy emperor, and no Regent. He had changed his mind.

13. 'A FATHER'S FEELINGS'

ALEKSANDR Guchkov and Vasily Shulgin, the two delegates sent to Pskov by the Duma Committee, now the Provisional Government, set off from Petrograd before news reached the capital that Nicholas had offered to abdicate— and therefore, in the minds of all those who heard of it, had abdicated.

Before setting off, and as the talks with the Soviet dragged on, Guchkov had set down the need for decisive action, regardless of any agreement with the Soviet:

In this chaos, in everything that goes on, the first thought should be to save the monarchy. Without the monarchy Russia cannot live. But apparently the present Emperor can no longer reign. An imperial order by him is no longer an order: it would not be executed. And if that is so, then how can we calmly and indifferently await the moment when all the revolutionary riffraff starts to look for an issue itself? They would destroy the monarchy...If we act following an agreement 'with them' it will surely turn out to be least favourable to us...[1]

Given this, Guchkov and Shulgin still thought that when they did arrive in Pskov, 170 miles away, their task would be to persuade Nicholas to abdicate. They expected a struggle.

The journey took them seven hours, so it was around 10 p.m. when their train pulled into the station and they were led across the tracks to the brightly-lit imperial carriages. Shown into a large saloon car, with a table set with *hors d'oeuvres*, they were met by the bent figure of old Baron Fredericks, the Tsar's long-time minister of court and keeper of the family's secrets.

Shulgin suddenly felt uncomfortable, conscious that he was 'unshaved, with a crumpled collar, in a business coat.'[2] Then Nicholas came in, wearing a grey Circassian coat, his face calm. He gestured and the two delegates sat down.

For Guchkov it was an extraordinary moment: for months he had been planning a coup in which Nicholas would be arrested on his train and made to abdicate. In Guchkov's mind he had pictured a scene not unlike the very one of which he was now part. It would have been two weeks later and there would have been no revolution, but otherwise there were uncanny resemblances between fact and ambition.

Yet Guchkov found himself curiously disconcerted as he faced Nicholas. He shook hands with him and sat down facing him across the polished tabletop. The Emperor — or past Emperor as he was now thought back in Petrograd — was sitting and leaning slightly back against the silken wall, his face blank and impenetrable. Guchkov, recovering his own composure, put his hand on his forehead as was his habit when speaking, and began his case, looking down rather than at Nicholas.[3]

As he did so, Ruzsky came in, bowed to Nicholas, and whispered to Shulgin to tell him 'that the matter has been decided'. However, he said nothing to Guchkov, who continued talking until he had finished what he had come here to say.

Expecting an argument he was astonished when Nicholas calmly replied: 'I have made the decision to abdicate the throne'.[4] Guchkov glanced at Shulgin. On the journey to Pskov he had rehearsed what he would say, making notes, and working out with Shulgin how best to counter Nicholas's rebuttal of their arguments. They expected a long night. Now, suddenly, it was all over.

The shock, in fact, was still to come. For after a pause Nicholas announced that he was abdicating not only for himself but for his son, and that he had therefore decided to name Michael as his successor.

Bewildered, Guchkov stared in disbelief. 'But we had counted on the figure of the little Alexis Nikolaevich as having a softening effect on the transfer of power.'[5] Replacing Nicholas with an innocent boy was the bedrock of their case for preserving the monarchy against those demanding a republic.

So why? Nicholas looked across the table. 'I have come to the conclusion that, in the light of his illness, I should abdicate in my name and his name simultaneously, as I cannot be separated from him.'

He leaned forward to Guchkov, as if seeking understanding. 'I hope you will understand the feelings of a father.'[6]

Fortunately for Nicholas — unfortunately for Russia — Guchkov still did not know of the earlier abdication cable, when Nicholas declared himself ready to abdicate provided that his son 'can stay with me until he comes of age', for had he done so he would have arrived in Pskov with a very different purpose. He would not have wasted his time in arguing for abdication, but rather concentrated on agreeing the terms under which Alexis, the new emperor, would remain in parental care for the next three years.

Nicholas could not abdicate twice. His first was binding on him— Ruzsky had a signed copy of that — and acceptance by the Duma Committee of some reasonable arrangement for Alexis's care would suffice to dispose of any conditional element in his abdication. The principle that an offer once made cannot be withdrawn if its condition is met would have been sufficient for Guchkov to have refused to consider the removal of Alexis from the succession. His difficulty was that he did not know that there had been an offer. And Ruzsky, knowing nothing of the political significance of the issue in terms of the struggle going on at the Tauride Palace, chose to remain silent about it.

However, the fact was that while waiting for the two delegates from Pskov, Nicholas had started to brood about giving up his throne but losing his son at the same time — a prospect which he pondered in dismay. The thought of his beloved son torn from his family and handed over to strangers was too terrible to contemplate, though it was probably no better to think that he might be handed over to 'Uncle Misha' as Regent and 'that woman'. A cynical view might well be that he also bitterly resolved that if 'they don't want me, then they won't get my son', but whatever was going through his tortured mind, he failed to recognise that what he was proposing was actually unlawful. The laws of succession drawn up and binding since the days of Tsar Paul I were designed to remove the right of one Emperor to choose or block the next.

Tsar Paul had good reason for introducing the law: his own mother, Catherine the Great, had intended to hand her throne to a grandson, not Paul, but died before that could be done. Previous sovereigns had also played fast and loose with the succession. No longer. Succession was to be by rank, not preference, and that was the law followed by the five emperors after Paul. There were to be no more palace coups.

This did not mean that an imbecile could demand the throne, for it was understood that someone clearly unfit to take the throne should not do so; however in ruling out such an heir there were independent procedures by which this should be shown to be in the interests of the nation, not merely an excuse based on the personal judgement of an Emperor.

Was Alexis unfit to become Emperor? The answer was No. Indeed, his parents had spent years hiding his illness from public knowledge so that when he did ascend the throne it would not be held against him. The issue here, never considered before, was separation. And that, in itself — while personally heart-breaking for his family — was not cause for ruling him out. After all, his brother as Regent was hardly likely to countenance such a course for his ailing nephew, and there had been no suggestion in the meetings at the Tauride Palace that removal of Alexis from his parents had been a condition of his inheritance.

Nevertheless that is what Nicholas in that afternoon of Thursday, March 2, decided would be the case, recklessly indifferent to the consequences for crown and country. To find excuse for his change of mind he called Professor Sergei Fedorov, the court physician to his carriage. Fedorov had always told him that Alexis's haemophilia was incurable, and he repeated that fact now. But that was not what Nicholas wanted to know: his question was whether he thought Alexis would be allowed to remain with the family after his succession. The correct answer to that was surely that Fedorov could not know: he was not a politician, he was a doctor. Instead, probably because he knew what answer Nicholas was looking for, he told him that he doubted if Alexis would be allowed to remain with his parents.[7] Where he could be more certain was that if separated, Alexis might not get the care he needed, given that his illness had been hidden from the world.

With that, Nicholas had the confirmation he needed to decide that he had sufficient cause for removing Alexis from the succession — contrary to the *Fundamental Laws* which bound all emperors. No one had a copy of these at Pskov but nevertheless Guchkov and Shulgin recognised the problem they faced, and retired to discuss it all with Ruzsky and his generals. Could an emperor change the laws of succession laid down in the past? After all, Nicholas was an autocrat and what one Tsar ordained perhaps another could set aside, a view which it seemed Nicholas had adopted. None of them could say with certainty that he was wrong.

Someone wondered if Michael's marriage to a commoner was a problem? They had no idea, but there was mention that Alexander II had married a commoner, though he was already then Emperor and she was his second wife.[8]

As the minutes ticked by the group came to the view that they had no choice but to accept the manifesto as it stood. Every hour counted and neither Guchkov nor Shulgin relished the idea of returning empty-handed to Petrograd, of lamely going back to the Duma to discuss whether a double abdication was acceptable. As things stood they reckoned they had no choice: they would have to accept Alexis being bypassed, and Michael as

Emperor. Filing back into the saloon they told Nicholas that they had agreed to his terms.

An abdication manifesto had been drafted earlier at *Stavka* and wired down to Pskov and it was this which Nicholas took into his study for amendment and signature. The original text drafted at Mogilev had been elegantly written, and the changes made by Nicholas in no way diminished the style. Beginning with a declaration about the need to continue the war 'to a victorious end' and 'the duty to draw Our people into a close union,' the remaining text, with the removal of Alexis, now read:

We have judged it right to abdicate the Throne of the Russian state and to lay down the Supreme Power. Not wishing to be parted from Our Beloved Son, We hand over Our Succession to Our Brother Grand Michael Aleksandrovich and Bless Him on his accession to the Throne of the Russian state...In the name of Our Dearly beloved native land, WE call upon all true sons of the Fatherland to fulfil their sacred duty to It by their obedience to the Tsar at this difficult time of national ordeal and to help Him, together with the people's representatives, to lead the Russian state onto the path of victory, prosperity and glory...'

A sealed copy of the abdication was handed over to Guchkov and another to Ruzsky for transmission to the army commands and to Petrograd and other key centres, including the garrison headquarters at Tsarskoe Selo.

It was then 11.40 p.m. but it was agreed that the manifesto should be timed as of three o'clock that afternoon — as stated on the draft sent from the *Stavka* when Nicholas had first decided to abdicate, albeit with Alexis as his successor.

It was also agreed that Nicholas should issue two other edicts, one naming Prince Lvov as prime minister of the new government, — the two delegates knew that had already been decided in Petrograd — and the other reappointing Grand Duke Nicholas in his place as Supreme Commander.

To give them legality, both were antedated to 2 p.m. when he was still Tsar.[9] It would have been better law if Nicholas had done the same in renouncing his son's claim to the throne on the grounds of ill-health citing independent medical evidence — the court physician was there to do that — and separating it from his own abdication. That said, it would have been better politics not to have done it at all.

But it was too late for any such comments. Just after midnight, when Guchkov and Shulgin, with their precious signed manifesto, amending the first, headed back to the capital the text of that second manifesto was being broadcast overnight to the world at large.

And with that, Nicholas left Pskov and headed back to Mogilev, the headquarters he had left with such confidence just 44 hours earlier. Throughout the formalities he had given no sign of distress. Guchkov was so astonished by the 'simple, matter-of-fact way in which the business was concluded that I even wondered whether we were dealing with a normal person'. Even with a person of 'the most iron control, of well-nigh unequalled self-control, one might have expected some show of emotion... but nothing of the sort'.[10] Others would also remark on his composure. 'He renounced the throne as simply as if he were turning over command of a cavalry squadron,' said one of his aides.[11]

Within himself, however, he was anything but calm. When he set off back to Mogilev, he went to his diary and revealed his private agony: 'At one o' clock this morning I left Pskov with a heart that is heavy over what has just happened. All around me there is nothing but treason, cowardice, and deceit!'[12]

As always, everyone was to blame but himself.

AS news reached the Tauride Palace in the early hours of Friday morning that Nicholas had removed both himself and his son from the throne, panic set in amongst the Duma leaders. The deal which they had thought settled with the Soviet had depended in great degree on the continuity of the legal order, and that the new Tsar would be a harmless boy.

Even so, the prospect of Michael as Regent had alarmed the mutineers more than it had frightened the political elements in the Soviet. Milyukov might try to persuade them that he was only 'a stupid man', but among the soldiery what was better known about him was that he had earned the two highest awards in the Russian army, and was a noted battlefield commander. They did not need to wonder what he would think about soldiers who killed their own officers. Talk of a general amnesty did little to reassure them when they thought he was to be Regent. When they found out that he was not that, but Emperor, the deal with the Soviets was not likely to survive the day.

When Milyukov had earlier gone to the Catherine Hall and a made a speech about the programme of the new government, before the issue had been finally settled with the Soviet, there had been protests when he announced the intention that Nicholas would be replaced by his son, with Michael as Regent. 'But that's the old dynasty', came cries from the crowd.

'Yes, gentlemen, that's the old dynasty, which you may not like and which I may not like, but…we cannot leave unanswered the question of the form of government. We have in mind a constitutional monarchy…but if we stop to quarrel about it now…Russia will drift into civil war, and we shall have a ruined country.'[13]

That evening as word spread that Michael was to be Regent, a frightened Rodzyanko, 'accompanied by a handful of officers who reeked of alcohol' came running up to Milyukov. 'In a quavering voice,' recalled Milyukov, a shaken Rodzyanko 'repeated their assertions that after what I had said about the dynasty they could not go back to their units. They demand that I retract what I had said. This I could not do, but on seeing the behaviour of Rodzyanko, who knew that I had spoken not only in my own name but in the name of the Progressive Bloc as a whole, I decided to issue a statement saying that I had expressed only my personal view.'[14]

The officers went in fear of retribution, but fear worked two ways and Rodzyanko was certainly one of those who was as scared of the revolution as the revolution was scared of the monarchy. Later, Milyukov would describe him as being in 'a blue funk' and this would become a significant factor in the next hours, for Rodzyanko would be the first to crumble when the news came, early in the morning, that Michael had become Emperor.

The Duma Committee as a whole had been willing to back Milyukov when they believed that Alexis would succeed to the throne, for that transfer of power was lawful and more importantly it faced the Soviet with the problem of waging war on a child. Little Alexis could not be compelled to abdicate because he was too young to sign anything, and they could be sure that Michael would never sign such a manifesto on his behalf. Alexis was also likely to attract the sympathy of the sentimental, God-fearing peasant soldiers, wavering between loyalty and rebellion, who so far had stayed in their barracks.

As written, the manifesto removed that advantage; furthermore it created confusion in the ranks of those who had been prepared to defend the lawful transfer of power, since in turn that would underpin their own claims to be the lawful government. The authority of the Duma men had been based in great degree on the continuity of the accepted order — and with a stroke of his pen Nicholas had swept that away.

Now it was the Duma men who saw their necks at stake. Fear is infectious and it was fear Rodzyanko spread through the Duma deputies and into the new government. No one was anxious to admit that, of course, and instead they thought up better reasons for their change of heart.

One easy excuse was Michael's morganatic marriage to a woman 'well known for her political intrigues'; another was that 'he had never been interested in affairs of state' — though that could hardly matter, given that it might be held an advantage in a constitutional monarchy where the Emperor was required not to interfere.

Even the republican Kerensky recognised them 'as irrelevant

arguments'; the real issue for the new government was whether it stood by the monarchy or caved into the Soviet. The test was courage, and there was not much of that about in those early hours.

Milyukov was one of the few who did not lose his head, arguing that 'what mattered was not who should be Tsar, but that there should be a Tsar'.[16] However, their nerves rattled by Rodzyanko, the abdication manifesto was seized upon as excuse for abandoning the very case which the Duma Committee had argued so strenuously with the Soviet. Kerensky, hearing his own case being made for him, thought that 'the decision of Nicholas II had really cut the Gordian knot.' Everyone on his side of the political divide 'felt with great relief that once the lawful and rightful succession had been broken, the immediate question of the dynasty had been settled'.[17] Nicholas had done for the Soviet what the Soviet did not dare to do on its own.

But that was later when all was known. The immediate imperative for the Duma men was to keep the manifesto secret until they had time to think what to do for the best. Could publication of the manifesto itself be stopped before it was too late? Rodzyanko was among those who desperately hoped so, and he drove off to the war ministry to wire Pskov and ask Ruzsky to hold up general distribution of it. It was 5 a.m. when Rodzyanko's tape, its own testimony to his blind panic, stuttered over the direct wire.

It is extremely important that the manifesto…should not be published until I advise you of it…it is with great difficulty that we managed to restraint the revolutionary movement with more or less bearable limits, but the situation is as yet far from settled and civil war is quite possible. Perhaps they would reconcile themselves to the Regency of the Grand Duke…but his accession as Emperor would be completely unacceptable…A mutiny of soldiers has flared up, the like of which I have not seen…little by little the troops were brought to order during the night, but the proclamation of Grand Duke Michael Aleksandrovich would pour oil onto the fire and a merciless extermination of everything that can be exterminated would start...[18]

An hour later he was sending the same message to Alekseev at *Stavka*. Alekseev, who had already sent out the abdication manifesto, was disturbed by his wire conversation with Rodzyanko, and at 7 a.m. he sent out his views to his other army commanders that 'there is no frankness or sincerity in the communications of Rodzyanko' and that 'there is no unity within the State Duma and the Temporary Committee'.[19]

Alekseev suspected that it was the Soviet which was dictating affairs in the capital. His response was to propose that the army should demand that the manifesto as written be implemented and that there should be a meeting of all army commanders to 'establish unanimity in all circumstances and in any eventuality'.

At the Tauride Palace, the new government knew that it could not delay much longer its meeting with Michael — whether he was Emperor or whether they could somehow return him to Regent. Everyone knew where he was. As they waited for Rodzyanko to return from his wire talks, Kerensky picked up a copy of the Petrograd telephone directory, flicked through the pages and ran his finger down the column to the name of Princess Putyatina. Her number was 1-58-48.* A few moments later, at 5.55 a.m., the telephone rang in 12 Millionnaya Street.

---

*As listed in Petrograd telephone directory 1916

PART III
The Last Emperor

14. EMPEROR MICHAEL

THERE was never any chance of keeping secret the succession of Michael as Emperor. In the four hours which had elapsed between the first telegraphed despatches from Pskov and the desperate call from Rodzyanko, the news had spread out not only to the army but to cities across Russia. At first light, thousands of troops in frontline units were swearing an oath of allegiance to Emperor Michael II, and in the Fourth Cavalry Division General Krasnov announced the succession to 'an enormous cheer'; over the next two days he decorated soldiers with the Cross of St George in the name of His Majesty Emperor Michael.[1]

At Pskov itself, with Nicholas gone, a *Te Deum* was ordered for the new Emperor in the cathedral. Dimitri's sister Marie went to the morning service, as did Ruzsky and his generals. The square beside the cathedral was crowded with soldiers, many of them wearing a red rosette, 'their faces agitated'. Inside, a packed congregation heard the manifesto of Nicholas read out, and then prayed 'for the prolongation of the days of the new Tsar'.[2]

As the morning wore on, even in far-off Crimea, and around the ex-Tsar's favourite home at Livadia, people celebrated Michael's succession. The American-born Princess Cantacuzène, granddaughter of US President Grant, and one of Petrograd's leading hostesses, was on holiday at Yalta at that time, and remembered that Nicholas's portraits disappeared 'from shop windows and walls within an hour after the reading of the proclamation; and in their place I saw by the afternoon pictures of Michael Aleksandrovich. Flags were hung out, and all faces wore smiles of quiet satisfaction. It was very bad; now it will be better, was the general, calm verdict. The supposition of a constitutional monarch was the accepted idea.'[3]

In Moscow, where the garrison had also gone over to the revolution, although without any of the excesses which had occurred in Petrograd, the succession of Michael was greeted with 'wooden indifference' on the part of the revolutionaries;[4] there were no marching protests or riots and no sign of resistance of the kind so feared by Rodzyanko in the hot-house of the Tauride Palace.

When Alexandra's sister Grand Duchess Ella heard the news at the Chudov Abbey of which she was abbess, her sole concern was the question of Natasha. Told by a monk that in the next service the liturgy would be changed to 'Our Right Orthodox and Sovereign Lord and Emperor Michael', she protested: 'What about…?' The monk broke in hurriedly. 'Ah, Matushka, there will be no mention of the lady.'[5]

There would be no prayers for Natasha, but otherwise the faithful crossed themselves and prayed for Michael. Even in Petrograd, the storm centre of the revolution, the news of his succession was greeted with cheers, at least outside the citadels of the revolutionaries.

At Warsaw station, when Guchkov and Shulgin arrived back from Pskov, the two delegates decided to make the first proclamation about Michael. '*Long live Emperor Michael*' they cried as they hurried from their train, cheered by the people as they went by. When Shulgin walked into the station's huge entrance hall, a transit battalion of frontline troops, surrounded by a curious crowd, was drawn up there as they waited to change trains. Shulgin read out the manifesto and, lifting his eyes from the paper, called for three cheers for 'His Majesty Emperor Michael II'. The battalion and the crowd responded with cheers that 'rang out, passionate, genuine, emotional'.[6]

Shulgin strode back into the station, the crowd making way for him as he went forward looking for Guchkov. Suddenly he was aware of an urgent voice telling him that he was wanted on the telephone in the station-master's office. When he walked in and picked up the receiver it was to hear the croaking voice of Milyukov. 'Don't make known the manifesto', barked Milyukov. 'There have been serious changes.'

A startled Shulgin could only stammer a reply. 'But how?...I have already announced it.'

'To whom?'

'Why, to all here. Some regiment or other. The people. I have proclaimed Michael Emperor.'

'You should not have done that', shouted Milyukov. 'Feelings have become much worse since you left...Don't take any further steps. There may be great misfortune.'[7]

Bewildered, Shulgin put down the phone, and looked around for Guchkov. He had gone off to a meeting of 2,000 men in some nearby railway workshops, he was told, intent on spreading the glad tidings of Michael's succession. Shulgin was about to go after him when he remembered that he still had the manifesto in his pocket. The railway shopmen had been staunch supports of the Soviet; if he went in, would he get out?

At that moment the telephone rang. This time it was Bublikov, the man whom the Duma Committee had appointed as Railway Commissioner. He was sending his own man to the station. 'You can trust him with anything...Understand?' Shulgin understood perfectly. A few minutes later Bublikov's messenger thrust himself through the crowd and Shulgin slipped him the envelope bearing the manifesto. The man took it and disappeared back to the transport ministry offices, where it was hidden under a pile of old magazines.

Shulgin then headed for the workshops, where Guchkov was standing on a platform above a dense mass of railwaymen, being harangued by its chairman, sneering protests about a new government led by a prince and full of landowners and wealthy industrialists.

'Is this what we had the revolution for, comrades? Prince

Lvov?' It was clearly not the time nor place to cry out 'Long Live Emperor Michael'.

As Shulgin joined Guchkov on the platform, the seething workers began to move forward menacingly. Here were two representatives of this bourgeois government, sent secretly to confer with the Tsar at Pskov. Whom did they really represent? 'Shut the doors, comrades,' cried the leaders.

The situation looked nasty, but then the railmen began to quarrel amongst themselves, with some shouting that the shopmen on the platform were behaving 'like the old regime'. Pushing, shoving, the crowd began to turn on its own, with voices calling out for Guchkov to be allowed to speak. He did so, briefly, defending the aims of the new government but prudently deciding not to mention Michael. As tempers cooled, the doors were opened again, and a shaken Guchkov and Shulgin were allowed to leave.[8]

By then the news of the proclamations read out at the Warsaw station had raced across the city. Lawyer Vladimir Nabokov, unaware that he was soon to play a critical role in the future of the monarchy, heard about Michael's succession twice over as he was walking to work from his apartment on the Morskaya, and when he reached his office he found 'great excitement, with crowds on the stairs and in the big conference hall'.[9]

Curiously, one of the last to discover the name of the new Emperor of All the Russias was Michael himself. When Kerensky telephoned the apartment at 5.55 a.m. he made no mention of the manifesto. The new government was not yet ready to tell him about that.

MILLIONNAYA Street was half-awake when Kerensky made his call. The apartment was spacious; even so, it was exceptionally crowded this Friday morning. Officers of the guard were sleeping in the study and Michael, his brother-in-law Matveev and Johnson were sleeping on settees and makeshift beds. Matveev had brought in fresh shirts and underwear since Michael had arrived in Millionnaya Street with only the clothes they were standing up in.

Johnson took the call from Kerensky and learned only that the 'Council of Ministers' would be arriving for a meeting in about an hour. Michael was not surprised for they were expecting formal news of Nicholas's abdication; but as Matveev would firmly record, 'in the light of the letter from the President of the State Duma Rodzyanko' delivered the evening before, they assumed that the delegation was coming 'to report on the Regency'. While they waited, Michael was 'therefore thinking over his appropriate reply expressing his consent'.[10]

The telephone call that ought to have been made to Millionnaya Street that morning would not have been at 5.55 but some two hours earlier, or just after 3 a.m. At Tsarskoe Selo that was the time that the garrison commander first tried to call Grand Duke Paul to tell him about the manifesto just received from Pskov; he thought it best if it was Paul who broke the news to Alexandra. Because he could not get through, an officer was sent to his palace. Paul came down in his dressing gown, and an artillery colonel, with a large red bow on his chest, read them the text of Nicholas's abdication. 'We realised at once that all was finished', said Paul's wife Princess Paley.[11]

Paul, in the event, could not bring himself to go to the Alexander Palace until 11 a.m. There he found Alexandra in her hospital uniform, still unaware that she was no longer Empress. After Paul told her what had happened, tears rolled down her cheeks, and she bent her head as if praying. 'If Nicky has done that, it is because he had to do so...God will not abandon us...As it is Misha who is Emperor, I shall look after my children and my hospital. We shall go to the Crimea.'[12]

That Alexandra would not know of the abdication until mid-morning was understandable; that the new Emperor was not formally told as soon as the news reached Petrograd was astonishing. The silence was deliberate.

One reason why the new government was anxious that Michael

should not know about the manifesto making him Emperor was that they did not want him better prepared than they were when eventually they did meet him. Kerensky would later gloss over the details of his telephone call to Millionnaya Street, but he would say of Michael that 'we did not know how much he knew' while adding that it was important 'to prevent whatever steps he was planning to take until we had come to a decision'.[13]

Whatever steps? There was only one action that Michael would have taken had he found out independently that he had been named Emperor, and that would have been to telephone Prince Lvov at the Tauride Palace and summon him to Millionnaya Street, with doubtless a few others, but not the entire Committee. The problem then is that he would have been asking the awkward questions, and Prince Lvov would not have had the answers.

If Milyukov, leader of the largest bloc in the Duma had insisted on accompanying Lvov to such a meeting — after all, Lvov was a man he had championed — that could have been awkward for those at the Tauride Palace who, led by Kerensky but also 'blue funk' Rodzyanko, were now more concerned about saving the new Provisional Government and themselves than saving the monarchy.

At 6 a.m. Kerensky, after his brief telephone call to Millionnaya Street, knew that Michael had not been told independently about the manifesto. Saying that the delegation would be with him in about an hour was more hope than reality. The hope was that the delegation, the majority of them already defeatist on the issue of the manifesto, could be with Michael before he had a chance to find out he was Emperor. The streets would be dark, the city scarcely awake, and with luck they could browbeat a stunned Michael into surrender before the Soviet had time to start browbeating them.

However, he had reckoned without Milyukov's resistance to any *fait accompli* as well as his insistence that they should wait until Guchkov and Shulgin — he counted on both as allies — got back to the Tauride Palace. As time went by, one question settled itself: that the manifesto had been circulated across the country and that the cat was well and truly out of the bag. The Soviet now also knew that Michael was Emperor, and the resulting clamour among the mutineers left the Duma majority in no doubt of what that meant for them. Impatient to get Michael out of the way, the transport minister Nekrasov set to work on drafting an abdication manifesto they would take with them to Millionnaya Street. By noon, the majority hoped that they would be bringing it back with his signature to the Tauride Palace. In presenting that to the Soviet, they could show themselves master of events — men of action, not chatter.

With no sign of Guchkov and Shulgin, held up by their adventures in the railway workshops, Milyukov could not delay the delegation any longer and by 9.15 a.m. it began to assemble in Millionnaya Street — later than Kerensky had hoped, but still time enough to believe they could be back triumphant in the Tauride Palace by noon. Michael, they accepted, must have heard the news that he was Emperor — since it was all round the city by now — but he would have had no time to think out what that entailed. He would also be alone, in a room packed with men determined in the main to get rid of him. How could they lose?

MICHAEL had found out that he was Emperor in the time in which he had been waiting to meet the delegation as Regent. The telephones were working, and as the news spread across the capital the line into Millionnaya Street was blocked with calls. Natasha, in Gatchina, could still not get through to Petrograd, but the local telephone system there was working as normal — there were 250 numbers on the Gatchina exchange — and that Friday morning her phone 'never stopped ringing' her daughter Tata remembered.[14]

. That was hardly surprising: the garrison commandant in Gatchina had his copy of the cabled manifesto at 3 a.m., the same time as at Tsarskoe Selo, and woke up the house to tell Natasha that she was now wife of the Emperor. The excitement was matched by the frustration at not being able to contact Michael, and find out what was going on in Petrograd.

The only personal caller at Millionnaya Street as the capital awoke that Friday morning was Bimbo, Grand Duke Nicholas Mikhailovich, who lived in the palace across the road. Two evenings before, Bimbo — whose brother George was staying with Natasha — had joined Michael for supper,[15] discussing his role as Regent, and as ever advancing his own liberal ideas on the shape of the monarchy to come. He returned early on Friday morning, for Princess Putyatina remembered him being there. Someone had called him with the news already racing around Petrograd. He was 'up-to-date with everything and he knew that the Emperor had abdicated', she wrote. According to her version, Bimbo said that 'I am very happy to recognise you as Sovereign, since in fact you are already the Tsar! Be brave and strong: in this way you will not only save the dynasty but also the future of Russia!'

In the excitement of the moment the princess did not recall Michael being in any way alarmed at developments before the first knock on the door announced the arrival of his prime minister Prince Lvov, and a quivering Rodzyanko. Putyatina, writing many years later, clearly failed to pick up or chose to forget the worries Michael had with that news. He had once been heir to the throne, and co-Regent with Alexandra for the baby Alexis. He was well versed in the laws of succession, for they had been drilled into him by constitutional experts at the time, and what he knew — as perhaps Bimbo, 24th in line to the throne when Alexis was born, ought also to have known— was that Nicholas could not bypass Alexis as he had done. There was no precedent for it, and it had left Michael in a very difficult position. It would be the reason why, when he did meet the delegation, that Kerensky remarked that he looked 'much perturbed'[17]

TWO miles separate the Tauride Palace and Millionnaya Street. On snow-covered streets a car could make the journey in about ten or fifteen minutes, driving down the street towards the Winter Palace, then turning into the archway leading to the large inner courtyard behind the Putyatin apartment. Once inside the courtyard the several cars arriving from the Duma building would be concealed from view as the cadet guards closed the heavy black courtyard doors behind them. The delegation had not told the Soviet executive about the meeting, and did not want them to have wind of it until afterwards, when they would be able to trump their protests by flourishing Michael's signed abdication.

Matveev, wearing his uniform as a reserve lieutenant in the Zemstovs Hussars,[18] was given the role of meeting the arriving delegates. The well of the staircase was crowded with armed cadet officers, and the Duma men threw off their fur coats there before climbing the shallow-stepped granite staircase, with its elaborate wrought-iron bannister, to the apartment landing and the waiting Matveev. They were then ushered into the drawing room, warmed by a roaring fire.

The room had been prepared to provide an informal setting. The settees and armchairs were arranged so that Michael, when he took the meeting, would be sitting in a tall-backed easy chair, facing a semicircle of delegates. Within fifteen minutes or so there were a dozen men gathered there. Seven of them were ministers in the newly-named Provisional Government and five were Duma deputies, led by Rodzyanko.

Before the meeting it had been agreed at the Tauride Palace that Lvov and Rodzyanko would lead the majority call for Michael's abdication, while Milyukov argued the minority view, that preserving the monarchy was essential if Russia was to be saved from extremism.

However, the great division between the two sides was that unless Michael did abdicate, none of those opposed to his succession would remain in the government. That left Milyukov in the position where he could make only a token defence of the monarchy. And if Michael refused to abdicate, he would find himself only with a foreign minister and — assuming Guchkov arrived in time to join in the meeting — war minister. The prime minister and the other seven ministers present would all resign; Rodzyanko, nominally still president of the State Duma, had promised not to take office in any replacement government.

However, as Rodzyanko would blandly comment that morning, the decision none the less would be one for Michael alone. Small wonder, then, that the majority of men in that drawing room were confident of being back in the Tauride Palace by not later than noon. What choice could Michael have but abdicate, abandoned otherwise by the new government and surrounded by mutinous troops who wanted him dead?

At 9.35 a.m., with the delegates deciding that they could no longer wait for Guchkov and Shulgin, Matveev was told that they were ready to begin.[19] The drawing room door opened, ministers and deputies rose to their feet, and in walked the man being hailed across the country as His Majesty Emperor Michael II. He moved around the room to greet each delegate individually. 'We shook hands and exchanged courtesies,' Kerensky would remember.[20]

Then Michael sat down in his tall-backed chair, looked around the men facing him, and the meeting began.

15. PLAYING FOR TIME

ONLY a couple of hours earlier, Michael had expected a meeting in which he would have been sitting in his chair as Regent, not as Emperor, for taking the crown was a possibility he had never considered, though neither had anyone else other than his brother after he decided that 'a father's feelings' came before everything else in deciding the fate of Russia. Michael was still struggling to come to terms with that, for removing Alexis from the succession was so contrary to every ambition hitherto held for him that it hardly seemed credible. Alexandra had been obsessed with 'Baby's rights', had fought like a tigress to protect them, and had brought Russia to the brink of ruin in consequence. Now, in a moment, Alexis had been swept aside.

But could Nicholas do that? It was not a question which bothered the troops and people cheering Michael's name across the country that morning, and in the midst of a great war and civil unrest, what mattered to them more was that the hated Nicholas had gone, along with the reviled government of Alexandra's lackeys.

There were many in the army who welcomed Michael on his own merits, and among the people at large those who knew of Michael approved, and among those who knew only his name, there was nothing they had heard to his discredit. Married not to a foreign princess but to a commoner from Moscow? If anything, that was reassurance, at least for those who were not committed republicans, that Russia would now have a new kind of monarchy and a constitutional Tsar who understood the concerns of the ordinary man-in-the-street.

If those relief forces which Nicholas had so confidently ordered to the capital had actually arrived, and the revolutionaries in the Tauride Palace had been driven out, then the frightened men of the Duma might have emerged as heroes, rather than cowards. But the troops had been turned back when Nicholas had been stopped, literally, in his tracks, and the battalion of heroes sent to Tsarskoe Selo had also turned back, for much the same reason. He wasn't there. He was on a train trundling back to Pskov, and he would not arrive back at *Stavka* until 8.20 that Friday evening.[1] Once again, in the midst of a crisis, he had vanished, leaving chaos in his wake.

The problem was not therefore whether Michael ought to be Emperor, but that he was, and as such the Petrograd Soviet and the frightened mutineers who gave them the only military power available in the capital, were joined together in their determination to get rid of him — the first, because it would destroy the monarchy, and the second because it would save them from the gallows. In turn, that decided matters for the new government. Michael had to go, and the question of whether his succession was lawful or not was of no account. He was the Emperor, and there was nothing that could be done about that. It was reality.

What was also reality was that when Michael began the meeting he was to find that everyone addressed him not as 'Your Imperial Majesty' but as 'Your Highness' — thus, not as Emperor but as Grand Duke. That had been a collective decision before the meeting: that they would signal their determination for his departure by using the title he would use after his abdication, rather than his title before he signed such a manifesto. It was intended as intimidation, and they thought it would also speed up the clock.

Michael made no comment about the form of address, though he could not but note it and understand the reason behind it. The majority of men were not here to support him. Looking around the room he could see that they were exhausted, unshaven, bedraggled and, as Prince Lvov would put it, unable even to think straight any more.[2] Kerensky would admit that he himself had been 'near collapse'. At dawn the previous day he had walked back to his apartment at 29 Tverskaya, and had fallen into bed, lying there for two or three hours in a 'semi-delirious state' for that was the only rest he had managed in the past five days.[3] Milyukov was so exhausted that he 'was falling asleep where he sat…He would start, open his eyes, then begin to sleep again'.[4]

In some cases it was not exhaustion but terror that marked the faces of the men from the Duma. Dread of the Soviet would be the recurring theme of the morning's discussions, and that fear would be heightened by Kerensky, the only man in the room who could claim to speak for the mob.

Kerensky, a master of the theatrical posture, would convince some there that he also was 'terrified' and that at any moment a gang of armed men might break in and murder the new Emperor, if not the rest of them.[5]

Fear was a weapon, and it was the principal weapon which Rodzyanko would use that morning. As he had done in his wires to Pskov and Mogilev he drew a black picture of the world outside the windows, where civil war loomed and a bloodbath threatened. Although as terrified as anyone else, he would forget that when writing from the safety of his memoirs; he would prefer history to believe that the only man fearing for his life that day at Millionnaya Street was Michael himself.

It was quite clear to us that the Grand Duke would have reigned only a few hours, and that this would have led to colossal bloodshed in the precincts of the capital, which would have degenerated into general civil war. It was clear to us that the Grand Duke would have been killed immediately, together with all adherents, for he had no reliable troops at his disposal then, and could not sustain himself by armed support. The Grand Duke asked me outright whether I could guarantee his life if he acceded to the throne, and I had to answer in the negative.[6]

This was self-serving nonsense. Rodzyanko was in no position to guarantee anyone's life, including his own, and certainly there was never reason for Michael, with Russia's two highest military honours pinned to his chest, to look to the quaking Rodzyanko for protection. He was better off with the cadets downstairs. However, Rodzyanko lived to write his memoirs and Michael did not.

Milyukov, with Guchkov not yet arrived, was the sole spokesman for those who believed that Rodzyanko and Lvov were leading the government to ultimate ruin, as would prove the case. Rousing himself, he argued that it would be immeasurably more difficult in the long term if the established order was simply abandoned, for in his reasoning the 'frail craft' of the self-elected Provisional Government, without a monarch, would soon be sunk 'in the ocean of national disorder'.[7]

As he advanced his case the combative Milyukov found himself fighting against a babble of angry voices; all idea of a measured debate had been swept away in a torrent of noisy argument. To latecomer Shulgin, now arrived with Guchkov, 'Milyukov seemed unwilling, or unable to stop talking…This man, usually so polite and self-controlled, did not let anybody else speak, and interrupted those who tried to answer him.'[8]

Milyukov would say afterwards that 'I admitted that my opponents may have been right. Perhaps indeed those present and the Grand Duke himself were in danger. But we were playing for high stakes — for the whole of Russia — and we had to take a risk, however great it was.'[9] In his view the better alternative early that morning would have been to confront the Soviet with the new manifesto and to have told them it would make no difference — that they would ensure that Michael endorsed the deal they had already struck and that the Soviet position and that of the mutineers was no different than before.

As it was, by concealing the manifesto in the hope of buying time, the Duma men looked as if they were hiding something when the Soviet found out anyway about Michael once the manifesto was proclaimed in the city; it made it look as if they were being double-crossed. This in itself was good reason for the Duma men's anxiety to get back to the Tauride Palace with the abdication, as evidence of their own good faith.

Until that was done, they were at risk. Tereshchenko, now the new finance minister, was one of those who feared the worst Late in the meeting he motioned Shulgin to leave the room for a moment. 'I can't go on anymore…I will shoot myself…what's to be done?' he moaned.

Shulgin, bewildered by the turnaround in the government's mood, asked him: 'Tell me, are there any units we can rely on?'

'No, no one.'

'But I saw some sentries downstairs…'

'That's only a few people. Kerensky is terrified…he is afraid… any moment someone could break in…there are gangs on the prowl. Oh, Lord!'[10]

Indeed, it was Kerensky, rather than Rodzyanko, who was now using the threat of Soviet violence to dominate proceedings. In effect their spokesman, his references to the risks of 'an internal civil war' appeared more menace than warning. There was also an oblique personal threat to Michael when he raised an arm and cried: 'I cannot answer for Your Highness's life'. [11]

When Guchkov interrupted him and attempted to support Milyukov, his intervention 'made Kerensky almost beside himself with passion, and provoked him to a torrent of invective and threats which terrified everyone there', Paléologue would record next day, after hearing reports of the drama at Millionnaya Street.[12]

During all this shouting and argument, Michael had sat sprawled in his chair saying nothing. To Kerensky he seemed 'embarrassed' by what was going on and 'to grow more weary and impatient'.[13]

That was hardly surprising as he listened to these quarrelling and frightened men, and this divided and helpless government. For these past years he had been told by men like these, by Rodzyanko and his ilk, that if granted a responsible ministry then they would know how best to conduct a government worthy of public respect. What he was seeing and hearing now made mockery of those claims. He had also heard quite enough, and saw no point in hearing more.

He rose from his chair and announced that he would like to consider the whole matter privately with just two of men in the room, and that he would then make his decision. The room fell silent. Kerensky stirred uneasily, thinking that Michael would retire with Milyukov and Guchkov, his two principal supporters as Emperor. To his surprise the choice fell on Lvov and Rodzyanko and 'a weight fell from my shoulders as I thought to myself that if he wants to speak to these two then he has decided to abdicate'.[14]

The delegates had agreed in advance that they would not support any private meeting, but since the majority believed like Kerensky that such a meeting was now to their advantage, they immediately supported the idea. Milyukov and Guchkov were dismayed, but there was little they could say to prevent it.

In Kerensky's later account of that meeting he portrayed himself as behaving with restraint and statesmanship, in accordance with the principle that the best history is the one you write yourself. However, it was not the story told next day to Paléologue, probably by Milyukov as foreign minister.

As Michael was moving to the door, Kerensky leapt to his feet and shouted: 'Promise us not to consult your wife!' Michael turned and smiled. 'Don't worry, Aleksandr Fedorovich, my wife isn't here at the moment, she stayed behind in Gatchina.'[15]

Michael's choice of Lvov and Rodzyanko for his private meeting did seem, however, to confirm Kerensky's view that he had decided to abdicate, given that both men had pressed him to do so that morning. Yet there was a more obvious reason for his choosing them: Lvov was prime minister and Rodzyanko was president of the State Duma, and thus they were the leaders of the two groups represented at the meeting, the government and the Duma. Given that, he had his own questions and there was little chance of getting answers to those in the noisy atmosphere of the drawing room. He had no wish to hear more dispute.

What he did want was to hear reassurance that the new Provisional Government was in a position to restore order and continue the war, and that they could ensure that the promised elections for a Constituent Assembly would be going ahead and not blocked by the Soviet, for otherwise then all that had taken place that morning was no more than hot air.

In his conversations with the two army commanders that morning, Rodzyanko had stressed that the commitment to a constituent assembly 'does not exclude the possibility of the dynasty returning to power'[16], and this is certainly a point he would have made strongly to Michael. Abdication was not the end of the monarchy but a short-term expediency until better times came along.

Convinced by their own arguments, Lvov and Rodzyanko returned to the smoke-filled drawing room, eyed curiously by the others as they took their seats, nodding as if all now was settled.

Michael stayed behind, conferring briefly with Matveev who had spent the morning with his ear pressed to the door of the drawing room. On the face of it the decision had already been made for him: if he abdicated, the war would go on, order would be restored, and democratic vote would determine the shape of its future status; if he stayed Emperor, the present government would collapse, there would be civil war, and the country ruined. Nicholas had given him command of a ship in which the crew had mutinied and the officers had taken to the lifeboats.

It could hardly be a surprise therefore when he walked back into the room and announced that he had decided to follow the advice of the two senior men present. Or words to that effect. Nothing was written down, and afterwards nobody could remember exactly what he said.[17] However, those present understood him to mean that he had decided to abdicate the throne, for in the black-and-white world of Petrograd it was a straight choice between stay and go and he was clearly not staying.

There were sighs of relief. Nekrasov fingered the abdication manifesto in his pocket: *We by God's Mercy, Michael II, Emperor and Autocrat of all the Russias...*[18] After that preamble the rest could be filled in simply enough. It would need a few flourishes, perhaps, to give the required sense of occasion, but essentially 'abdicate' was the word that mattered. Allowing five minutes or so for regretful comments and funereal courtesies, Michael's manifesto could be in the Tauride Palace by lunch-time, with the Soviet obliged to hail their success. By late afternoon it could be posted all over the city. In fact, it would turn out to be rather more complicated than that. Michael was not going to give them 'abdicate'.

AFTER Michael's statement the meeting came to a stop. The delegates crowded around him had assumed that the next step would be that Michael would sign their prepared manifesto, but he seemed in no hurry to do anything else for the moment, and had waved that notion aside, saying that he would deal with that after lunch. After lunch? Faces stared at him blankly; however, the call demanding that they settle matters immediately never came, for at that moment, as if on cue, the drawing room door opened and Princess Putyatina emerged on the scene as hostess, inviting anyone who wished to do so to join her in the dining room.[19]

It was a wholly unexpected development but in their surprise no one seemed able to voice a protest. The delegates looked at each other, unsure what to do, and then realised that there was nothing that could be done about it. About half the men in the drawing room accepted the invitation and shuffled in to sit at the lunch table. They included Prince Lvov, Kerensky, Shulgin, Tereshchenko, and Nekrasov, his unsigned abdication manifesto tucked back in his pocket. Princess Putyatina sat at the head of the table, with Michael at her right hand; Matveev and Johnson were seated together at the end of the table. [20]

Rodzyanko and the other ministers and deputies, confused, left the building and went back to the Tauride Palace, their victory delayed. Since the Soviet was still unaware that there was a meeting with Michael, and as yet the returning delegates could not wave his abdication manifesto, there was nothing they could do but keep out of the way and fend off questions.

The impatient Soviet in consequence took their own steps to deal with the issue of Michael and the monarchy by ordering 'the arrest of the Romanov family'; in Michael's case this was not to be house arrest but 'an actual arrest', which in turn came to mean that 'he is subjected only to the surveillance of the revolutionary army'.[21] A bluff to put pressure on the Duma men to deliver Michael's abdication and quickly?

Back in Millionnaya Street there seemed no haste to do so at the lunch table. Michael's greater interest appeared to be in finding out what had happened at Pskov. 'Tell me', he asked Shulgin, 'how did my brother conduct himself?'

'His Majesty was very pale but at the same time very calm and resigned…amazingly calm.'[22]

Shulgin then told him the full story, including Nicholas's reasons for bypassing his son. The whole table listened attentively, for it was the first account any of them had heard of the abdication scene at Pskov. Despite the drama of their own day, what had happened at Pskov had changed everything, and no one thought of interrupting Shulgin as he described the scene in the imperial carriage. Michael made no criticism of his brother and in front of Michael no one else did so either.

After that, conversation was polite, with no mention of the reason for their all being there, until lunch was finished and Princess Putyatina rose from the table and withdrew. The delegates then looked at Michael, waiting for the moment when he would formally provide his abdication; Nekrasov fingered again the manifesto in his pocket.

Matveev, having sat throughout lunch in silence, then asserted himself, asking Nekrasov to let him see what he had written down. Nekrasov handed it over, and Matveev read through it, then returned it with the air of a man who had found it wanting.

Nekrasov glanced down at the paper: he had no experience of drafting a manifesto of this kind; had he missed something? This Matveev did not seem to be quite the nonentity they had taken him for when he was acting as doorman. His manner was that of advisor, acting for Michael, not servant.

That became clear in moments after Michael suggested that Matveev 'should help set down in proper form what had taken place'.[23] Oh dear, he was a lawyer. He was also trouble, for nodding towards Nekrasov, Matveev announced to the table that in order to prepare a proper manifesto for Michael's signature they would first need to have a copy of the original abdication manifesto signed by Nicholas, as well as a copy of the *Fundamental Laws*.

An embarrassed Prince Lvov knew from Shulgin that he had handed the manifesto over at the Warsaw station to some man from the transport ministry, but no one at the table had any idea what had happened to it thereafter — that it was actually still hidden under a pile of old magazines in the office of Bublikov, the transport commissioner. As for the Code of Laws — where could they get a copy of those?

The lunch table was now in disarray, any thought of a quick exit with a signed manifesto now abandoned. Somehow the lawyers were going to have to take over and since Michael had his own in Matveev they were going to need one themselves. The man they settled on was Vladimir Nabokov, and Prince Lvov volunteered to call him. For Michael he was a welcome choice: for Nabokov's sister Nadine was one of Natasha's closest friends, and her daughter was a playmate of Michael's seven-year-old son George.[24]

Prince Lvov first tried Nabokov's office in the General staff building, and then his home; he was not there either but his wife offered to trace him, which she did promptly. He was at another of his offices, and he promised to leave immediately.

With that, Kerensky and the Duma men other than Lvov and Shulgin, decided to return to the Tauride Palace. There was nothing they could do here, and it was clearly going to be a long afternoon. Assured by Prince Lvov that they would be told as soon as the manifesto had been signed, they left looking rather more subdued than when arriving so confidently almost six hours earlier. They were not sure how it had happened, but somehow Michael now seemed to be in charge.

At almost that very moment a telegram was sent to Michael from Sirotino, a railway station some 275 miles from Pskov. Nicholas, having 'awoken far beyond Dvinsk,'[25] had suddenly remembered that he had neglected to mention to his brother that he was the new Emperor. He hastily scribbled out a telegram, despatched at 2.56 p.m. and addressed to 'Imperial Majesty Petrograd'. It read: *To His Majesty the Emperor Michael: Recent events have forced me to decide irrevocably to take this extreme step. Forgive me if it grieves you and also for no warning — there was no time. Shall always remain a faithful and devoted brother. Now returning to HQ where hope to come back shortly to Tsarskoe Selo. Fervently pray God to help you and our country. Your Nicky.*[26]

As so often during the past days, Nicholas had acted when it was too late to matter. However, at least it was delivered, unlike the last telegram sent to him, and returned Address Unknown.

THERE were no cabs or cars available to Vladimir Nabokov, but hurrying along the crowded Nevsky Prospekt he reached Millionnaya Street just before 3 p.m. After briefing him on the events of that morning, Prince Lvov explained that 'the draft of the Act had been outlined by Nekrasov, but the effort was incomplete and not entirely satisfactory, and since everyone was dreadfully tired…they requested that I undertake the task'.[27]

But as Matveev had pointed out earlier, they could not proceed without the Code of Laws and the original Nicholas manifesto. However, since the manifesto was lost somewhere in the transport offices, there was no dispute about its meaning and it had been proclaimed all over the city. That being so, what Nabokov agreed as essential was having the *Fundamental Laws* in front of them.

Who would have a copy? Nabokov telephoned the

constitutional jurist Baron Nolde —'that astute and exacting specialist in state law'[28] — at his office in nearby Palace Square, asking him to come at once and to bring with him a first volume of the Code of Laws. He arrived ten minutes later.

He, Nabokov and Shulgin now retreated into the bedroom of Princess Putyatina's young daughter, with only a small school desk at which to write. The immediate problem which confronted the two lawyers was precisely that which had exercised Michael when he had first learned that he had been named Emperor: was that lawful?

Nabokov and Nolde did not need any prompting on that issue: both recognised from the outset that Nicholas's manifesto contained 'an incurable, intrinsic flaw'. At best it was doubtful law, and as Nabokov would say, 'from the beginning Michael must necessarily have felt this'. Rightly, he judged that 'it significantly weakened the position of the supporters of the monarchy. No doubt it also influenced Michael's reasoning.'[29]

That said, Nabokov and Nolde were left in the same position as Michael: the political fact that Alexis had been bypassed and could not be restored in any practical sense, given the peril of present circumstances. Michael had been abandoned by the new government and they did not want to hear the lawyers telling them that Michael was not the Emperor in fact, and that Nicholas's abdication manifesto was wrong and would have to be done all over again so that Alexis was Emperor and Michael the Regent.

They did not need Lvov and Shulgin to spell out the consequences of that: the Soviet would not only march into the apartment and arrest Michael, as they threatened to do, but arrest the whole government, leaving Kerensky to put together another one.

When Nabokov and Nolde began their task, handing out drafts of the manifesto to Matveev for perusal and approval by Michael, they began with the same preamble used by Nekrasov: *We, by God's mercy, Michael II, Emperor and Autocrat of all the*

Russias... They started off therefore on the premise that Michael was lawful Emperor, and that in abdicating he 'commanded' the people to obey the authority of the Provisional Government in which he was vesting his powers until a constituent assembly determined the form of government.

This formula gave legitimacy to the new government, which otherwise was simply there by licence of the Soviet. No one had elected the Provisional Government which represented only itself, and in that regard it had arguably less authority than the Soviet which could at least claim to have been endorsed by elected soldier and worker delegates.

Michael could make the new government official and legal, as no one else could, and therefore it was important that his manifesto be issued by him as Emperor. If he was not Emperor, he had no power to vest, and no authority to 'command' anyone. Of political necessity the new government needed Michael to give up the throne, but first they needed him to take it.

However, it was not going to be that simple. Michael was clear in his own mind about the position in which he had found himself. He had not inherited the throne. Alexis had been unlawfully bypassed and Michael proclaimed Emperor without his knowledge or consent. He had not willingly become Emperor and Nicholas had no right to pass the throne to him.

At the same time, there was nothing that could be done about that. The wrong could not be righted; it was far too late for that. The only issue therefore was how best to salvage the monarchy from the wreckage Nicholas had left in his wake.

For Michael there were two imperatives: keeping the monarchy in being until the Constituent Assembly decided the future status of Russia in six months' time; and secondly, acting as Emperor for the single but vitally important purpose of providing legitimacy to the Provisional Government, and thereby ensuring the restoration of order and the continuation of the war.

That the government was demanding his abdication in order to appease the Soviet was a serious complication, but even so, he was not going to abdicate. Besides, if he did, who was going to succeed *him?* The throne 'was never vacant' — the law said that — and it followed therefore that if he abdicated, someone else would immediately become Emperor in his place. Kirill?

Nobody that morning seemed to have thought of that, but Nabokov and Nolde understood perfectly his argument. The problem was how to express all of it in a manifesto. Tearing up their first draft, and thereby consigning Nekrasov's manifesto to the dustbin, they started again, with Michael darting in and out of the schoolroom to make sure that their new draft stayed in line with his wishes.

There was not much time, but fortunately they were both very good lawyers, and with Matveev they worked as a team which knew the difference between the small print and the telescope to the blind eye. The result was a manifesto which would make Michael Emperor without it saying that he had accepted the throne; that as Emperor he would vest all his powers in the new Provisional Government; and with that done he would wait in the wings until a future Constituent Assembly voted, as he hoped, for a constitutional monarchy and elected him. Meanwhile, he would not reign, but neither would he abdicate.

Despite the intense pressure on Michael and the lawyers in Millionnaya Street as evening drew in that day, his final manifesto said exactly what he wanted it to say, and it bore no resemblance whatsoever to the manifesto which Nekrasov had drafted that morning and which he had handed over after lunch. It said:

A heavy burden has been thrust upon me by the will of my brother, who has given over to me the Imperial Throne of Russia at a time of unprecedented warfare and popular disturbances.

Inspired like the entire people by the idea that what is most important is the welfare of the country, I have taken a firm decision to assume the Supreme Power only if such be the will of our great people, whose right it is to establish the form of government and the new basic laws of the Russian state by universal suffrage through its representatives in the Constituent Assembly.

Therefore, invoking the blessing of God, I beseech all the citizens of Russia to obey the Provisional Government, which has come into being on the initiative of the Duma and is vested with all the plenitude of power until the Constituent Assembly, to be convoked with the least possible delay by universal suffrage, direct, equal and secret voting, shall express the will of the people by its decision on the form of government.

MICHAEL.[29]

By this manifesto Michael made clear that the throne had been 'thrust upon me' not inherited, and that he was passing all his powers to the new Provisional Government until the future status of Russia was decided by a democratically-elected Constituent Assembly. He had changed the imperious word 'command' in the first version to 'beseech' and had removed all use of the imperial 'We', as well as the description of him as 'Emperor and Autocrat', but he had signed with the imperial *Michael*, rather than the grand ducal *Michael Aleksandrovich*.

There was no precedent for a manifesto in these terms, and the Code of Laws, seemingly so essential a few hours earlier, had been closed and put aside as irrelevant to the necessity of the moment. But as Nabokov later commented, 'we were not concerned with the juridical force of the formula but only its moral and political meaning'.[30]

In so saying, the credit for that went to Michael and his refusal to do what he was told by the new government. A lesser man would have meekly given in to the threats and intimidation of that morning. Michael did not, and while he would be powerless to affect what was to come, nonetheless he had pointed the country in the right direction. It would be for others to make sure they stayed on course.

As for the 'abdication manifesto' itself, curiously, for those who took the trouble to read it carefully, of the 122 Russian words meticulously written out at the school desk by Nabokov 'in his beautiful handwriting'[31] the one word which did not appear, as it did in Nicholas's manifesto, was 'abdicate'.

12 Millionnaya Street

The meeting place on March 3, 1917 was in the drawing room of Princess Putyatina's apartment, with its pedimented window, two floors above the main entrance. Cars drove in through the gates to the left, and there were sentries on the door. Michael woke up there that morning thinking he was Regent, only to find that he had been proclaimed Emperor.

The exhausted men with the fate of Russia in their hands

Left to right: Kerensky, Prince Lvov, Rodzyanko, and Milyukov

Most members of the Provisional Government expected to leave Millionnaya Street with Michael's abdication in their hands...what they got instead was a manifesto in which the word 'abdicate' would not appear

KERENSKY and Rodzyanko had returned to Millionnaya Street by the time the manifesto had been finalised, and they were present when Michael sat down at the school desk and put his signature on the document which, as Nolde would recall, 'was in essence the only constitution during the period of existence of the Provisional Government'.[32] Nabokov also recognised it as 'the only Act which defined the limits of the Provisional Government's authority'.[33] When the British ambassador later asked Milyukov where the government derived its authority, he replied: 'We have received it, by inheritance, from the Grand Duke'.[34]

To Nabokov, standing beside the school desk, Michael 'appeared rather embarrassed and somewhat disconcerted' as he came into the room, sat down and took up the pen. 'I have no doubt that he was under a heavy strain,' said Nabokov, 'but he retained complete self-composure'.[34] Nolde was also impressed, declaring Michael to have 'acted with irreproachable tact and nobility'.[35] Shulgin, watching him sign, thought to himself 'what a good constitutional monarch he would make'.[36] Even Paléologue, once persuaded by the Tsarskoe Selo camp to think him a weakling, would praise him next day, writing in his diary that 'his composure and dignity never once deserted him' and that his 'patriotism, nobility and self-sacrifice were very touching.'[37]

The theatrical outburst, predictably, was left to Kerensky. 'Believe me,' he cried out, 'that we will carry the precious vessel of your authority to the Constituent Assembly without spilling a drop of blood'.[38] In fact, he would spill it all, but that no one could then foresee.

IT was only after the delegation returned to the Tauride Palace that the arguments began over the meaning of the manifesto. At Millionnaya Street there had been no time to study it. Professor Lomonosov had turned up from the transport ministry, belatedly bringing with him the original Nicholas manifesto hidden there; the intention was that it be published jointly with Michael's. But should these be presented as Acts of two Emperors? Since the word 'abdicate' was missing from Michael's, how was his manifesto to be described?

Because it was a political rather than a legal document, at midnight there was still no clear answer to the question of whether Michael had refused the crown or had abdicated, though no attention seems to have been paid to the point that he had done neither.

'Foaming at the mouth, Milyukov and Nabokov tried to prove that the abdication of Michael could only have legal meaning if it was recognised that he had been Emperor.'[39] It was not until 2 a.m. that agreement was reached — that he was Emperor — and Nabokov set about the final form in which the manifesto would appear, in the form judged best to appease the Soviet. At 3.50 a.m. it was taken away to the printers.[40]

Michael, the country would be told, having succeeded to the imperial throne after Nicholas's abdication, had in turn abdicated. He had been Emperor, and was Emperor no more. That was simple. People could understand that, and one of them that evening was his brother in Mogilev.

He was just settling down after his return from Pskov when Alekseev came in with Rodzyanko's wired version of what had happened in Millionnaya Street. Afterwards, Nicholas wrote in his diary:

Misha, it appears, has abdicated. His manifesto ends up by kowtowing to the Constituent Assembly, whose elections will take place in six months. God knows who gave him the idea of signing such rubbish.[41]

Given the wreckage which he had mindlessly left behind him and the impossible position in which he had placed his brother, his effrontery had an epic quality about it. Certainly, when he said much the same to his brother-in-law Sandro a few days later, Sandro confessed himself to be 'speechless'.[42]

But what, finally, did Michael wearily say himself of that day as he prepared to retire to his makeshift bed? His diary entry for that Friday, March 3, was breathtaking in its brevity.

At 6 a.m. we were woken up by the telephone. It was a message from the new Minister of Justice Kerensky. It stated that the complete Council of Ministers would come to see me in an hour's time. But actually they arrived only at half-past nine a.m...[43]

And that was all, from the man who had woken up that morning thinking he was Regent, and went to bed having been proclaimed Emperor.

16. RETREAT TO GATCHINA

MICHAEL left Millionnaya Street next morning, Saturday March 4, at eleven o' clock, the first time he had set foot outside the apartment for four days. The previous afternoon, while waiting for the final draft of his manifesto, he had sent off a courier with a hastily-pencilled note to Natasha to tell her that he expected to return next morning. 'Awfully busy and extremely exhausted,' he had scribbled. 'Will tell you many interesting things. I kiss you tenderly. All yours, Misha.'[1]

There was certainly no point in remaining in Petrograd. He had no further role to play, and was not likely to have one until and if a constituent assembly decided to support a constitutional monarchy, and that could not be for several months hence. The new government had its mandate, and needed no more. In essence, Russia now had a caretaker government and a caretaker emperor in a caretaker monarchy.

As Michael left the apartment and stepped out on to the landing, the first sight to greet him was as a surprising as it was agreeable. Lining the staircase leading down to the street was a guard of honour made up of the officers and cadets stationed in the building. There was an order to present arms and as Michael, saluting, walked down the stairs and outside into his waiting car, a cry of 'Long Live Russia'.[2]

But what might follow? Would there be hostile demonstrations at the station, agitators demanding his arrest, as the Soviet executive had done only yesterday? Michael's manifesto, or rather the gloss the Provisional Government had put on it, was sufficient to strike out the Soviet threats against Michael, though not against his brother; passions were calmed and instead, Michael found himself going home in something akin to triumph.

Followed by another car filled with armed cadets, he and Johnson were driven off to board a special train arranged for them at the Baltic station. Joined by General Yuzefovich, his old chief of staff, he stepped out of his car and into a station 'overcrowded with soldiers…everywhere were machine-guns and boxes of ammunition'. Flanked by his armed escort he walked to his waiting train and to another reception of the kind he had not expected. 'A military detachment was lined up by my carriage and I greeted them, and a gathered crowd cheered me.'[3]

The scene at the Baltic station, with saluting mutineers and applauding bystanders, was not without its irony. Here was its own evidence that the manifesto drafted at Millionnaya Street had served its purpose, at least in the short term. His 'abdication' — perception being nine-tenths of politics — had put an end to the revolution. Now Michael was being hailed, not hunted, and if Lvov, Kerensky and the others had been present at his departure, it would have given them immense satisfaction. 'It seems that order in general is being established', he would write that night in his diary.[4]

The previous evening, in explanation of his manifesto, he had told Princess Putyatina that it would 'calm the passions of the populace, make the soldiers and workers who had mutinied see reason, and re-establish the shattered discipline of the army.'[5] He said much the same on his return to Gatchina on Saturday afternoon. Bimbo's brother George, still taking refuge in Nikolaevskaya Street, wrote afterwards that Michael feared that if he were to reign as Emperor 'without knowing the wishes of the country, matters will never calm down'.[6]

For the moment, however, he was simply glad to be home and away from the madness of Petrograd. It was hard to credit everything that had happened since he had set off for the capital only five days earlier, when his brother was Emperor and Supreme Commander in Mogilev, and he had gone to the Marie Palace to discuss what could be done with a government that had vanished that same night. Five days? It seemed a lifetime.

Inevitably Natasha, thrilled to have him back safely, would pour scorn on Nicholas. The excuse so often had been that he was doing Alexandra's bidding, but she had not been at Pskov and had no hand in the decision to bypass Baby. How could he have been so stupid, so selfish, so blind to the consequences? There was no answer to that, and never would be. How different everything would have been — for the wider world, as it turned out, not just Russia — if Michael had come home that weekend as Regent, not as the newspapers were announcing, as ex-Emperor. Natasha could clench her fists in rage, but there was nothing that could be done about it. Nicholas had ruined the Romanovs and in ruining them had ruined Russia.

OFF the streets that week because of strikes, the Petrograd newspapers returned with their first reports of the dramatic events of the past few days. With only one notable exception* they presented Michael's abdication in the way the government intended. Nicholas's manifesto was followed immediately by Michael's, their intentional juxtaposition helping the headlines which linked both as equal abdications.

In four newspapers — *Birzhevye Vedomosti, Den, Petrogradsky Listok*, and *Petrogradskaya Gazeta* — the headlines were identical: 'Abdication of Grand Duke Michael Aleksandrovich'.[7] There was nothing in the text itself to justify that, but the accompanying statement by the Provisional Government included the word 'abdication' and that in turn justified the headlines over the manifesto.* Eyes glazed over the lawyer-speak below, their minds already made up by the headlines.

*Only *Rech*, the newspaper supporting the Kadet party, of which Milyukov was leader, avoided the word 'abdication'. Its headline correctly called the manifesto a 'Declaration'.

From 'abdication' grew the assumption, fed by triumphant Soviet propaganda, that the monarchy was finished. Even the British and French ambassadors seemed to think in consequence that Russia was now a republic. Both were to be corrected by Milyukov, the new foreign minister. 'The Constituent Assembly alone will be qualified to change the political status of Russia', he told Paléologue;[8] and when he heard Buchanan referring to the new government as republican, 'he caught me up, saying that it was only a Provisional Government pending the decision of the future Constituent Assembly'.[9]

Correcting the impression gathered by two experienced and senior ambassadors was one thing; it was quite another with the country at large. Michael had been wasting his time at the school desk it seemed. What he had signed was not his suspension of imperial power until the decision of a future constituent assembly, but his abdication. What was intended as temporary was taken as permanent. Everyone knew that, because it said so in the newspapers. Some people, reading the manifesto, would say that he had 'refused the crown' rather than abdicated, but the effect was the same. Michael had given up.

There were exceptions to this generally negative response. In *The Times* of London, for example, the judgement of Robert Wilton, their respected correspondent in Petrograd, was that 'perhaps in the end it will be all for the best'. Accepting that while 'at present we must be content to go on with the Provisional Government until quieter days supervene,' he concluded that were it possible to bring about the Constituent Assembly 'there could be little doubt as to the election of Grand Duke Michael to the Throne by an overwhelming majority'.[10] Following events in Yalta, Princess Cantacuzène took much the same view — 'we looked forward to the probability of the Constituent Assembly being in favour of a constitutional monarchy'.[11]

Besides, as Michael might wryly have reflected, the idea of having his succession confirmed by being 'elected' was exactly how the Romanov dynasty came into being. The first Romanov, his namesake Michael I, had been elected by a national assembly in 1613. After 300 years, a second 'election' of a second Michael would change the Romanovs from autocrats into constitutional monarchs, like the British. No one on March 3, 1917 could know that a future assembly would vote to retain the monarchy, but equally no one could know that it would not. Six months is a long time, and if Russia won great victories in the summer, and the public mood improved, the picture could well look very different. Re-reading Michael's manifesto then, what it actually said might be better understood. However, that appeared a vain hope in the immediate aftermath of its publication.

Some people would never forgive Michael for becoming Emperor but not being Emperor. Grand Duke George wrote to his wife that while 'Misha's manifesto seems to have calmed the republicans, the others are angry with him...'[12] The right-wing Duma member Vasily Maklakov, who was not at Millionnaya Street, called the manifesto 'strange and criminal...an act of lunacy or treason, had not the authors been qualified and patriotic lawyers.'[13] In Tsarskoe Selo, Grand Duke Paul's wife Princess Paley, damned Michael as 'a feeble creature' and 'a weakling',[14] though there was no surprise in her saying that.

In short, in some quarters it would be Michael who would be blamed for the fall of the House of Romanov. 'Not us' they would cry, 'it was him'.

One exception in Michael's corner was A. A. Mossolov, former head of the Court Chancellery, who observed that when Michael 'became Emperor, those Grand Dukes who were in Petrograd failed to rally around him'. Bimbo apart, that was true, although the excuse would be that either they could not get near him that day, or they did not know where he was.

But in casting blame, the ultimate responsibility for all that happened lay with Nicholas, and above all, Alexandra.

Brooding over events in faraway Persia, Dimitri was in no doubt about that. 'The final catastrophe,' he judged, 'has been brought about by the wilful and short-sighted obstinacy of a woman. It has, naturally, swept away Tsarskoe Selo, and all of us, at one stroke.'[16]

MICHAEL'S manifesto, in empowering the Provisional Government as lawful, also bound it to do what it promised to do, and which limited its role to that of restoring order, continuing the war, and exercising its powers only until such time as the Constituent Assembly determined the status of Russia. In particular it had no rights to pre-empt any decision reserved to the elected Assembly when it came into being.

So it seemed on March 3. The reality was very different. Michael did not surrender the Romanovs, the new government would do that for him, yielding to the clamouring pressures of the Soviet. There would be no place in the new order for Grand Dukes: their rank, privilege, wealth, land and even liberty were now at the disposal of a government in hock to the Soviet. The meeting at Millionnaya Street had not intended it, but long before any constituent assembly could come into being, the Romanovs would be out of business. Indeed, that seemed to be the case almost immediately, such was the weakness of the new government.

On his return to Gatchina Michael had assumed that he would continue with some role in the army, or at least do so when conditions allowed it. Technically he was still Inspector-General of Cavalry with the rank of colonel-general, but he was willing to serve in any capacity. He was to be immediately disappointed; there would be no job for him or any other Grand Duke.

'They do not allow us to go the front fearing that we might start a counter-revolution,' wrote Grand Duke George from Gatchina, though no such idea has 'even crossed our minds.'[17] Perhaps so, but in Petrograd the government knew that the Soviet would never believe that.

On April 5, one month after he signed his manifesto, Michael noted with scarcely concealed bitterness: 'Today I received my discharge from military service,' adding caustically 'with uniform'.[18] It was another pointer to the way reality had overtaken the meeting at Millionnaya Street.

Next day, Michael and Natasha, together with cousin George, went by train to Petrograd, Michael's first visit to the capital since his manifesto. There was no imperial carriage now; they would have to travel like everyone else, buying tickets, and finding seats where they could. They were intent on organising the removal of his furniture from his mother's home at the Anichkov Palace before it was 'liberated' by the workers.[19] It would be the first and only time that Natasha would ever set foot in the palace in which Michael had been born 38 years earlier.

As Michael settled down in his carriage at Gatchina, 'a soldier came running to the compartment in which Misha sat by the window, and taking off his military fur cap, made a deep bow'. At the same station, a group of soldiers stood to attention as Grand Duke George came up to them. 'They seemed delighted to talk to me,' he wrote. 'I could do anything with these soldiers who now want a republic with a Tsar!'[20]

For a Grand Duke to think it worth mentioning that soldiers had stood to attention when he approached them, or that one had bowed to Michael, was a measure of just how greatly discipline had deteriorated in the army over the past month. The cause of the collapse in ordinary standards was not the revolution itself, but the notorious Order No 1 which had been issued by the Petrograd Soviet on March 1 before the formation of the Provisional Government. Intended at the time to apply only to the Petrograd garrison, the 'order' had become widely interpreted as applying to all troops, including those in the front-line.

Guchkov, war minister in the new government, found out about Order No 1 only after it was published and he had failed to get it rescinded. On March 9, just a week after taking up his post, he had cabled Alekseev in Mogilev: 'The Provisional Government has no real power of any kind and its orders are carried out only to the extent that this is permitted by the Soviet...in the military department it is possible at present to issue only such orders as basically do not contradict the decisions of the above-mentioned Soviet.'[21]

The effect was disastrous, for it essentially made officers subservient to the dictates of 'soldier committees' established in every military formation, which took away the control of arms from officers, and in some instances dictated what military action might, or might not, be taken against the enemy.

Off-duty soldiers were to be treated as civilians, with no requirement to salute or stand to attention; officers were 'prohibited' from speaking to soldiers 'rudely'. In some units, 'soldier committees' insisted on electing their own officers, and expelling those they judged to be too strict or who were suspected of wanting to get on with the war. No wonder, then, that there was no place in this new 'democratic people's army' for Michael or any other Grand Duke, including 'Uncle Nikolasha', reappointed Supreme Commander by Nicholas before he abdicated. The new government had simply sacked him.[22]

Paléologue estimated that there were well over a million deserters roaming Russia. 'Units have been turned into political debating societies,' reported the British military observer Alfred Knox after a tour of the northern front. Front-line infantry refused to allow the artillery to shoot at the enemy in case the enemy shot back, and fraternised daily with the Germans facing them. As for the troops in Petrograd, 'the tens of thousands of able-bodied men in uniform who saunter about the streets without a thought of going to the front…will be a disgrace for all-time to the Russian people and its government'.[23]

Michael thought the same, and said so in a letter to a British friend, Major Simpson. 'I want you to know that I am very much ashamed of my countrymen, who are showing too little patriotism ever since the revolution, and who are forgetting their agreement with the Allies, who have done so much to help them. But nonetheless I hope that the return of their good feelings will prevent them becoming traitors.'[24]

One consolation for Michael was that his own Savage Division had remained immune to the breakdown in discipline. Officers and men were as rock-steady after the revolution as they had been before. He would also have been proud to know that when an officer returned from Petrograd to his Muslim regiment, he found that 'one question seemed to interest the men most — the fate of Grand Duke Michael'. When he replied that he was in Gatchina and that he was 'safe for the moment' the men would shake their heads and mumble, 'Allah preserve him — he is a real *dzhigit*. Why didn't he come to us when it all happened: we would never have given him up.'[25]

SITTING in Michael's house, Grand Duke George decided that he could no longer stand living in this new Russia. He had accepted the emergence of the new government 'but what he had seen after that,' he wrote to his wife in England, 'is enough to make your hair stand on end. I would like to leave the country at once.' He was also tiring of Gatchina: 'Misha is so nice but his wife is so vengeful about the Romanovs'. [26] George was not sure how much more he could take of her outbursts.

His natural hope was that he would go to England, where his wife, the daughter of the late King George of Greece, had been stranded since the outbreak of war. Accordingly, three weeks after the new government came into being, he went to see Buchanan to seek permission to travel to England.

Although he was not directly connected to the British royals, his wife Marie was a niece of the Dowager Queen Alexandra, as was Michael. So, in the hope of increasing his chances, he told Buchanan that Michael was also keen on going back to his waiting estate in Sussex. He told Buchanan that he saw no hope for Russia with the Soviet pulling the strings. 'Everything was being confiscated…and to think that these brutes will probably govern the country…it will become a country of savages…every decent person will leave.'[27]

George's inclusion of Michael as being his co-applicant was

not entirely as he presented it to Buchanan. Walking in the palace park, George had talked to Michael about getting away, and Michael had told him that he was also thinking of going to London. The difference between the two was that George wanted to get out altogether, whereas Michael was thinking only of a short trip, without his family, and with the intention of getting back as soon as he could.

The reason in his case was that, freed of all responsibility, Natasha had urged him to get specialist treatment for his 'damned stomach pains' which had so often laid him low in the past. There had been previous discussions in the last couple of years about having treatment in Britain but because of his military duties it had been 'impossible for him to get to the great specialists who could have dealt with it radically,' his stepdaughter Tata recalled. Now, with time on his hands, Natasha saw the chance for him to get the treatment he needed.

In those early days of the new government, Michael assumed that there would be no difficulty in getting permission to go abroad for a few weeks perhaps. After all, he would be leaving his wife and family behind, and that in itself would be sufficient surety that he would be coming back. The Soviet might bark protests, but surely Kerensky would satisfy them that it was for genuine medical treatment, and nothing more than that. In the event the refusal he feared did not come from the Soviet, but from his cousin King George V at Buckingham Palace. The king had shut the door on any Romanovs coming to Britain. He had enough problems with his own throne.

THE Romanov who posed the greatest difficulty for King George was ex-Tsar Nicholas, notwithstanding the close family ties and long friendship, and the loyalty he had shown as an ally. His fall from power had been welcomed by liberals worldwide — by American President Woodrow Wilson as well as by British prime minister Lloyd George. But liberal sentiment was not the problem. 'Bloody Nicholas' was a hated figure among British socialists, holding as they did an idealised view of the Russian revolution; and what they were not prepared to accept was any idea that he might be offered refuge in Britain.

On March 9, six days after his abdication, Nicholas had returned to Tsarskoe Selo, escorted by Duma deputies on his imperial train. With that he began what was in effect a prison sentence. He and his family — the children no less than their parents — were confined to their apartments in the palace and restricted for exercise to a small area of the park outside. They were guarded day and night, and while the bayonets were protection from potential attacks by Soviet extremists they were also a bar to the outside world. The family were captives, under threat that they face worse than house arrest. The Soviet continued to clamour for their confinement in the fortress of St Peter and St Paul.

There were endless petty humiliations. Soldiers enjoyed taunting them; crowds of spectators at the outer railings would peer in, hissing and booing. It was an ordeal borne with dignity, and in the confidence that it was only temporary — that they would very shortly be sent abroad into exile. Pierre Gilliard, the Swiss tutor employed at Tsarskoe Selo, would remember that 'there was endless talk about our imminent transfer to England'.[29]

The Provisional Government, worried by Soviet threats, encouraged that idea as the best way of keeping the family out of reach of vengeful revolutionaries. The British government quickly signalled that it was willing to take them, assuming in doing so that the king, Nicholas's first cousin, would surely support that — they were family.

Buckingham Palace, however, was aghast at the prospect. King George was alarmed not just by the inevitable left-wing protests which would greet any move to give 'Bloody Nicholas' sanctuary but that the British royals were themselves facing increased hostility over the fact that, although British by birth and upbringing, they were all of German descent. When even a dachshund risked being kicked in the street the British king, with a German father-in-law, and German relatives all around him, was understandably sensitive about being damned as a German. British republicanism was not deep-seated but it was very noisy.

It would not be long before anti-German sentiment would be so great that the British royals in the House of Saxe-Coburg-Gotha, as Queen Victoria thought it to be, would reinvent themselves under the more agreeable name of the House of Windsor. By Order-in-Council of July 17, 1917, Alexandra's eldest sister Victoria, of Hesse-Darmstadt until she married Prince Louis Battenberg, disappeared, to be replaced by the terribly English-sounding Marchioness of Milford Haven, though she had never been there. Other Battenbergs were translated into Mountbatten and Carisbrooke; the Duke of Teck found himself converted into a Scotsman, as the Earl of Athlone.

With this looming ahead, King George was not pleased to find himself caught up in the problems of a Russian autocrat with a German wife and for whom there was almost no sympathy in any quarter. However, his objections were at first set aside by the British government on the grounds that the offer having been made, it could not be withdrawn.

It was at this point on March 23 that the cable came into London from Buchanan asking that the names of Grand Dukes Michael and George be added to the list of those seeking refuge in London.

Now two ex-Emperors knocking on the door? It gave opportunity for Buckingham Palace to re-open the case for barring Nicholas. 'I do trust that the whole question…will be reconsidered,' wrote the king's private secretary Lord Stamfordham to the foreign secretary Balfour. 'It will very hard on the King and arouse much public comment if not resentment.'[30]

More shots came in from Buckingham Palace. 'The residence in this country of the ex-Emperor and Empress…would undoubtedly compromise the position of the King and Queen… we must be allowed to withdraw from the consent previously given.'[31] Yet George V was fully aware of the dangers facing his cousin if he was not granted refuge. 'I fear that if poor Nicky goes into the Fortress of St Peter and St Paul he will not come out alive,' he later wrote in his diary.[32]

Could the problem be avoided if Nicholas went instead to France? The reply from the British ambassador in Paris was that 'The Empress is not only a Boche by birth but in sentiment... she is regarded as a criminal or a criminal lunatic, and the ex-Emperor as a criminal from his weakness and submission to her promptings.'[33]

As the British agonised, the Provisional Government itself stepped away from the idea of sending Nicholas abroad. The Soviet would have none of it, and with that the new government pledged that it would not again give permission for any member of the imperial family to leave Russia without the agreement of the Soviet. That conveniently allowed the British to let their invitation to wither on the vine. The Romanovs were stranded.

17. FAREWELL MY BROTHER

UNLIKE the miserable house-arrest suffered by Nicholas and his family in Tsarskoe Selo, Michael and his family in Gatchina lived very much as before. In many respects his own day-to-day life changed little as the weeks went on. He was free to move within the Petrograd area, though not beyond without a permit. He could drive into the country in his Rolls-Royce or his new Packard — ordered before the war, but which had unexpectedly turned up at his house a year earlier; he could have friends to stay, and afford staff and a houseload of servants. Walking about the town, people still bowed to him in the street,[1] and while there were now guards posted in Nikolaevskaya Street they were there only to keep away hooligans and looters. As even George admitted in one letter to his wife, 'the government is trying to be as polite as possible with us, I must own that they have been quite correct towards us'.[2]

Although Michael's annual income from the imperial purse had stopped, as it had for all Romanovs, and his imperial yacht requisitioned along with his train carriage, he still had ample cash in the bank. He also continued to receive some income from his retained private holdings, including his Ukraine sugar factory and his Brasovo estate. His real concern about Brasovo was that he was not permitted to go there to look after its affairs and its people as he usually did. The government in deference to the Soviet had refused a permit.

The man a future constituent assembly might therefore confirm as Emperor was thus virtually a prisoner in his own country, even though he was not confined as was his brother and his family in Tsarskoe Selo. Nonetheless, in itself that made a mockery of the promises given by the Duma men on March 3. The powers he had vested in them to ensure orderly and responsible government had clearly been hijacked by the disorderly and irresponsible men in the Soviet.

Yet otherwise he could not complain about his life in Gatchina. He had bought another house for his staff, on Baggout Street where Natasha had lived when she was married to Wulfert, and at the end of April he rented another in Kseniinsky Street, by the Priorate. 'The house has two floors, we're thinking of it for our servants,' he noted in his diary for May 5, 1917.[3] He had spent the day inspecting the house, planning to enlarge the garden, and discussing with Natasha the final furnishings, due for delivery nine days later.[4]

But would they be left alone as they had been? There were worrying signs that the Soviet was becoming ever more assertive and demanding, now that the Bolsheviks were back in Petrograd and challenging them. Lenin and Trotsky, returned from exile by the Germans in the hope of stirring up even more trouble, were formidable rivals to the Soviet. That did not bode well, and while Michael had no intention of leaving Russia permanently, it seemed prudent to have some sort of insurance policy in case matters worsened.

An exit permit to Finland —the gateway to Sweden, Norway and then England— suggested itself. To get one, he would need to pull strings and do so discreetly, without the comrades finding out. General Polovtsov, his old friend from the Savage Division, had recently been appointed commander of the Petrograd garrison and on an official trip to Gatchina in June he was contacted by Michael's ADC Prince Vyazemsky.

'It was completely out of the question that I should openly visit the Grand Duke, whom I liked so much,' said Polovtsov. 'A plot would have at once been suspected, but I was delighted to think that a secret meeting with his ADC could be arranged.' It took place in the Gatchina palace. In the course of this meeting Vyazemsky asked if Michael could be given a permit to cross into Finland with two cars.

Back in Petrograd, Polovtsov casually approached Kerensky. 'By the way, I have had a request from the Grand Duke Michael to deliver him a permit for crossing the frontier into Finland with his family in two cars. You always say that you admire him so much for his correctness and straightforwardness, so I expect you will have no objection...'

Kerensky looked at him through half-closed eyes. 'If I were not in Petrograd at the moment, what would you do?'

'I would deliver it on my own responsibility.'

'Then deliver it on your own responsibility,' Kerensky replied.[5]

There were, however, no such discreet concessions for Nicholas. After three months' imprisonment at Tsarskoe Selo no solution had been found to the question of what to do with the ex-Tsar and his family. In July, an attempted coup by the Bolsheviks in Petrograd was to force a decision. The uprising, crushed by loyal government troops after two days of serious disorders, was a serious setback for the Bolsheviks, and a humiliation for its leadership with Lenin, shaving off his beard as disguise, fleeing by car to Finland.

But it also settled the immediate future of Nicholas. Believing that the Bolshevik failure might encourage a monarchist counter-revolution, Kerensky decided to remove the ex-Tsar from the political chess board while there was opportunity to do so. He chose Tobolsk, in the far-off Urals; his reason, he would say, was that it was 'an out-and-out backwater'.[6] The move was fixed for August 1.

Michael heard of this 'only by accident' in the afternoon of the previous day. With only hours to spare, he drove at once to Petrograd with Natasha and Johnson, going directly to the Winter Palace, home and office to the all-powerful Kerensky, now master of both the Provisional Government and the Soviet which, with the Bolshevik threat, had come to find itself needing him as much as he had once needed them. It was difficult in these days to distinguish one from the other.

While Michael and Natasha waited in their car, Johnson was sent into the Winter Palace to find Kerensky and to persuade him to allow Michael to see his brother that night.[7]

Kerensky had taken to working at the desk of Michael's father Alexander III and sleeping in his bed. The red flag flying over the Winter Palace was also lowered whenever he was out of town, as had happened when the Tsar would leave in imperial days.[8] It was as if Kerensky had become Tsar, which in a sense he had: he was the virtual dictator and as much autocrat as Nicholas had ever been.

The Provisional Government which had met Michael in Millionnaya Street was largely dissolved. Only three of the 12 original ministers remained in office — Kerensky as prime minister, war minister and navy minister; Tereshchenko, formerly finance minister was now foreign minister; and Nekrasov who remained transport minister. Milyukov and Guchkov had resigned in disgust within the first two months; Prince Lvov had quit as prime minister after the abortive Bolshevik uprising in July, which left him at best as no more than a figurehead in a government dominated by Kerensky. The others had just vanished, to be replaced by men from the Soviet, though no Bolsheviks joined the government for they had refused to 'collaborate'.

This was no longer the Provisional Government, bound by the constitution handed to them by Michael — it was the Kerensky Government, bound by no one save himself and his lackeys. The so-called Kerensky Offensive, launched against the Germans in June, had failed. If anything, that meant that his grip had to tighten; since there was no victory, other than against the Bolsheviks, his eyes had turned inwards. The enemy, he believed, was now within.

It was around 7.30 p.m. when Johnson was led in to see

Kerensky. Yes, he understood, and saw no objection. A meeting was arranged for midnight at Tsarskoe Selo, which was the earliest that Kerensky could be there, and he insisted on being present.

After Johnson re-emerged into the palace square, Michael drove to Matveev's apartment on the Fontanka, where they all had dinner. At 10 p.m. Michael and Natasha drove north to Tsarskoe Selo, stopping at Grand Duke Boris's English-style villa on Town Street. From there, at midnight, Michael was taken alone to the Alexander Palace by the Guard Commandant, Colonel Eugen Kobylinsky.[9] Entering through the kitchen, they went through the basement to the stairs leading to Nicholas's study. In the anteroom they were met by Kerensky.

It was some five months since the brothers had seen each other, the last occasion being in February 1917, when Michael had gone to Tsarskoe Selo to beg Nicholas to make the concessions necessary to save the throne. Nicholas had then dismissed his arguments as alarmist, as he had dismissed all those before. Now he was an ex-Tsar, a prisoner, unable to command anyone, and helplessly awaiting despatch with his entire family into distant exile.

Kerensky, making small talk, accompanied Michael into the study, and then retreated to a side table and pretended to be absorbed in a book.[10] As the door closed behind them, 13-year-old Alexis, the boy who should have been Emperor, came into the anteroom and asked Kobylinsky: 'Is that Uncle Misha who has just come in?' Told that it was, he hid himself behind the door. 'I want to see him when he goes out,' he said, peering through a crack in the door at the study beyond.[11]

Although Kerensky sat with his head seemingly buried in his book, privacy was impossible. However low their voices, Michael and Nicholas knew he could hear everything they said, so they did not say much in consequence. There had been an awkward silence at first, then ten minutes of polite conversation, neither sufficiently at ease to think of anything that actually mattered. *'How is Alix? How is mother?'* Their conversation never rose above the trite. 'They stood fidgeting all the while, and sometimes one would take hold of the other's hand or the buttons of his uniform,' Kerensky, sneaking glances over his book, would say later.

After ten minutes, Kerensky motioned that the meeting was over. 'May I see the children?' asked Michael, not knowing that Alexis was outside the door, looking in.

'No,' answered Kerensky. 'I cannot prolong the interview.'[12]

Michael and Nicholas clasped hands, and murmured their goodbyes. Then Michael, his eyes filled with tears,[13] turned and left as he had come. Alexis, waved away by Kobylinsky, retreated out of sight, hoping that some call would come for him from Uncle Misha. But there was no call; Michael had not known he was there.

That night, all he said to his diary was that 'I found that Nicky looked rather well'.[14] He would never see his brother again, though of course he could not know that it was Nicholas who would briefly outlive him.

Nor could he know, as he drove back to Gatchina in the eearly hours of August 1, that he was about to become a prisoner himself.

18. KERENSKY'S CAPTIVE

THREE weeks later, on Monday, August 21, Michael stayed at home while Natasha, with Johnson as escort, went off by train to Petrograd. Shopping, with lunch afterwards at the Astoria? He preferred a stroll around the town, and pottering in the garden. At seven o'clock that evening, as he was awaiting their return, a column of trucks roared into Nikolaevskaya Street, and braked at his front door. Armed troops, some 60 in number, jumped down and surrounded the house, bayonets drawn, as Andrei Kosmin, deputy chief of the Petrograd District, accompanied by the local Gatchina commandant, walked to the front door, to be met by a startled Michael. Kosmin, brandishing an order for his arrest on the orders of Kerensky, told him that he was now confined to his house, under guard.[1]

Half an hour later, a car drew up and Natasha and Johnson, alarmed by sight of the troops, hurried into the house. The waiting Kosmin stiffly nodded, told them that they too were under arrest, and then marched off, leaving the guard to the local and somewhat embarrassed commandant. He could only shrug at Michael's questions; there was nothing he could do about it — the written order was signed by Boris Savinkov, a former revolutionary terrorist who was now 'Director of the War Ministry'. The order read:

To the Commander-in-Chief of all Forces of the Petrograd District. Based on the resolution of the Provisional Government an order is given to arrest the former Grand Duke Michael Aleksandrovich as a person whose activities are a threat to the defence of the country...

and to the freedoms won by the revolution. This person must be kept under the strictest house arrest... This order must be declared to the former Grand Duke, who should be kept under arrest until a further special order.[2]

A bewildered Michael, now styled a 'former' Grand Duke, though there had been no decree to that effect and nor could there lawfully be since it was not within the power of the Provisional Government to pre-empt any decision reserved to the future Constituent Assembly, could not understand what any of this was about. There had been no warning, no hint of trouble, so why was Kerensky suddenly turning on him?

In fact, the order was a panic measure by a government now fearful of a 'counter-revolution' in favour of the monarchists. That being so, Michael was a threat, a rallying point for those who wanted to be rid of Kerensky and his discredited, oppressive and incompetent government. Yes, Kerensky had scored a victory over the Bolsheviks in July, with its leader Lenin in flight to Finland, but that was in-fighting between one brand of socialists and another, and for monarchists there was not much to choose between either.

A week earlier General Lavr Kornilov, the recently-appointed Supreme Commander, had been given a hero's reception by the rightist delegates at the State Conference held in Moscow, and in consequence Kerensky had become convinced that 'the next attempt at a blow would come from the right, and not from the left'.[3]

His suspicions were fuelled by reports that Mogilev was a hotbed of monarchist conspirators, a view encouraged by complaints that 'in the evenings, in order to tease the local democrats,'[4] the officers opened the windows and played on the piano the old national anthem, *God Save The Tsar,* and not the *Marseillaise*, which the revolutionaries had adopted in its place.

Michael was arrested in this climate of an imagined monarchist counter-revolution, though the immediate cause three days earlier had been a farcical 'plot' to rescue Nicholas and his family from

Tobolsk. The central figure was Margarita Khitrovo, a former maid-of-honour at the imperial court. The blindly-devoted Margarita journeyed to Tobolsk taking to Nicholas and Alexandra a large number of letters concealed in a pillow-case; within hours of her arrival on August 18, her hotel room was searched and the letters discovered. Arrested, she was sent back to Petrograd the following day.[5]

Although the letters turned out to be merely innocent correspondence, in the frantic atmosphere of Petrograd the news of her detention at Tobolsk was taken as evidence of a major counter-revolutionary plot.' Highly exaggerated tales of this conspiracy reached the government', admitted Kerensky later, but that was not enough to change his attitude towards Michael.[6]

Angry rather than alarmed, since he knew nothing of any so-called plot, Michael wrote a letter of protest to Kerensky demanding an end to his arrest and the withdrawal of the guards, but was told in reply only that 'the present position of democracy and the state is such that it was found necessary to keep me in isolation'. They had been caught up, as he put it four days later, 'in a plot which never existed'.[7]

As it happened, they were now to be embroiled in another plot which never existed, the so-called 'Kornilov Affair', an event which this time was to prove more tragedy than farce.

At 3 a.m. on Tuesday, August 29, eight days after the order placing them under house arrest, Michael and Natasha were awaked by an excited Gatchina commandant and told that they had to be ready to leave for Petrograd in an hour's time with their family. The house was to be evacuated. Wakening the children and staff, and quickly packing suitcases for the unknown ahead, they trooped downstairs only to find that the military drivers could not get Michael's cars started.

Michael watched them struggling for a while, and then suggested that it would be best if they called out his chauffeur to help. Eventually they did so, and he started the cars for them, his face saying what he thought of these bungling drivers. In consequence it was not until 5.10 a.m., 70 minutes later than ordered, that the convoy set out for Petrograd.[8]

From the viewpoint of their nervous guards it was just in time. The Supreme Commander General Lavr Kornilov had ordered his crack Third Cavalry Corps to advance on the capital and Michael's 'private army', his beloved Savage Division, was marching on Gatchina, and was so close it would be in the woods around it within hours.

GENERAL Kornilov had intended to strengthen the government, not rebel against it. He had replaced Brusilov in mid-July after the failure of the 'Kerensky Offensive' launched on June 18, and he was determined to restore discipline in the army, including the reimposition of the death penalty. No army could wage war when regiments refused to advance or simply deserted to the rear whenever the enemy counter-attacked. The 'Kerensky Offensive' had shown that 'the world's first democratic army' would, when tested, vote with its feet.

Kornilov, the son of a Cossack peasant, and the man who had formally placed Alexandra under house arrest at Tsarskoe Selo in March, did not think of himself as a rebel—'I despise the old regime', he said[9]— but he wanted a strong government which could free itself of its dependency on the dictating policies of the Soviet and the Bolsheviks.

On August 7, he ordered General Aleksandr Krymov on the Romanian Front to move his Third Cavalry Corps northwards so that it could deal with any attempted coup by the Bolsheviks in either Petrograd or Moscow. He was prepared, he told his chief-of-staff, to disperse the Soviet, hang its leaders, and finish off the Bolsheviks.[10]

As they headed north there came intelligence reports that the Bolsheviks, Lenin having quietly returned, had regrouped and were planning another attempt at seizing power in the capital. On August 22 Kerensky asked Kornilov to send a cavalry corps to defend the government, but intending that this corps, when in the capital, would then come under his direct control, not Kornilov's. It would then give him a force not only able to deal with the Bolsheviks, but with any attempt by the right to mount a counter-revolutionary attack against him. He would cover a threat from either or both.

This ploy backfired. The Third Cavalry Corps, which included the Savage Division and two Cossack divisions, as well as artillery, was what he would be getting and not the 'democratic' and biddable divisions he had expected. The Third Cavalry Corps, commanded by General Krymov, the 'political' general who had been one of the key figures in the Guchkov conspiracy which had been intent six months earlier on capturing Nicholas in his train, was staffed by monarchist officers, and its men were immune from Soviet and Bolshevik indoctrination. Kornilov, it seemed, was sending a Trojan Horse.

Certainly, Boris Savinkov, Kerensky's emissary at Mogilev, saw it that way. He urged that Krymov be replaced and he also sought to have the Savage Division, known to be loyal to Michael, and commanded by his old friend Prince Bagration, removed from the corps.[11] Kornilov ignored him. There was no point, he said, in sending a corps 'acceptable' to the Soviet and Bolsheviks. If Krymov and the Savage Division scared Petrograd, then that was precisely what was required. As he told his chief-of-staff, they might not like it, but they would thank him afterwards.[12]

Kerensky was now caught between a determined Kornilov and a clamouring Soviet, and unable any longer to claim the middle ground. Persuading himself that Kornilov's real intent was to arrest him and the rest of the government, he decided to brand Kornilov a traitor and to present his advancing columns as a counter-revolution. The fact that Kerensky himself had ordered him to send troops was no longer the point: Kornilov's crime was that he had sent the 'wrong' troops.

In the early hours of August 27, after a Cabinet meeting called to deal with 'the emergency' Kerensky demanded and was given dictatorial powers and what remained of the Provisional

Government in all practical sense ceased to exist. After sending Kornilov a cable sacking him as Supreme Commander, Kerensky asked the Soviet to help in defending the revolution; they promptly set up a military committee which almost at once fell into the hands of those who were Bolshevik in all but name. On their authority some 40,000 weapons were issued to the workers so that they could defend 'democracy'.[13] Kerensky, as he would soon find to his cost, had armed the very people determined to overthrow him and replace the Soviet with themselves.

Kornilov, enraged by his dismissal, defiantly declared his intent to 'lead the people to victory over the enemy to a constituent assembly where it will decide its own destiny and choose its own political system'[14] — precisely the aims set out in Michael's manifesto six months earlier. Unfortunately this last-minute rebellion made it look as if he had intended to rebel from the outset. His generals were sympathetic but confused. The army as a whole would not support what looked like a counter-revolution. Kornilov was on his own.

The Third Cavalry Corps in the event was also hesitant. At his own headquarters in Luga, 70 miles from the capital, Krymov did not know, with Kornilov sacked, if he was obeying or disobeying his orders. Two days later, on August 29, as his columns reached Tsarskoe Selo, and his Savage Division arrived at Gatchina, he received a telegram from Kerensky claiming that Petrograd was calm, no disorders were expected, and 'there is no need of your corps'. He was 'commanded' to stop the advance ordered by the sacked Kornilov.[15] Krymov was stopped in his tracks. Two days later he went to Petrograd at Kerensky's invitation and met him at the Winter Palace. Denying any intent to rebel, he pointed out that he had been advancing in support of the government, not against it, as ordered by Kornilov and at the request of Kerensky himself. Unjustly accused, he left the meeting in despair, all hope gone of a fresh start for Russia. Going to a friend's apartment, he wrote a letter to Kornilov and another to his wife; that done he put a revolver to his head and shot himself.[16]

Next day, September 1, Kerensky appointed himself Supreme Commander and declared, in open breach of the very constitution he had sworn to Michael to defend — 'to carry the precious vessel of your authority to the Constituent Assembly without spilling a drop' — that Russia was now 'a democratic republic'.

ON that first day of the new 'republic' the man who was still its last Tsar remained under arrest in Petrograd, seventy-two hours after being taken from Gatchina. Michael and Natasha, their two children, their British governess Miss Neame, and the faithful Johnson, had been taken first to military headquarters, and then told that they were be housed under guard in a small apartment on the Morskaya. Escorted by 65 soldiers, packed into a convoy of trucks, they were taken in their cars and led into their new 'prison'. Michael immediately protested. 'The premises were absolutely unfit for our stay, without any elementary convenience, and with only three beds', he complained.[17]

Faced with a furious Natasha — never one to keep silent in any circumstances —and a stubborn Michael, the officer in charge seemed incapable of simply locking the door and leaving them to make the best of it. Instead, he looked helplessly from one to another, not knowing what to do. Michael took over. Johnson was sent out to find a telephone and call Matveev. Fortunately he was at home, and offered to put them all up in his spacious apartment.

That settled matters. The officer gave in, went off to telephone his superiors, and came back to say that permission had been granted, provided that a guard was stationed outside Matveev's door. With that, they all trooped downstairs to their waiting cars, and followed by their truckloads of armed soldiers, drove off to the Fontanka.

Having been awaked in the middle of the night, they were all exhausted by the time they reached Matveev's apartment in the early evening, the children fretful, and hungry. As the door closed behind them, and the sentries took up their position on the landing outside, Michael was outraged. 'That is how dangerous criminals are guarded!' he wrote angrily in this diary that night. 'We cannot find out anything about ourselves and we are frustrated and melancholic.'[18]

What made his situation worse was that in the next days his stomach problem flared up again, and Natasha always frantic about his health, insisted on specialists being allowed to see him. Three of them arrived the following Monday, September 4, and after examining him recommended a strict diet, hot-water bottles, and complete rest— 'but where can one find that under present circumstances?' he asked.[19] That evening, at 9 p.m., Kerensky's ADC Grigorev arrived, with the welcome news that Michael was to be released shortly.

This change of heart appears to have been after an intervention by the British ambassador, Buchanan, to whom Johnson had been despatched in the hope that he could help. Buchanan in turn saw Tereshchenko, the foreign minister in this rump Provisional Government. Buchanan then also reported matters to London, in a cable to Lord Stamfordham, the king's private secretary, circulated to the Cabinet.

'The poor Grand Duke Michael has, I am afraid, had rather a bad time of it lately…I protested strongly to Tereshchenko against the treatment to which HIH has been subjected and Tereshchenko in turn spoke to Kerensky. From what Tereshchenko has since told me I hope that the Grand Duke will be released at once.'[20]

He was not, in fact, released, but Tereshchenko did agree that Michael and his family could go back to Gatchina, subject to remaining under guard. After nine days locked into an apartment in Petrograd, they were back home by midnight on Wednesday, September 6, 1917.

'Our cortege consisted of five cars, two of them ours,' Michael recorded. 'Natasha, children, Kosmin and I were in the Packard, in the front were Neame, Johnson and the Commandant, at the rear —the Rolls-Royce with the guard. As soon as we arrived I went to bed. It was so nice to be back home at last.'[21]

Though he would never know it, three days before his arrest in Gatchina on August 29, Tereshchenko had gone to see Buchanan to tell him that it had been decided to allow Michael to go abroad though, as Buchanan duly reported to London, he 'begged me that what he had told me might be kept secret.'[22] That was unlikely to have been kindness, for there was none of that around in August 1917. Almost certainly, Kerensky's aim was to get Michael out of the country, and remove him as a potential figurehead for the counter-revolution he so feared. If so, it was too late for that. The following day, he was facing the prospect of Kornilov's corps advancing into the capital, and 24 hours after that the Savage Division was almost in Gatchina. Arresting Michael, not freeing him, was the only option then for a desperate Kerensky.

Would Michael have been allowed into England if he had been freed to go there? Buckingham Palace had shut its doors to him and any other Grand Duke back in March. But with their own House of Windsor in place, and their German roots buried under new titles, had cousin George V relented?

The answer was that he had not. Buchanan could plead as he had done, but he was wasting his time. The doors of Buckingham Palace remained not merely shut, but locked and bolted. Michael was a Romanov and for that, he was damned.

IT would not be until the following Wednesday, September 13, three weeks after his first arrest, that Michael was told he was free at last. 'But why we were under arrest is unknown, and of course, no accusations were made, there couldn't be. Where is the guarantee that this won't be repeated?' It seemed that there was no intention of that. Two days later, 'quite unexpectedly,' an apologetic Kosmin returned to Gatchina and 'brought me a written permit to go to the Crimea whenever we wished'.[23]

After all that had happened, that was cheering news. Perhaps they should go there for the winter? Maybe better times were ahead after all. Michael had shrugged off Kerensky's announcement that Russia was now a republic — republic or monarchy, what did it matter, he wrote, 'if only there is order and justice in the land'.[24] And perhaps there would be: elections for the new Constituent Assembly had been fixed for November 12 and the resultant Assembly was due to convene on November 28. Whatever Kerensky and his Soviet allies did in the next weeks, their time of arbitrary rule was drawing to a close. The Russian people would decide the future, and there would be a new and elected government, not these men who had made such a botch of affairs in the past months. For years the leading politicians of the day had clamoured that they were best placed to take the country forward, but having been handed the torch by Michael, they had proved incapable of keeping it alight. It was very dispiriting.

Anxious friends urged him to leave at once. There were many Romanovs who had sought sanctuary in the Crimea, where the reach of the Soviet was hardly noticeable, but Michael refused even to think of that. No, he would stay where he was until the future of Russia was settled. After all, he was the architect of those elections: he had made the calling of a constituent assembly a condition of his vesting his powers in the then seemingly promising Provisional Government. He would stick it out in Gatchina until the Assembly decided what was to be. It was his duty. Hope must triumph over experience.

Some of that hope reached the banished Dimitri in Persia. Taken under the wing of the British ambassador in Teheran, and made an honorary officer in the British army, Dimitri received an unexpected letter from Natasha in early October 1917. In his diary he wrote that he was 'surprised that she suddenly decided to make contact and wrote favourably and touchingly — this might mean that things have taken a little turn for the better in Gatchina'.[25.]

In fact, they were about to get much worse. On October 25, 1917, Petrograd fell to the Bolsheviks — the men dedicated to creating a Russia in which there could never be either an emperor or a democratic republic. The best Michael could hope for now was to be left in peace as Citizen Romanov.

19. CITIZEN ROMANOV

KERENSKY had blundered badly in arming the Bolsheviks in the face of Kornilov's advancing columns. He had sacked him as Supreme Commander and placed him under arrest, but in humbling Kornilov he had lost the trust of the other generals. He had made his bed in the extremist camp and he now had to lie on it. Declaring a republic on September 1 had done nothing to win over the workers. That month, there were strikes across Russia, and mass unemployment as industrial plants closed and manufacturing slumped. As Kerensky's stock fell, that of the Bolsheviks rose. 'Down with the war', they cried, a call that was echoed throughout the Petrograd garrison and beyond.

The Bolshevik coup, rumoured for mid-September, came later but when it did come Kerensky had no Savage Division, no Krymov, and no Kornilov to crush it. Kerensky was on his own, as he discovered when the three Cossack divisions he had ordered to the defence of the capital refused 'to saddle up'.[1] The bulk of the Petrograd garrison also refused to rally to him, and for the defence of the Winter Palace—which he had made the centre and symbol of his power — he had to rely on officer cadets and a 'women's battalion'.[2]

At Gatchina, the Bolshevik threat dominated discussion from October 19, when Michael noted that 'an action...is expected daily'. Five days later he wrote that 'all bridges in Petrograd are swung apart because of the action expected every moment by the Bolsheviks'. The next day, Monday, October 25, Petrograd fell. 'The Winter Palace is occupied by the Bolsheviks...The

Council of the Republic is dismissed by the Bolsheviks and the military staff of the District is in their hands. There is shooting in some streets. The whole garrison went over to the Bolsheviks… Kerensky has gone to Dno to summon help.'[3]

The following day he recorded that 'all power is in the hands of the Military Revolutionary Committee. All the banks, ministries are seized. The Winter Palace, which was heavily bombarded was defended by cadets and the Women's Battalion and many lives were lost. All Cabinet ministers were arrested and are in the Kresty prison. In short, the Bolsheviks have won a complete victory…but for how long?' [4]

Although Petrograd had fallen, Gatchina was still in the hands of loyal government troops, reinforced by artillery and tough-looking Cossacks. The local Bolsheviks fled at the first sight of them. Kerensky, having abandoned the capital, now turned up at Gatchina Palace, defiantly promising a counter-offensive.

Walking about the town, Michael and Natasha were briefly encouraged. There were reports of more troops on their way. Cavalry, guns, and armed soldiers seemed to be everywhere, though there were not yet enough for General Peter Krasnov, commander of the diminished Third Cavalry Corps; even so, he seemed confident.

In his own show of confidence, and as signal to the townspeople that all would be well, Michael and Natasha went to the local cinema, in the evening of Friday, October 27 — two days after Petrograd fell — to see the film *She Put Him To Sleep Forever*, starring the Italian actress Franchese Bertini.[5] It was a curious place to find the last man proclaimed Emperor of All the Russias, but sitting in the packed cinema, surrounded by soldiers and townsfolk, it was a gesture intended to show Michael's contempt for the Bolsheviks and his faith in Krasnov, now marching to Tsarskoe Selo to do battle with the enemy.

In the event, it would be a disaster. Heavily out-numbered, Krasnov was soundly beaten, retreating with the remnants of his Corps after what would be the only battle between loyal troops and the triumphant Bolsheviks. It was the end for Kerensky, no longer dictator but a hunted man. It was also the end of any hope that Michael had that the Bolshevik uprising would leave him untouched in Gatchina. He had to get out before they came for him.

He still had his Finnish permit for two cars, but how much time had he? On Monday, October 30, Johnson was sent to the palace to find the answer to that. He returned at 11.30 p.m., his face grim. 'The position of Gatchina is critical,' he reported.[6] It was now or never.

With that, the household began packing valuables, working until 4 a.m. with the ever-practical Natasha 'sitting down and prising out the precious stones from various Oriental orders' which Michael had been awarded over the years.[7] After a few hours' sleep they resumed packing and continued doing so for the rest of that day. Michael went out and returned to report that a truce had been declared 'until midday tomorrow' — Wednesday, November 1.[8] It was going to be touch-and-go.

The plan was that the children and Miss Neame, would leave early in the morning in the Packard, and go to Batova, an estate owned by Natasha's close friend Nadine Vonlyarlarskaya, sister of the lawyer Vladimir Nabokov, 15 miles to the south of Gatchina. Nadine and her young daughter would go with them, and they would wait there until Michael and Natasha arrived in the second car.

Arriving safely, the car started back to Gatchina to pick up possessions and provisions while the children, Nadine and Miss Neame sat down to breakfast. 'Suddenly the manageress of the estate came hurriedly in to say that Bolshevik centres were being formed in all surrounding villages; that our car had been seen coming to the house; and that the Commissars intended to arrest the occupants, thinking that they were members of the Provisional Government trying to escape.'[9] All telephone lines to the house had already been cut.

Knowing that Michael had to be warned if he was not to fall

into the same trap, Nadine quickly saddled a horse and rode off to the local hospital and used their telephone to call him. There was only one line working but she got through to Nikolaevskaya Street. Speaking in English to confuse eavesdroppers she told Michael what had happened. He replied that he would send the Packard back with a message.

The little party waited anxiously all day but it was not until 8 p.m. that the Packard returned, with an armed Bolshevik sitting next to the chauffeur.[10]

The plan was in ruins. Even before the truce deadline passed, Gatchina had fallen into the hands of the Bolsheviks, and sailors had turned up at Michael's house and confiscated both the Packard and his Rolls-Royce.[11] Their only concession was that, Michael having persuaded the new local Bolshevik commandant Semen Roshal that the children had gone only on a day trip, to permit the Packard to return and bring them home.

At least they still had a home. Kerensky at that moment was a refugee, hiding in a peasant's cottage. The Provisional Government, born on March 3, was no more.

THREE days later, on Saturday November 4, the Bolshevik commandant Roshal returned to Nikolaevskaya Street. Roshal was a prominent figure in the Petrograd party, and a leader of the Kronstadt sailors whose revolutionary fervour had made them the 'shock troops' of the Bolshevik coup. Roshal produced an order of the Military Revolutionary Committee that Michael was to be taken to the Bolshevik headquarters in Petrograd. Michael protested, and after a long argument Roshal compromised: Michael could select his own accommodation in the capital and he would be free to go out, provided he stayed in the city. [12] Once more Michael was under arrest, but on rather more generous terms than had been the case under Kerensky ten weeks earlier. Yes, he would wait, said Roshal, until Michael could arrange something. He would come back tomorrow.

Michael telephoned 12 Millionnaya Street. Princess Putyatina had gone to Odessa, but her sister was staying there with her husband and brother. They would be delighted to have Michael and Natasha join them, but there was no room for the children. Michael called Matveev. The children and Miss Neame would stay with him.[13]

The following afternoon, Sunday, Roshal re-appeared with both of Michael's car and a squad of sailors. At 5.30 p.m. the household set off in convoy, followed by Roshal and two truckloads of guards.

Having seen the children safely into Matveev's apartment, Michael drove to Millionnaya Street, where Princess Putyatina's brother-in-law came out to greet them. Michael put a finger to his lips, as warning to him to be careful what he said in front of the two armed sailors standing behind him, flanking Roshal, 'a tall man, with dark, piercing eyes', and dressed in a soldier's tunic and fur cap. Roshal motioned them to go into the building, and once inside repeated his instructions on the terms of his 'arrest'. He then left, leaving the two sailors as sentry on the door.[14]

Although officially 'under surveillance', the Bolsheviks left him alone over the next days. He walked around the city, going first to the square in front of the Winter Palace where he 'admired its appearance' as he caustically put it. 'All the walls were spotted with bullets, and also the windows'.

Bolshevik propaganda would later portray 'the storming of the Winter Palace' in heroic terms as if a triumphant victory against a determined enemy, but it was nothing like that. There were only enough defenders to guard three doors, and the Red Guards, soldiers and sailors massed in the palace square simply broke in through the undefended doors and disarmed the tiny garrison once inside. The government ministers who had been working there, including Tereshchenko, were arrested. Three cadets were wounded, and six sailors were said to have been killed in the square earlier, but storm it was not.

On his return to Millionnaya Street, Michael and Natasha entertained friends. The conversation inevitably turning to politics, it became so heated with Natasha and the others so 'worked up and shouting', that 'we had to employ drastic measures', Michael suggesting that he should be given 'a chairman's bell to restore order' and if that failed, 'a revolver'.[15]

Eight days later, on Monday, November 13, Michael was told that he could go back to Gatchina under 'house arrest', though again the conditions were so lax that the order seemed not worth the paper it was written on.[16]

Although Michael was returning with everyone else, Natasha decided to stay on in Millionnaya Street for a few more days, though her motive was wholly practical: she was determined to go into the State Bank and rescue her valuables held there in a strong-box. The bank had been closed because of a strike, but it was due to re-open in two days' time. She would be back on Saturday.

When he got home he dashed off a letter to her in Millionnaya Street, laconically addressing the envelope to 'Comrade Nathalie Sergeyevna Brasova from Comrade MAR'. He reported that 'two of our people kept watch in the house during the night because our guard had been removed, but, as of tomorrow, we are supposed to have a guard again. Everything is quiet and comfortable here, it was a great pleasure to return home and breathe the wonderful fresh air. Johnnie is going to town tomorrow and will call at Millionnaya for a minute, and will come back with you on Saturday. It is now 9.30 p.m. and he and I are going for a little sledge ride in the wonderful moonlight...'[17]

Natasha got what she wanted at the bank. Telling officials that she needed access to her strong-box in order to examine papers, she was escorted into the vault and the box given to her. When she left the bank her muff was 'stuffed full of some of her more valuable and portable jewellery'.[18] She would need it all in the days to come.

Although Michael was released from his notional 'house arrest' shortly after his return to Gatchina, he would not be free from minor harassment. On November 25, 1917, a party of soldiers arrived at the house with an order authorising them to confiscate wine and provisions. They took '80 bottles of our wine and a quantity of sugar...some bottles were drunk and smashed on the spot'.[19]

Determined to put an end to such petty looting and hooliganism, and to obtain some form of guarantee that the Bolsheviks would 'leave me in peace', Michael went back to Petrograd next day and walked into the party headquarters to confront one of Lenin's henchmen, Vladimir Bonch-Bruevich, Secretary of the Soviet of the People's Commissars. After Michael's protestations, Bonch-Bruevich drew up a permit on official paper declaring Michael to have 'free residence' as an ordinary citizen.[20]

For the next three months the Bolsheviks left Michael Romanov in peace. He walked around the town unmolested, with people still bowing to him in the street. What he had not realised was that local volunteers had organised a discreet watch over him in case of trouble, and were also guarding his house against hooliganism.

When he did find out about this private protection, he made it known than he did not need it and that 'nobody will touch me here. I do not have the right to give orders, but I want the guard to be removed.'[21]

One change for the better at Gatchina was the appointment of the young Vladimir Gushchik as palace commissar. Destined one day to be a celebrated writer, Gushchik still thought of Michael as a Grand Duke, and he would say of him that he had 'three rare qualities: kindness, simplicity, and honesty...None of the parties were hostile towards him. Even socialists of all colours treated him with respect...'[22]

Gushchik became a close friend of Johnson and so trusted that he even became guardian of confidential papers which Michael did not feel it was safe to keep in his house. He proved himself a valuable friend and ally, and did what he could to make life as tolerable as the situation allowed. To protect Michael he would later burn the confidential papers entrusted to him;[23] what they would have revealed about Michael and Natasha's political contacts and activities is unknown.

But that would be later. Outwardly, life in Nikolaevskaya Street had settled down to so ordinary a routine that it might almost have been that the revolution had passed him by. When Christmas came 'we lit the tree, danced around it, and played cat-and-mouse. The children made masks and danced around the room in a comical way...' On New Year's Eve 'we sat down to eat at 12, not so much to greet the New Year as to say goodbye to damned 1917 which brought so much evil and misfortune to everyone'.[24]

THE New Year brought no sign that 1918 was going to be any better. The delayed elections for the Constituent Assembly, which the socialists had insisted should go ahead as the price of their support for the Bolsheviks, got them the victory they had expected, with the Bolsheviks capturing less than 25% of the vote and winning only some 170 of the 700-plus seats.[25]*

This was a mandate for a democratic republic, not a constitutional monarchy. Subject to a formal resolution, Michael's caretaker role as Emperor appeared to be over. But when the Assembly met for its opening session on January 5, the Bolsheviks closed it down that same day by sending in armed and drunken troops, and that was the end of that — the last hope that Russia would decide its own future as Michael had decreed in his Millionnaya Street manifesto nine months earlier.

Two prominent liberal members elected to that Assembly — Aleksandr Shingarev and F. F. Kokoshkin, both sometime ministers in the Provisional Government — were murdered immediately afterwards. Russia was no longer a monarchy, a republic, or a democracy; henceforth it was to be ruled by

*Socialist Revolutionaries emerged as the largest group, with around 375 seats. Estimates of the number of votes cast vary between 36.2 million and 41.7 million. Of the 815 seats in a full Assembly, more than a hundred had not been awarded at the opening. Whatever its final complexion, the Bolsheviks would have been a minority.

Bolshevik *diktat,* with opponents shot or arrested. Murder and robbery became commonplace.

For most ordinary people, including Michael's staff, though not Michael himself, the war had ceased to matter. The very British governess Miss Neame was as patriotic as anyone, but 'it had come to such a pitch of terror,' she said later, 'that we were all praying and waiting anxiously for the arrival of the Germans, as we then knew we would be safe'.[26]

Fighting their own people, the Bolsheviks could not afford to continue fighting Germany. Over the next two months Michael's diary would be dominated by the negotiations with the Germans for a separate peace. 'What a disgrace to Russia!' he wrote when he first heard of the talks.[27] They would stop and start and in the end the peace terms agreed would be worse than the ones first on offer. The Treaty of Brest-Litovsk, signed on March 3*, ended the war between Russia and Germany, and cleared the way for a civil war. Russians would now concentrate on killing each other.

For the nervous servants at Nikolaevskaya Street, the regret was that the advancing Germans had stopped short of Gatchina. 'Everyone was in despair,' wrote Miss Neame. It would quickly prove to be more than justified.

Four days later, at 11 a.m. on Tuesday, March 7, Michael was on his bedroom balcony, overlooking the snow-covered street beyond his garden. It was a beautiful morning, with bright sunshine. Troubled by his 'damned stomach pains' he was lying on his couch, beginning his diary for the previous day, noting that he had been playing the guitar in the afternoon. As he started to write: 'In the evening…'[27] he was interrupted by the sight of a group of armed men running up the road towards the house. Minutes later they were on the path, and forcing their way into the house itself.

Michael heard them running up the stairs, and then they were in his bedroom, the officer in charge bursting onto the balcony.[28]

*From February 1, 1918, the Bolsheviks adopted the Western calendar, February 1 becoming February 14. All dates hereafter follow the new calendar

In his hand he carried an order for the arrest of Michael and Johnson.

The order was signed by Moisei Uritsky, the head of the feared Petrograd Cheka — formally the Extraordinary Commission on the Struggle Against the Counter-Revolution, Speculation and Sabotage — and which was designed as an instrument of terror, with powers which in effect made it a law unto itself.

Miss Neame, cowering downstairs, would never forget Michael's arrest. This time his protestations were ignored. This time there would be no negotiations, no compromises, no acceptance that he could make his own arrangements for accommodation in Petrograd, no opportunity even to pack a bag. He was pulled from his couch, and pushed out to the stairs with shouts and brandished bayonets. The cries of Natasha and the rest of the household were ignored as they were thrust aside, and Michael and Johnson marched down the path and into the trucks which had driven up to the house.

Watching him go, Miss Neame was struck by the 'sad look in his eyes —so tired and ill, he was hurt at all the injustice'.[29] He would never come home ever again.

Driven to the capital, he was taken to the Smolny, once an exclusive girls' school, a few streets beyond the Tauride Palace and now Bolshevik headquarters. Michael would quickly find that he was not just under arrest as before — he was a prisoner of the revolution.

A distressed Natasha, quickly packing a suitcase, followed Michael to the capital, catching the train, and spending the night at the home of her friend Maggie Abakanovich on the Moika. Having telephoned Millionnaya Street, she met up with Princess Putyatina next morning and together they walked to the grey-painted Smolny. Passing through the colonnaded entrance, past machine-guns and guards with fixed bayonets, they were given permission to see Michael; they found him in a large room, furnished now with eight beds and a few chairs. He was standing in a window recess, talking to Johnson as armed guards stood around, smoking and laughing loudly. When Natasha walked in, he came quickly over to her and 'kissed her hand without speaking'.[30]

As they all sat down in the chairs and began talking quietly, a door opened and Uritsky came in, dressed in a leather jacket, high boots and a grey fur hat. Princess Putyatina remembered 'a man of under-average height, with a prominent, fleshy nose, large lop-ears, small ferrety eyes with an expression of cold cruelty'. He gave a short nod, pulled up another chair, sat down and lit a cigarette. He refused to answer any questions about the reason for Michael's imprisonment, and after a few vague promises about improving conditions, he got up and left.

The following day, Thursday, Natasha and Princess Putyatina returned again, but were allowed to see Michael for only thirty minutes. Desperate to do something, Natasha decided to go directly to Lenin, who was somewhere in the same building. 'Noticing that there was a sentry in front of one of the doors, we presumed that must be his office. Natasha brusquely opened the door without giving the sentry time to bar the way,' and marched in. Lenin, sitting at his desk, looked up startled, as Natasha firmly closed the door behind her.

The confused sentry outside made no attempt to follow her in, though he did bar the princess from doing so. She collapsed on a bench. 'I do not know how long I waited, but I do know that I got up several times and paced the corridor nervously'. At last the door opened and Natasha peeped out, beckoning her in. The sentry hesitated, but stepped aside as the princess swept by him.

Natasha was standing in the office on her own. Lenin had disappeared through another door, promising to look into the matter, but 'saying that it not only depended on him'. After a long wait, the inner door opened and instead of Lenin his friend Bonch-Bruevich walked in, nodded a greeting, and tried to sound reassuring. The question of Michael's arrest would, he promised, be reviewed later in the day. No, he could not say more. [31]

It was all they could get out of him, and with that Natasha and the princess left and walked back into the capital. Was there hope? They could only reassure each other through their tears that there must be.

That evening, as Natasha waited anxiously for news, twenty-four party leaders met at the Smolny, among them Lenin and Joseph Stalin, the man who would one day succeed him. Fearing that Petrograd was too near the German lines, and the counter-revolutionary movement in Finland, the meeting was to finalise the decision to move to the greater safety of Moscow.

One of their last decisions was to decide the fate of the 'former Grand Duke M. A. Romanov'. Given his prominence, and the potential threat he posed as a rallying point for counter-revolutionaries, not least the monarchists, the meeting was in no doubt that he could not be left behind. The answer was that he was to be exiled 'until further notice' to the distant Urals. Johnson was also to be exiled, but 'shall not be accommodated in the same city'. The arrangements were 'entrusted to Comrade Uritsky'.[32]

Next morning, Friday, a protesting Natasha was refused permission to see Michael. With that she and Princess Putyatina hurried away to find Uritsky. It was a very long walk back into the centre of the capital, and down to 2 Gorokhovaya Street at the bottom of the Nevsky Prospekt; the building they were looking for, formerly the offices of the City Governor, beside the Alexander Gardens and opposite the Admiralty, was now the headquarters of the Cheka.

Natasha waited by the steps, and the princess went inside to find Uritsky. He was in his office, and motioned her in, telling her that she had come 'just at the right time'. Michael, he told her, was to be exiled to Perm, a thousand miles away.

Shocked, the princess hurried out to the waiting Natasha, and broke the news. 'It was a terrible blow, but she bore it with courage and resignation'.[33]

Late that night Michael sat down in his prison room at the Smolny and wrote his farewell letter to Natasha.

Uritsky has just read to us the resolution of the Soviet of People's Commissars ordering our immediate move to Perm. They gave us half an hour to be ready...everything has happened so unexpectedly... Don't be disheartened, my dearest — God will help us to go through this dreadful ordeal. I kiss and most tenderly embrace you. Your Misha.[34]

At 1 a.m. that Saturday, March 11, Michael and Johnson were driven out of the Smolny through the darkened, freezing and snow-covered streets to the dimly-lit and near-deserted Nicholas station. After three shivering hours, with no means of keeping warm, they were marched to the train which would take them into exile and to a fate it was best they could not know.

20. PRISONER OF PERM

IN peacetime the twice-daily standard trains from the capital took two days to reach Perm, and the twice-weekly Siberian express got there in 37 hours. The train on which Michael and Johnson left at 4 a.m. that Saturday would take eight days, crawling along at less than five miles per hour. By Tuesday, and after some 80 hours, they had got only as far as Vologda, 371 miles from Petrograd.[1] The weather was bitter and they were housed in a battered carriage attached to a freight train, sitting in a grubby unheated compartment grandly marked 'First Class' but which had all its windows broken or missing.[2]

The armed six-man escort — Latvians commanded by a Russian — treated them with indifference at first but by Sunday evening, impressed at finding that their imperial prisoner made no complaint, their attitude changed. As they were getting ready to settle down to sleep, 'two of the escort even took off their coats and hung them over the windows to keep out the draughts,' Johnson reported later.[3] They began to address Michael as 'Michael Aleksandrovich' and after that 'they did their best to take care of us'.[4]

As the train dragged itself into Vologda, the guards agreed when Michael asked for permission to send a telegram. It was as reassuring as it could be, and Johnson took it for despatch to a frantic Natasha. *Everybody well. Fellow-travellers are nice. Moving very slowly by freight train.* At his final meeting with Uritsky he had been told that Natasha and the family could travel to see him whenever she liked. In his telegram he said 'it will be quite impossible to travel with children...Must take food for entire journey.'[5] That said much about what might be expected at the stopping stations *en route*; even at Vologda, the first large town they had reached, there was barely anything to buy in the station restaurant.

What irked Michael particularly was that he and Johnson were to be separated when they got to Perm. At their next stop at the small station of Sharya the following evening he fired off a protest telegram to Lenin, using his ill-health as justification, and asking him to revoke that particular order. He did.[6]

Finally, on Sunday March 19, the train reached Perm at the end of its eight-day journey and Michael and Johnson — unshaven, filthy, exhausted and ravenous — were taken under guard to the *Hermitage Hotel* where they were given a small room in which they could at last wash, and look forward to sleeping in a bed.[7]

Perm, with a population then of 62,000, was the capital of a regional government of the same name, which also included Ekaterinburg, 235 miles to the south-east. The gateway to Siberia, and standing above the broad River Kama, it was normally a thriving city with 19 churches, a new university, and fittingly, since it was the birthplace of Diaghilev, boasted the largest theatre outside Petrograd and Moscow. There were worse places to be in exile; Michael was resolved to make the best of it.

The first shock came two days later when the local authorities, having had no instructions about Michael, decided to put him in prison, and keep him in solitary confinement, a move explained away by a Bolshevik newspaper in Petrograd which said that he had 'become insane' — a story published worldwide and reported even in *The Times* in London.[8] Johnson was also put behind bars.

Before being taken away, Michael had been allowed to send a brief telegram to Natasha, telling her that he was 'to be kept until further notice in solitary confinement'.[9] He also managed to dash off three other telegrams — to Petrograd Commissars Bonch-Bruevich, Lunarcharsky and Uritsky — demanding that the local Soviet be instructed to release him at once. 'Urgently request issue of directives immediately,' he wrote on March 20.[10]

Five days later Michael's valet, Vasily Chelyshev, and his chauffeur Borunov, who had arrived in Perm on a 'proper' train just as Michael was being imprisoned on March 21, reported to Natasha that there had been 'no reply to the telegrams of our "boss"…very important the local authorities receive directions…' Chelyshev also told her that 'Uritsky was being evasive'.[11] Natasha had sent the two men to provide moral and practical support —there would be no car for Borunov to drive — and they had brought clothes, books, and a variety of toilet and medical supplies packed by Natasha, but they were not being allowed to see Michael.[12]

Natasha banged on doors across Petrograd but it was two long weeks before finally the order came for his release. Robert Wilton, *The Times* man, helpfully filed the story in London, making it difficult for the Comrades to retract that order;[13] even so the local Perm Soviet dragged its heels, as if determined to show its independence, continuing to keep Michael in prison while the world was reading on Saturday, April 6, that he was free. It was not until 11 p.m. the following Monday that the prison gates opened and he walked back into the world.[14]

The resourceful Chelyshev had arranged rooms for Michael in the *Korolev Rooms* at the end of Siberia Street not far from the embankment of the Kama river. The handsome three-storey hotel, opened 11 years earlier in 1907, prided itself on providing the most luxurious accommodation in the city. Though taken over by the local Soviet — and renamed *Hotel No. 1* — its guests were entitled to a three-course dinner every day, with tea or milk.[15] The hotel was a long, flat-fronted building painted yellow ochre, with tall arched windows; inside were elegant columns and stucco mouldings.

Michael was given a large room on the first floor, number 21, with a wrought-iron balcony overlooking the busy street outside, and immediately above the main entrance.[16] It was the very best on offer, and after what Michael had endured, over the past five weeks, a joy to behold. Johnson, Chelyshev and Borunov also found rooms in the same hotel. Once in his room Michael immediately wrote to Natasha.

My very own, dearest Natasha. At last I can write to you openly, as up to now, i.e. up to last night, we were under arrest and all my correspondence was being checked by the local Soviet. I did not want to write letters, knowing they would be read by all and sundry… Yesterday morning we were told that we would be released and we have spent a wearisome day awaiting the results.

Thanks to the insistence of Vasily,, we were at last released at 11 p.m. and went straight to the rooms we have rented in the Korolev Rooms. My head is going round and round — so much I want to tell you, as I have lived through so much in the last five weeks of my arrest.

My dearest Natashechka, I thank you from all my heart for the lovely letters and also for all the trouble you have taken to help me. Thank God, the first step was successful, and we are free. This is already a great relief. The second step would be to get away from here and go home, but I am afraid that this won't be soon. I am terribly lonely without you, my darling, come here as soon as possible.

As from today, I will start looking for some lodgings for us and as soon as I find something suitable will send you a wire…Adoring you, all yours. Misha.[17]

After five weeks of suffering it was a letter that made the best of the position he was in, and which offered hope that somehow the worst was really over.

THE arrest of Michael was immediate evidence enough for Natasha that the Bolsheviks could not be trusted to leave them alone — and that therefore their son, seven-year-old George, might also be at risk. Arrest a child? She had seen enough of the arbitrary power exercised by the Cheka not to doubt that they might, if it suited them, do just that. Her daughter and Michael's step-daughter Tata was less of a worry — her birth certificate gave her name as Mamontov, not Romanov, so it was George who had to be sent to safety. But how? Natasha could not go with him, not only because there was little chance of her getting across the frontier, but because she would not leave Michael behind, and no less could she leave Tata. George's nanny was the British Miss Neame, an enemy alien in German eyes.

The Danes provided the answer. Their embassy was across the road from the Putyatin apartment in Millionnaya Street, and Michael was a cousin and friend of Denmark's King Christian, so little George was 'family'. The plan was for George and Miss Neame to travel together on a Red Cross train, with Miss Neame using a false passport in the name of Silldorf, and posing as the wife of a repatriated Austrian officer, with George as her son; a Danish officer would accompany them to Berlin.

It was a daunting prospect; neither Miss Neame or George spoke a word of German, and once on the train they would have to remain absolutely silent. What would happen if they were directly challenged was something that did not bear thinking about.

On March 16, three days before the train carrying Michael reached Perm, Miss Neame and seven-year-old George were taken into Danish protection, and hidden until permission for the journey had been received from Copenhagen.[18] It was forty days before they were ready to move on April 25.

The ruse worked. The Bolsheviks took no notice of her or George as they passed across the border into German-controlled territory. Arriving safely in Berlin, they were taken immediately to the Danish embassy, where the American-born wife of the Danish ambassador took them into her care. They were there for a week while the ambassador delicately set about the task of disclosing the truth to the German foreign ministry about George and his British nanny, in Berlin on false papers.

The son of Grand Duke Michael Aleksandrovich? That was a matter which went straight to the Kaiser and his brother Prince Henry — married to the sister of both the ex-Empress and

Grand Duchess Ella. Whatever was to be said about Natasha, George was their nephew. But that apart, a favour to Michael had potentially strategic benefit. In helping little George there might well be advantage to Germany,

The Kaiser and his High Command intended one day to have a reckoning with the Bolsheviks whom for the moment they had to tolerate. They had sent Lenin back in April 1917 in the hope, now realised, that he and the Bolsheviks could take Russia out of the war, but they had no intention of leaving him or they in power. Berlin's view was that when the war in the West ended, either with imperial Germany victorious or on terms which left Germany with a free hand in the East, they would turn on the Bolsheviks, clear them out, and re-establish monarchy in Russia. Michael, on all the evidence available, was the Romanov best placed to take back the throne. They needed him.

On the authority of the Kaiser, orders were therefore immediately given that George and his nanny — notwithstanding that she was an enemy alien who ordinarily would have been interned — were to be allowed to go through to Denmark without impediment of any kind. 'He not only kindly allowed us to go on, but we had a reserved first-class carriage', an astonished Miss Neame reported afterwards.[19]

Having left Berlin in style, with orders passed forward that they were to cross the frontier 'without we or our luggage being searched,' they were met on arrival in Copenhagen by a court official, taken to the palace, and invited to stay with the king and queen. 'You and the boy must settle down and be happy with us', King Christian told Miss Neame. 'I admire you for undertaking such a dangerous journey.'[20]

Danish help did not stop there. The embassy in Petrograd decided to 'rent' part of Michael's house in Gatchina to protect it from the attentions of hooligans. Every day, to keep up the pretence, two Danish officials would go there to make it appear that they were in residence. To add further protection, a Danish flag fluttered above the house.[21]

BY mid-April, 1918 — and before son George was to be smuggled out of Russia into Denmark — Michael's position had begun to look more than tolerable, compared with what had gone before. The latest orders from Petrograd, signed by both Bonch-Bruevich and Cheka boss Uritsky, were that he and Johnson 'are entitled to live in freedom under the surveillance of the local Soviet authorities';[22] surveillance amounted only to a requirement that Michael reported each day to the militia headquarters next-door to the hotel — irksome but a very minor inconvenience in practice. Otherwise he was at liberty to do as he pleased.

He had tagged himself as the 'Prisoner of Perm' in a photograph taken of him with Johnson in a muddy street just after his release from prison, where he had grown a beard which he vowed not to remove until he was entirely freed,[23] but he was more cheerful now than at any time since his arrest on January 5.

His obvious popularity among the townspeople at large did not endear him to the more fervent members of the Perm Soviet, but for the moment they did no more than grumble about it.

One 'refugee' from nearby Ekaterinburg and who also had booked into the *Korolev Rooms* remembered that 'I was at first afraid of staying there' because the presence of Michael 'would attract the attention of the Soviet authorities' but he quickly discovered that Michael, seemingly blessed by Moscow, was 'at complete liberty and walked around the town without anyone following. Even the local Soviet commissar who ran the hotel as if he owned it, was careful to treat Michael 'quite correctly'.[24]

Sometimes in a shabby raincoat, tweed cap and boots, and on fine days in a grey suit, soft hat and carrying a stick,[25] Michael became a familiar figure as he strolled around town. Princess Putyatina in Petrograd would hear reports that people meeting him in the street 'treated him with great respect' and they brought him 'all sorts of delicacies'. *The Times* man Robert Wilton, in Perm some months later, would report that his rooms 'were always full of provisions'. He also learned that when out walking Michael 'found himself running the gauntlet of popular ovations'.[26]

Michael, reviewing his position in those early days of relative freedom could afford a degree of optimism. With Johnson, Chelyshev and Borunov there as practical support, and still with enough cash to meet his needs despite the loss of his income, all that he now wanted was for Natasha to join him as quickly as possible. As she badgered the Petrograd authorities for a permit to travel to Perm, his main concern was finding an apartment in which they could live out their exile. However, that proved more difficult than he had thought. 'We can live in our hotel,' he cabled her towards the end of April. 'Waiting impatiently.'[27]

What Natasha had not dared tell him, in telegrams and letters that could be read by Cheka agents or informers, was that she had sent little George out of Russia. Those were anxious days until she heard from the Danish embassy in Petrograd, firstly that he had arrived safely in Berlin, and then finally in early May that he was in the palace in Copenhagen. With that worry off her shoulders, she was free and cabled him to say that she was on her way, and would be in Perm in time for Easter — Good Friday that year falling late on May 10*. Delighted, Michael cabled back: 'My darling, beloved and very dearest Natasha, thank God that we, nevertheless, are able to celebrate Easter together, if not at home.'[28]

With Tata being looked after in Gatchina by Princess Vyazemskaya, Natasha arrived, after a two-day journey from Petrograd, with her friend Maggie Abakanovich and Prince Putyatin as escort, though both would return after a few days, their duty done. On the evening of Easter Saturday, May 11, they went to a packed 1,500-seat opera house where the French actress Beauregard was playing in *Dream of Love*. Michael's party included two of Perm's best-known society figures, Sergei and Olga Tupitsin, neither of whom had anything other than contempt for the Bolsheviks; afterwards Beauregard joined them

*The Russian Orthodox Church did not adopt the new Western calendar so the date was April 27 under the old Julian calendar; it also celebrated Easter much later that year than was the case elsewhere — March 29 in Britain.

in their crimson-and-gold box,[29] with the ever-elegant Natasha holding court, as oblivious to the sullen stares of the new Bolshevik 'aristocracy' as previously she had been to the disapproving eyes of imperial society.

On Sunday they went to the Cathedral of St Peter and St Paul; the scene was one which outraged the Bolshevik workers at the arms factory at nearby Motovilikha. 'The blatantly monarchist ceremonies of the bourgeoisie and the new Tsar-Saviour's almost daily procession to the cathedral along roads covered with carpets and fresh flowers angered the working class,' Cheka agent A. A. Samarin complained bitterly.[30]

To men like these it was as if Citizen Romanov was not 'the former Grand Duke' but treated as if he were actually the Emperor. They sneeringly referred to him as 'His Imperial Majesty' [31] but yet seemed unable to do anything about it other than shout furiously amongst themselves.

With Natasha's arrival she and Michael began immediately the hunt for an apartment. During that first weekend together they looked at various places, including an apartment and a 'nice house' in the same street as their hotel. As Michael had said, it was not easy; however, what was encouraging was that acquaintances from Gatchina — Colonel Peter Znamerovsky and his wife — had found a good apartment at 8 Kungurskaya Street and it heartened Natasha.[32]

Znamerovsky, former commandant of the Gatchina railway gendarmerie, had been arrested shortly after Michael, and likewise exiled to Perm. They would become close friends, bound as they were by common misfortune.

Inevitably, with Natasha in town, there was not an evening when they were not being entertained, for there was no shortage of invitations from the 'smart set' in Perm, only too happy to play host and hostess not just to the Grand Duke but to the woman who had been talked about ever since their runaway marriage. Everyone was curious to meet her and to have Michael and Natasha at their dinner table, or to be invited to join those who did. Each day was as crowded as the next. There were also plenty of public occasions, when the two would be ogled by the many, not the few.

Michael and Natasha went back twice to the opera house in the coming week, to a piano recital and to a concert by a group of artists from the Maryinski, the imperial theatre in the capital before the Soviet had struck that word from the dictionary. Each time, Michael and Natasha sat in the same left-side box, as if that now belonged to them.

On other evenings in that crowded week they gave dinner parties for the Tupitsins and the Znamerovskys, and during the day they went for walks along the river bank, or strolled into the marketplace on the Monastyrskaya and into some of those shops still open for business.[33] Eyes followed them everywhere; people eagerly ran forward to catch even a glimpse of them as they walked by.

Then, suddenly, it was all over. The real world caught up with them again. A large armed force of Czechs had taken control of Chelyabinsk, a town 390 miles to the south. The local Bolsheviks, alarmed by the unexpected emergence of a new enemy so near to them, took fright, and in so doing forced Michael and Natasha to the realisation that their hopes of making a new life for themselves in Perm had ended. Some two weeks after arriving in Perm, Michael insisted that Natasha had to leave, and leave urgently, while she still could.

CHELYABINSK was the junction for the Trans-Siberian railway from Moscow to Vladivostok; the Czechs were former prisoners-of-war who had agreed to change sides and fight their old masters, the Austro-Hungarians. Under the terms of the peace treaty between Russia and Germany they had been released from their camps and were travelling to Vladivostok, with the intention that they would then be shipped out to join the Allied armies. Under the same treaty, Austrian prisoners-of-war were being shipped westwards to rejoin their army. The two sides came up against each other when their respective trains met at Chelyabinsk. An Austrian soldier threw a slab of concrete at the jeering Czechs, injuring one of them. The Czechs lynched the offender, and when the local Bolsheviks attempted to intervene the Czechs took over the town. Shortly, the entire 50,000-strong Czech Legion, strung out along the line to Vladivostok, would turn and decide to fight the Bolsheviks, adding a new and dangerous dimension to the civil war being waged elsewhere in Russia.

The news brought panic to the Perm Bolsheviks. Only a day's journey from Chelyabinsk, the fear was that the Czechs would move on them next. For Michael the question was how the Bolsheviks would then react, and the answer to that was that the quicker Natasha was out of the city the better. The first available train was expected in Perm on Saturday morning, May 18. She had to be on it.

On their last day together, on Friday the day before her she left, they took an afternoon stroll, and then had a quiet and gloomy dinner in the hotel before Natasha packed to go home. 'It is very sad to be left alone again,' wrote Michael in his diary that night.[34]

Next morning, miserable at parting, but little knowing that they would never see each other again, they left the hotel at 9.30 a.m. and took a cab to the station. 'We waited for a long time for the train on the platform there because the Siberian Express was late...Natasha found a seat in a small compartment of the international carriage, sharing with another lady.' The train left at 12.10 p.m. He stood staring down the line as the train pulled out and waited until it was out of sight. He took a cab back to the hotel, and that night he wrote in his diary that 'it has become so sad and so empty now that Natasha has gone, everything seems different and even the rooms have changed...'[35]

BEFORE leaving Perm Natasha made clear that she would be going back to fight for his release from exile. If Perm was no longer a safe place to keep an ex-Tsar, then what was he doing there? He should be sent home again, or if that was out of the question, Moscow would be better than Perm. It was an argument she saw no point in making to Uritsky in Petrograd; she would go to Moscow and bang on Lenin's desk again.

After his move to Moscow on March 10, Lenin made the Kremlin his seat of government, choosing for himself one of the buildings of the old Court of Chancellery, opposite the Arsenal, taking a five-roomed apartment on the second floor, with offices on the same floor. The Kremlin bells now played the *Internationale* instead of *God Save the Tsar,* and the double-headed Romanov eagles mounted on the gates had been stripped of their crowns, but otherwise it was the same Kremlin Natasha knew well from her childhood.

Arriving in Moscow she went directly to her parents' apartment at 6 Vozdvizhenkan, only a few hundred yards from the Troitsky Gate and the Kremlin immediately beyond. They were both relieved and alarmed to have her home again — relieved because she had returned safely, alarmed because of her determination to challenge Lenin head-on. 'They'll never let you in', was their view.

With guards blocking entry to the Troitsky Gate and on every building within the Kremlin, entry without authority or permit was impossible. The Kremlin was a fortress, and the Bolsheviks intended to keep it that way. However, 'impossible' was not a term which Natasha recognised. Somehow, one set of guards passed her through to the next set of guards, so confident her manner, so persuasive her claim that she had an appointment with Comrade Lenin.

Finding Natasha yet again at his desk, Lenin was no more forthcoming than he had been at the Smolny.[36] It was not his decision. She left his office empty-handed, but refusing to give up she then went on to badger other members of the Bolshevik regime, among them Trotsky — who had been 'ill-tempered and answered rudely' when tackled by Natasha in Petrograd.[37] He was no better tempered this time.

One by one the doors opened then closed after her, leaving her to return back to her parents with nothing to show for her desperate persistence.

'She imagined that personal intercession with the Red chieftains would move them to let him go,' commented *The Times* man Wilton. 'Of course, it was an illusion excusable only in a distracted wife'. [38]

In the early summer of 1918 the Bolsheviks faced too many threats to think it was safe to release Michael. On the contrary, what they were going to do, without the world finding out about it, was to murder him, and murder him long before any of the other Romanovs. The last Emperor was to die first.

21. EITHER HIM OR US

ON Tuesday, May 21, as Natasha was heading into Moscow, Michael and Johnson appeared by order at 33 Petropavlovskaya–Okhanskaya, the Perm offices of the sinister Cheka. Until then they had reported only to the local militia, next door to their hotel. However, because of the growing Czech threat, the Perm Soviet decided that it could no longer be responsible for Michael's 'safety'; responsibility was transferred to the provincial Cheka.[1]

The change seems to have coincided with a resolution by the workers in nearby Motovilikha that if the Perm Soviet did not arrest Michael, they would 'settle with him themselves'.[2] The Bolsheviks at Motovilikha, some two and a half miles away, were largely employed in the huge government munitions factory there, and were noticeably more militant than those in Perm. In his diary afterwards, Michael wrote that at the Cheka offices 'I was given a piece of paper ordering me to go there every day at 11 o' clock (good people, tell me what this means)'.[3]

The switch to the Cheka seemed at first merely an irritation. Whereas at the militia office Michael had simply popped his head around the door at whatever time suited him, now the officious Cheka demanded that he present himself at precisely the stated time; they also took delivery of all letters and telegrams to him, and read them before handing them over.[4] It was an unpleasant reminder of his real position.

Nevertheless Michael continued otherwise to go about the town without restriction. In the week after Natasha left Perm, he listened to a string orchestra in the City Garden, saw 'a dreadful farce' in his box at the Opera House, spent an evening at the Triumph Cinema, visited a waxworks exhibition, and went in search of walking boots, buying a pair of 'simple soldiers' lace-up boots'.[5]

At one of the shops in Siberia Street the manager asked him why it was, in view of his comparative freedom, that he did not escape. Michael only laughed. 'Where would someone as tall as I am go? They would find me immediately.'[6]

The Cheka was not quite so sure of that. Perm was now more crowded, as thousands of people trying to make their way eastwards found themselves stranded in the town, with the railway line to Chelyabinsk cut. Among these unexpected newcomers were 'two Americans' who called on Michael after dinner on Saturday, May 25. Identified by Michael only as 'Mr O'Brien' and 'Mr Hess',[7] they were the kind of visitors the Cheka looked upon with suspicion, as possible messengers for plotters intent on rescuing him.

Unlike his brother held in close confinement under heavy guard in Ekaterinburg, Michael was free to go anywhere in town and meet anyone. The Cheka knew where he was at 11 o'clock in the morning, but otherwise there was no watch on him, and with the town so crowded there was little they could do to check out the papers of everyone; moreover, that would have done little to help them.

Plotters would make sure they had the right papers — or least papers that looked right — and a plausible story to go with them. Mr O'Brien and Mr Hess could be anyone. They came, they went, and the Cheka was none the wiser.

Colonel Znamerovsky certainly had ideas of escape, and given the worsening position in Perm it would be odd if he had not; with good reason he feared that the 'Motovilikha workmen might be goaded into violence'.[8] The problem was not escape in itself, but making good that escape by getting out of Perm to safety.

Curious messages arrived at the *Korolev Rooms* in those anxious days; two survive, though their meaning is lost. *The mignonette is*

not a flower of brilliant beauty, but its fragrance is divine, says one.
The other is equally mysterious: *Turkeys are yours.*[9]

On Tuesday May 28, a week after Michael's first visit to the
Cheka, the city was declared to be 'in a state of war'.

THE Czech threat had also heightened fears among the Bolsheviks
in Ekaterinburg, half-way between Perm and Chelyabinsk,
and therefore at even greater risk of finding itself under attack.
Nicholas and Alexandra had been transferred there from Tobolsk
four weeks earlier, arriving on April 30. They had been taken to the
ominously-named 'House of Special Purpose' — formerly, until
they seized it, the two-storey home of a wealthy local merchant,
Nikolai Ipatev. Their five children, kept behind because Alexis
had been ill, rejoined them three weeks later.

The house had been hidden from curious eyes by the erection
of a tall wooden fence on all sides. Five rooms on the upper floor,
their window-panes painted white so that no one could see in
or out, were to serve as prison for the family. The lower floor
became a guardroom. Other than being allowed to walk in the
garden in the afternoon, the family spent their days confined
to their rooms, with nothing to do except to read and sew and
make up their own games to pass the slow days. It was tedious,
humiliating, and with their Red Guards marching to and fro as
they pleased, deliberately oppressive.

But they were not the only Romanov captives in Ekaterinburg.
Alexandra's sister Ella, aged 54, was there also, confined in a hotel
along with Grand Duke Serge Mikhailovich, the three grown-up
sons of Grand Duke Konstantin Konstantinovich, who had died
in 1915, and, the youngest of the group, Vladimir Paley, the 21-
year-old half-brother of Grand Duke Dimitri. They were allowed
no contact with Ipatev House, and Alexandra was never told that
her sister was in the town.

The locally-based but powerful Ural Regional Soviet —
commanding Perm as well as Ekaterinburg — had no intention
of evacuating Nicholas and his family, notwithstanding the threat

from the Czechs. With the railway line to Moscow blocked at Chelyabinsk, their options were limited in any event. What to do with the family would be a decision they were not ready to make.

However, at the end of May their second group of six Romanov captives were told that they were being moved 'for safety' to Alapaevsk, a bleak mining town some 180 miles to the north-east of Ekaterinburg, and roughly the same distance from Perm. There they would be confined in a small simply-furnished schoolhouse, with no more than five or six rooms, guarded by Latvians and local Red Guards. They were allowed to walk into the town, and talk to locals, but in the evenings there was nothing to do but sit in their rooms, and pass the time as best they could. It was a dreary existence, in which one day was indistinguishable from the next; with no prospect of escape, they could only endure the grinding monotony in the hope that somehow better times lay ahead.

Had they known of it, they would have been astonished at the freedom enjoyed by Michael — and the seeming concern of the Bolsheviks to treat him as they treated no other of their Romanov prisoners. Nights at the opera, dinner parties with friends, shopping in town, his own staff of retainers — that was a privileged world they could barely imagine still existed. On the face of it, and whatever the reason for his special treatment, Michael was a very lucky man indeed.

Sadly, that luck was about to run out.

AS Ella and the other Romanovs in her group were preparing for their move to Alapaevsk, Michael noted in his diary that 'it is difficult to work out what is going on, but something major is brewing'.[10] There were rumours everywhere as he walked about town, heads still bowed as he passed by. A few days later, on Monday June 3, he wrote to Natasha to set out his views on his own position, his spirits low.

'My dearest sweetheart, my own darling Natasha...it is now 16 days since you went away. I can't describe how I feel— depressed and desperate from all the surroundings here, from this dreadful town where I am in absolute uncertainty and living an aimless life. Why do I write this when you know it so well yourself?' One practical complaint was that the *Korolev Rooms* were becoming increasingly expensive, and a drain on his reserves of cash. 'The price for the rooms is going up all the time and the cook serves us with enormous bills,' he added.

The good news was that he had found an apartment at 212 Ekaterinskaya Street with 'a nice view from the balcony over the river'.[11] That would save money, for it was privately owned by his friends the Tupitsins, and the rent would be almost nominal. It would be free in a couple of weeks, and when Natasha could get back to Perm it would be a home for them. Given the military situation he feared that 'we will not be able to see each other for another two months, which would be dreadful', though if matters improved, 'I will hope that you can come here sooner'.

To this letter he added a separate postscript, jokily headlining it as *The Recent Political Review* and signing off as *Correspondent-on-Tour.*

Everything here is outwardly calm, but the authorities admit that things are rather acute and serious. We have to continue to give our signatures daily in the Committee of 'Charms'. In the town squares the railwaymen and party-workers are receiving military training, drill and similar body exercises... The town is full of rumours and disturbed by news that in the east — not very far away, in 'Katia's Burg' [Ekaterinburg] there are activists of either 'Czech-Slovaks' or 'Slovak-Czechs'... What their further plans are, nobody knows, but our town is now declared under military law.[12]

Shortly after sending off this letter Michael suffered another bout of his 'damned stomach pains', the first for some time. Next day he went as usual to report to the Cheka, and 'had a bit of a run in with one of the "comrades" there who was very rude to me'.[13] The 'comrade' was Gavriil Myasnikov, former chairman of the Motovilikha Soviet, who had been appointed ten days earlier to the Perm Cheka, taking over responsibility for dealing with 'counter-revolutionaries'.[14]

With his arrival, the local Cheka changed from being offensively officious to menacing. Before the 1917 February Revolution Myasnikov had spent four years in a labour camp for terrorist acts. In the six years before that he had been arrested and imprisoned for various violent crimes, his life a series of escapes, periods in hiding, and prison until in 1913 he went to a labour camp.[15] Now 29, Myasnikov hated what Michael represented and bitterly resented the freedom he was allowed in Perm.

Among his Bolshevik members in Motovilikha there had been fierce criticism of the benign treatment afforded Michael and the way in which the 'bourgeoisie' would bow to him in the street, and lay flowers in his path when he went to the Cathedral.

There had been nothing Myasnikov could do about that from Motovilikha, but now as head of a Cheka department he was determined to come down hard on Michael and show him who was master in Perm.

A fellow Bolshevik, the secretary of the Perm Party Committee, thought Myasnikov to be 'a bloodthirsty and embittered man, and not altogether sane...'[16] Other local Bolsheviks were also frightened of him, believing him capable of utter ruthlessness. In turn, he suspected some members of the Perm Soviet of being in awe of Michael and too ready to protect him. He was also convinced that there is 'an organisation of officers attempting to liberate him'.[17]

There appears to have been some effort by the 'moderates' to remove Myasnikov from the city Cheka, for only a week after his appointment they tried to get rid of him by 'promoting' him to the Ural Regional Cheka in Ekaterinburg. But after he refused to go, the appointment went to the local Cheka chairman, F. N. Lukoyanov[18] whose removal left Myasnikov more powerful than before. Lukoyanov was no saint; Myasnikov was a cold-blooded killer.

Michael, of course, knew nothing of Myasnikov other than

he was rude and unpleasant; after his first 'run in' with him at the 'Committee of Charms' he simply shrugged off the row and went off on the Kama in a motor boat. In the afternoon he had 'wonderful coffee and cake' with the landlady at the *Korolev Rooms*, and in the evening walked to the City Garden to listen to a string orchestra.[19]

What troubled him more was that over the next three days he would spend much of his days in bed, suffering from stomach pains. On Saturday, June 8, 'I ate nothing after midday because I was in pain all the time'. On Sunday he 'spent the whole day in bed by the window' and in the evening Znamerovsky arrived 'and told me much of interest about rumours circulating in the city'.[20]

On Monday he was on his feet all day 'but felt very poorly'; he also had a telegram from Natasha to report that she had arrived back in Gatchina from Moscow 'last Wednesday' after two weeks of fruitlessly banging on doors in her efforts to have him released. She saw no hope of that now, but she would be cheered by news that he had found an apartment. At least they would have somewhere to live together when next she could get to Perm.

The following day, Tuesday, Michael felt much better and the pains were 'not as intense and did not last long'. Znamerovsky with Michael's godson Nagorsky came to tea, and at 10 p.m. Nagorsky popped back to say goodbye , for as Michael wrote in his diary next morning, 'he is going to Petrograd today.' [21]

It was Wednesday June 12. The last day of Michael's life.

MICHAEL could not have known it, but he had been secretly 'sentenced to death' a few days earlier. There was no signed order and no paper trail to identify the names of those who decided his fate. In Perm itself, where the murder necessarily had to take place, there would be attempts many years later to pretend that it was entirely a local decision, taken under the pressure of the immediate threat from the Czechs and 'Whites' — ex-Tsarist officers and soldiers who had declared their own war on the Reds and were advancing from the east. But Perm was less at risk than Ekaterinburg or Alapaevsk, both of which were far nearer to the approaching enemy. Moreover, it would be another five weeks — July 17/18 —before the Ural Regional Soviet, which commanded all, would order the deaths of Nicholas and his family, and the other six Romanovs held in Alapaevsk. The decision to 'execute' Michael on June 12 was not therefore for the same reasons as the others. Moreover, officially, Michael was not to be killed at all — he was to escape.

Escape? That was its own proof that Moscow and not the mindless thugs in the Perm Cheka, or their counterparts in Ekaterinburg, were behind his murder. The local Bolsheviks were well able to kill Michael in secret; it was far beyond their wit to understand why, having done so, they should then promote afterwards the story that he had escaped — a story that could only, on the face of it, encourage the very counter-revolutionaries Michael's death was supposed to dismay. Why kill him and then hand the enemy a propaganda victory by telling them he was alive, free, and had outwitted his captors?

The Kremlin knew perfectly well the purpose of that — wanting him dead, but also wanting him alive. Confusion in the ranks of their enemies suited them well, and unlike the men in the Urals they faced west, not east; the Germans were almost on their doorstep. In June 1918, with the British driven back to the sea, and a German army approaching Paris, Berlin could be optimistic about success in the West — if not victory, then forcing an armistice which would leave them a free hand in the East. For its part, Moscow could be in no doubt what that would mean for them, and possibly sooner rather than later.

After the Treaty of Brest-Litovsk in March 1917, imperial Germany made very clear what its ambitions were in Russia. Monarchy was to be the natural order and a republic unthinkable. Poland in September 1917 had been declared an independent kingdom and a three-man Regency was established while Germany and Austria tried to agree on who would get the crown;

the most popular candidate was the Austrian archduke Charles Stephen, in that he was a Catholic, spoke Polish, had two Polish sons-in-laws. The three former Russian Baltic states —Estonia, Latvia, and Lithuania— were declared to be Grand Duchies, though in the summer of 1918 Lithuania would go on to declare itself a kingdom, electing as sovereign the Württemburg Duke Wilhelm of Urach; Finland became independent in December 1917 with the help of 40,000 German troops and would shortly elect the Kaiser's brother-in-law Prince Frederick Charles of Hesse-Cassel as king.*

The Ukraine, which declared itself independent in November 1917, came under effective German control in April 1918 when a German-backed Russian general seized power as a prelude to a monarchy. Although Austria hoped that the crown would go to one of their archdukes, the Germans saw it as being part of a restored Russian monarchy. The man they had their sights on as Emperor was Michael.

There was no interest in the ex-Tsar, despite appeals on his behalf by those who had never resigned themselves to his abdication; both British and German intelligence agreed that the only possible candidate was Michael.

Hence the decision to kill Michael, but also to keep him 'alive'. For then no other Romanov could step forward and claim his inheritance as Emperor. Lenin had boasted that he would not leave the Romanovs as a 'live banner' for counter-revolutionaries. So instead what he would leave them was a ghost. The last Emperor was to remain the last Emperor.

The subsequent testimony of those involved in Perm, emptied of any reference to the Kremlin's strategic purpose, followed the simple line that Michael was killed because he was a rallying point for counter-revolutionaries. Myasnikov would claim the discovery of a plot by an organisation of officers to rescue him. He had to be killed because 'he was the only figure around whom

*Neither in the event would reign since, contrary to their high hopes of early summer, Germany would lose the war before they could do so.

all the counter-revolutionary forces could unite', and that the 'danger to Soviet power if Michael escaped and became the head of the counter-revolutionary forces would be immense'.[24]

This was supported by another local Cheka chairman, Pavel Malkov, who said that Michael had been killed because of the advance of counter-revolutionaries, and also because of his 'suspicious behaviour'.[25] Another leading Bolshevik, A. A. Mikov, described a meeting attended by Malkov, Myasnikov and others in a *dacha* outside the city. Malkov told the assembled group that 'it was dangerous to "keep" Michael any longer; he might escape even though he was being watched closely'. Mikov suggested killing him. 'I was sure they were all in favour'. He dated the meeting as 'in the middle of June…I remember it well, it was a Sunday evening.'[24] If so, it was Sunday, June 9, when Michael was laid up in the *Korolev Rooms* with his 'damned stomach pains'.

However, the impression that the Perm Cheka and the City Soviet were acting on their own initiative does not survive scrutiny. More credibly, the Perm Bolsheviks met that Sunday evening to discuss how best they could carry out the order to kill him, and then promote the cover-up. What certainly they agreed between themselves was the identity of the man who would organise and carry out the murder. That man, and the man most eager to take on the role of executioner, was Myasnikov. He was also the man most likely to be approved by their superiors in Ekaterinburg. The president of the Ural Soviet there was Aleksandr Beloborodov, a former clerk in Perm, and whose family still lived in the city. He knew Myasnikov well; they were close friends.

On the morning of Wednesday, June 12, Myasnikov was told to go ahead with the murder immediately. Everything else essential to its success was in place. Michael was about to 'disappear'.

22. DEATH IN THE WOODS

ONCE the weekend decision to kill Michael had been confirmed, Myasnikov acted with considerable speed. His first task was to recruit an execution squad. 'I needed hard men who had suffered from the autocracy...men who were prepared to bite through someone's throat with their teeth. I needed men who could hold their tongues, who trusted me more than they did themselves, and were ready to do anything if I told them it was necessary in the interests of the revolution.'[1]

The four men who met this criteria were all from the Motovilikha arsenal.

Nikolai Zhuzhgov, aged 39, and a friend of Myasnikov for many years, was a member of the Perm Cheka and also assistant chief of the Motovilikha militia. A small man, with sunken eyes, he had spent seven years in labour camps, some of that time with fellow prisoner Myasnikov.

Vasily Ivanchenko, aged 44, was head of the Perm militia and a deputy in the local Soviet; in 1906 he had been given a 15-year prison sentence for the murder of two Cossacks, and like Myasnikov he had been freed in the February revolution.

Andrei Markov, aged 36, was the Perm 'commissar for nationalisation' and worked as a foreman in one of the Motovilikha workshops. A thickset man, he again had spent some time in prison with Myasnikov, who regarded him as someone who could be relied upon to do whatever he was told.

The fourth member of the death squad was Ivan Kolpashchikov, a powerfully-built man with a curiously squeaky high-pitched voice, and like the others a veteran of the prison camps; when not working at the Motovilikha arsenal, he served as a Red Guard.[2]

On Wednesday evening, June 12, Myasnikov called the four men to a meeting in the projection room of the cinema in Motovilikha. There he set out the reasons why Michael had to be killed. If 'His Imperial Majesty' is not dealt with, then 'tomorrow he may not be here, tomorrow he may be standing at the head of the massed forces of the counter-revolution.'

But there was something very important that they had to understand. Nobody was to know about it. The official story was to be that Michael had escaped, for then Lenin and the Bolshevik leaders would not have to defend themselves against 'the bourgeois governments' and 'we will not compromise them'.[3]

The four men having vowed silence, Myasnikov then told them that in order to ensure secrecy the murder would have to take place that night; Michael would be seized from his hotel room, taken to a wood and shot. As cover for the abduction, he would be presented with a forged order, and told that he was being 'evacuated for security reasons' because of the threat posed by advancing 'Whites'. On the morrow it would be announced that he had escaped, and his entourage would be arrested for complicity and shot.

The time was now 9.30 p.m. The abduction was set for midnight. The chosen execution spot was a wood near a place called Malaya Yazovaya, not far beyond Motovilikha. If all went according to plan, 'His Imperial Majesty' had four hours to live.

AT the beginning of June, in accordance with an order from Moscow, the clocks in Bolshevik Russia had been advanced by two hours. It was a fuel-saving device, and accordingly it did not become dark in Perm on June 12 until after eleven o'clock. On that date, darkness lasted for six hours and 13 minutes, so that with sunset at 10.52 p.m., sunrise would be at 5.05 a.m.[4] The distance between the hotel and the wood was six-and-a-half miles (10.5 km), and by horse-drawn carriage, travelling slowly over bad roads in darkness, the journey would take about an hour. There would be no difficulty in finding the wood for it was well known to Bolsheviks as a favoured meeting place in the days when they held illegal gatherings there.[5] Allowing an hour or so for digging a grave, the execution squad would be back in Motovilikha long before dawn.

There was a great deal to do. Myasnikov telephoned the arsenal and arranged horses for the two phaetons to be used in the abduction. At ten o' clock they were ready and he and the four-man death squad set off for Perm's Cheka offices.[6]

On arrival Myasnikov drafted 'the order' intended to fool Michael into thinking it was official. The wording was that *In view of the approach of the front, Comrade Nikolai Zhuzhgov is hereby instructed to evacuate Citizen Michael Romanov to Central Russia.* The order was to be triple-signed, ostensibly by the Cheka chairman Malkov, the Cheka secretary, and by Myasnikov as head of the counter-revolutionary department. Myasnikov signed for himself; Markov and Kolpashchikov forged the two other signatories.[7]

During Markov's typing of the document Myasnikov later claimed that they were interrupted by the unexpected arrival of Malkov and of Sorokin, chairman of the Provincial Executive Committee. He would say that they saw what was being written, guessed its purpose and appeared 'confused and frightened'; he had to swear them to silence.[8] That was untrue, though it is its own evidence that even seventeen years later, when Myasnikov set down his account of events,[9] he still felt bound to cover up the role of some of those involved.* Malkov, Sorokin, and the other local Bolshevik leaders were wholly complicit in the decision 'to shoot Michael Romanov immediately in complete secrecy'. Myasnikov was their agent.

What is therefore more probable is that Malkov feigned

*Myasnikov's account is that given to the Soviet embassy in Paris in 1935 after he had fled Stalin's purges. His statement was intended to win him a pardon, and permission to return. He was successful.

surprise when he walked into the Cheka offices, for officially he did not know anything about the plot, given that his role was to pretend afterwards that Michael had escaped. In the meantime he stayed where he was, and would no nothing more until he received a telephone call from Myasnikov to confirm that Michael had been successfully abducted and taken to his death.

At 11.45 p.m. Myasnikov and his men were ready to leave. Marching out of the Cheka offices, with Zhuzhgov folding the typewritten order and thrusting it into his pocket, fifteen minutes later their two phaetons clattered into Siberia Street and stopped outside the *Korolev Rooms*. While Ivanchenko and Kolpashchikov turned the carriages round so that they would be facing in the right direction for the abduction, Zhuzhgov went to the hotel entrance and banged hard on the door. A Red Guard opened it, then stood back as Zhuzhgov flourished his order and pushed his way inside.[10]

MICHAEL had spent that Wednesday much as any other day, walking in the town and strolling by the river. However, most probably he went to Ekaterinskaya Street at some point to look at an apartment he had agreed to rent from his friends the Tupitsins, for Johnson had an appointment with them that day to conclude negotiations.[11]

Certainly he was back in the hotel by 6 p.m. for his old friend Colonel Znamerovsky joined him then and stayed with him until 9 p.m.[12]

Michael may well have then returned to his letter to Natasha, which he had started the previous day; the first pages, beginning as always with *My darling, beloved Natasha*, would be on his writing desk. At midnight he was in his dressing gown, talking to Johnson, when his valet Chelyshev interrupted him to tell him that his bath was waiting for him.[13]

What happened then in the *Korolev Rooms* chiefly depends on the evidence of four men. They are the accounts subsequently provided by Myasnikov and squad member Markov, as well as the statements of Michael's valet Chelyshev, who was present throughout the scene, and of a witness called Krumnis, a guest in the hotel. On the main points they broadly agree.

Krumnis was playing cards in the hotel when he heard raised voices in the hallway. He went out to find three armed men standing in the office of Ilya Sapozhnikov, the hotel commissar. Myasnikov, Zhuzhgov and Kolpashchikov were telling the commissar that they had orders to evacuate Michael. The commissar insisted that he should first telephone the Cheka offices for confirmation, but the armed men refused to allow him to do so.[14]

Leaving the others in the hallway to continue their argument. Zhuzhgov approached a kitchen maid and asked her to take him to Michael's room. The girl led him upstairs to Room 18, occupied by Michael's chauffeur Borunov.[15] Chelyshev was then in Michael's room and when he came out, followed by Johnson, to find out what the shouting was all about, they found Borunov 'talking to a man in a soldier's greatcoat' who was waving a piece of paper and demanding to know where 'Michael Romanov lived'. Told it was Room 21, he stepped forward, brandishing a revolver when Chelyshev attempted to bar his way.[16]

Pushing past Chelyshev and Johnson, Zhuzhgov marched into Michael's room and thrust the order into his hands. Michael stood up, read the paper, but refused to comply until he had spoken to the Cheka chairman Malkov. Zhuzhgov, staring up at a man eight inches taller than himself, had a gun and an order but neither seemed to impress Michael, as he continued to demand that he telephoned Malkov.[17]

Zhuzhgov left the room and called for help; and Kolpashchikov rushed upstairs to his aid.

Michael still stubbornly refused to go with them, and as the argument went on another of the squad arrived — Markov, who had been waiting outside the hotel, expecting Michael to have been quickly bundled downstairs and into the street.[18]

Even with three armed men in the room Michael continued to insist that he telephone Pavel Malkov, unaware that he was in the plot. It was the burly Kolpashchikov who ended the stand-off. Grabbing Michael roughly by the shoulder he snarled, 'Oh, these Romanovs. We are fed up with you all.'[30]

Realising that it was futile to go on, Michael began to get dressed. Johnson insisted that he accompany him, and after a brief discussion between them the three men impatiently agreed. Telling Michael that his effects would be sent on afterwards, the men pushed Michael out of the room.

As they were leaving, Chelyshev remembered about Michael's medicine and ran forward, holding out the bottle. 'Please, Your Highness, take it with you', he called out.[20] The men roughly shoved him aside as they hauled Michael onto the stairway, motioning Johnson to follow.

Downstairs, Krumnis watched as three armed men and their prisoners came towards him in the hall. Michael and Johnson, he remembered, 'were dressed in the everyday suits that they usually wore when they went out walking. They did not have coats with them, but carried sticks in their hands.' He did not notice 'any particular agitation on their faces.'[21]

Myasnikov, who had stayed in the lobby, led the way into the street. Chelyshev, watching from the balcony, saw Michael 'violently pushed' into the first phaeton. Zhuzhgov clambered in after him, with Ivanchenko on the reins. Johnson climbed into the second phaeton, with the two other members of the squad. Because they had not allowed for Johnson's inclusion there was no room now for Myasnikov in the three-seater phaetons. Nevertheless he told them to go ahead — 'I will catch you up. If I don't, then wait for me at Motovilikha.'[23]

As the two carriages clipped away towards the Siberian Highway, Malkov and Sorokin came running up from the Cheka offices and then went with Myasnikov into the militia office next door to the hotel, where they went over the plan they would put into operation as soon as they had telephone confirmation that Michael was dead. They would then circulate the story of his escape, and arrest his servants and associates.[24] That done,

Myasnikov ordered a militia carriage to take him to Motovilikha. Going at a fast trot he caught up with the others just as they arrived at the militia offices there. Zhuzhgov climbed down and came over to him. Yes, they had spades. No, there was no need for Myasnikov to follow, they could manage on their own.[25]

Myasnikov stood in the darkness and watched as the two phaetons set off and disappeared into the darkness. Satisfied that this was the end of Michael he then went into the militia offices and telephoned Malkov at the Perm Cheka. Malkov told him that the escape story would now be circulated, search parties organised, and telegrams sent out to the world at large to say that Michael Romanov had been abducted by counter-revolutionaries.[26]

By this time the phaetons had reached the paraffin stores some three miles beyond Motovilikha. Michael had sat silently on the journey to Motovilikha but when they moved off again he had begun to question Zhuzhgov about their destination. The first place that came into Zhuzhgov's head was Mogilev, adding quickly that they were heading for a railway crossing to be put on a train there to avoid the attention they would have had in 'a busy station'.[27]

It was not a reassuring answer: Mogilev was 1,400 miles to the west, and the carriages were heading east. Michael made no comment, but he 'didn't seem frightened', said Zhuzhgov afterwards.

Six hundred yards past the paraffin stores[28] the carriages slowed and then stopped as they reached the wood selected for the execution. Michael and Johnson were told to get out, and then led into the wood. To the obvious question of why, Zhuzhgov roughly replied that it was a short cut to the railway crossing. They did not go far before stopping, and pushing Michael and Johnson aside.

What followed was cold-blooded murder. There were no explanations, no ceremony, no macabre ritual of a last cigarette and blindfold. Zhuzhgov simply lifted his Browning and aimed it at Michael, standing a few feet away, and simultaneously

Markov shot Johnson, but only wounding him. Zhuzhgov's gun either misfired or he missed for Michael, knowing that he was about to die, ran forward his arms out wide, 'begging to say goodbye to his secretary'.[29] As he did so Zhuzhgov fired again but because he was using home-made bullets his gun jammed, as did Kolpashchikov's gun as he attempted to fire a second bullet at the staggering Johnson. With Michael still moving forward with his arms outstretched he was shot in the head at close range. Markov later boasted that he did so; Zhuzhgov claimed that when Michael fell he 'pulled Johnson, who had been shot by Ivanchenko, down with him. I went up to them. They were still moving. I put my Browning to Michael's temple and shot him. Ivanchenko did the same to Johnson'.[30]

The time was approximately 2 a.m. on Thursday June 13.

With four men armed with the axes and spades taken from the carriages 'it didn't take very long'[31] to dig the single grave into which they then threw the bodies. Before burying Michael and Johnson their bodies were stripped of all their clothes and possessions, which were put into the phaetons and taken back to Motovilikha, seemingly as proof that they were dead. They had been told not to touch personal effects but the temptation of trophies proved too much for them. From Michael's pockets they took a watch, a cigar case, a penknife and a tobacco tin.[32] Johnson's pockets yielded among other things a handsome silver watch which Markov kept for himself and which he would go on wearing for the rest of his life.*

At Motovilikha the killers took the bloodied clothes, poured kerosene over them and set them on fire. Myasnikov, lighting a cigarette, looked at his watch. It was 4 a.m.[33]

No one would ever find the graves.

THE first telegrams from the Perm Cheka announcing the 'escape' of Michael Romanov had already been despatched.

---

*He was still wearing the watch in 1965, when as an old man his statement about Michael's murder was lodged in Perm archives.

The Korolev Rooms in Perm (left}. Michael's room was immediately above the front door on the right. It was from there that he was abducted on June 12, 1918 and driven off to his death.

Prisoner of Perm, April 1918
The last known picture of Michael with Nikolai Johnson, taken by a street photographer in Perm just after their release from prison. Michael wrote on the back of the photo, 'Prisoner of Perm' and vowed not to shave off his beard until he was free again

The Killers

Left to right:

Markov, Kolpashchikov, the leader Myasnikov, Ivanchenko, and Zhuzhgov.

They posed together after the murder

Malkov telephoned Myasnikov at 2.20 a.m. to confirm that he had cabled the Soviet of People's Commissars at Moscow, for the attention of Trotsky and Feliks Dzerzhinsky, the Cheka supremo. A copy was also sent to Petrograd and to the Ural Soviet and the regional head of Cheka in Ekaterinburg. The message read: *Last night Michael Romanov and Johnson were abducted by persons unknown in military uniform. Search as yet unsuccessful, most energetic measures taken.*[34]

That was code for Michael is dead. No alarm bells sounded in the Kremlin, as would have been the case if Michael had actually escaped and was on his way to lead the 'Whites'. No vengeful tribunal descended on Perm to exact punishment for those charged with Michael's security. No one demanded an accounting by the local leadership, or the arrest of those whose negligence had permitted the rescue. There was no enquiry, no scapegoat, no consequence.

Moreover, the 'energetic measures' to find the 'escaped Michael' involved no more than despatching token search parties, sent out everywhere except the road to Motovilikha and beyond. What the Cheka did do, and promptly, was to arrest Chelyshev and Borunov as 'accomplices'.[35] Chelyshev would later recount what had happened in the *Korolev Rooms* to a fellow prisoner, Aleksandr Volkov, a former valet in the Tsarskoe Selo household. He told him he was in no doubt that Michael had not been rescued by friends but abducted by enemies.[36]

Nevertheless, the story of the 'escape' was spread so convincingly that most ordinary people accepted it as fact. In the local Soviet newspaper, the Perm *Izvestiya,* Michael was said to have been abducted 'soon after midnight' by 'three unidentified armed men in military uniform…Orders were immediately given for Romanov's arrest and mounted militia units were despatched along all highways, but no traces were found.'[37]

Many of Perm's townspeople saw 'the hand of God' in Michael's disappearance. Prayers led by the archbishop were said for him in the cathedral, 'for the health of God's servant Michael';

rumour had it that he would reappear at the head of an army and restore order.[38]

One of the few who wondered if all was as it seemed to be was Krumnis in the *Korolev Rooms*. He noted that 'everything about the escape seemed strange, all the more so because there were no house searches'.[39] The sister of the senior Cheka man Lukoyanov, so recently promoted to Ekaterinburg, admitted that the news 'had been received rather strangely at the Cheka; they weren't particularly worried'.[40]

The telegram to them apart, Moscow had full details of the murder shortly afterwards. According to Myasnikov, a local Bolshevik leader, M. P. Turkin, was immediately sent to the Kremlin to report on what had happened to Yacob Sverdlov, President of the All-Russian Congress of Soviets, and so powerful he was known as the 'Red Tsar'. Sverdlov was said to be 'very, very pleased'; he then telephoned Lenin, 'who was also very pleased'.[41] Given that in 1935, when Myasnikov recounted this at the Soviet Paris embassy, he must have known that to be true, for otherwise it would not have done him any good to say so. It might also be one of the reasons why he was allowed to return to Russia: he clearly knew too much.*

However, there is independent evidence that Turkin was indeed in Moscow at that time, for he is listed as a delegate to the All-Russian Congress held there at the beginning of July, and presided over by Sverdlov.[42] Moreover, shortly after the murder, Myasnikov went to Ekaterinburg, to a meeting of the Ural Regional Soviet at the *Hotel Amerika* on Pokrovsky Prospekt. Those present were the leaders of the Ural Soviet, headed by Myasnikov's old Perm friend, Beloborodov. The purpose of the meeting was to draw up a resolution for the execution of their Romanov prisoners. Although they knew Michael was already dead, his name was included as one of those the Regional Soviet 'considers it indispensable to execute...' However, the resolution

---

*He would have been better to have stayed in Paris. Back in Russia he was executed by the Soviets in 1945.

recognised that 'for reasons of foreign policy' it might be necessary to keep that 'absolutely secret'.[43]

The meeting also agreed that the Ural Soviet should send immediately two envoys to Moscow to obtain the endorsement of the Bolshevik leadership for their decision. The first envoy was a very senior figure in the ranks of the Ural Soviet: secretary and war commissar Filipp Goloshchenkin; the other was a man with no position at all — Myasnikov, who it was said was carrying 'a personal report' for Lenin. The two envoys* were instructed to return 'not later than July 15'.[44]

The man who had been Emperor Michael II was dead. Now the question was how best to deal with the other Romanovs in the custody of the Ural Soviet. Five weeks after the murder of Michael, the world would have the answer to that.

---

*The two envoys travelled separately. Myasnikov was also escorting his friend Beloborodov's wife and family, travelling to Moscow. Although he survived, they drowned in a cross-river ferry accident. That would explain why he did not return with Goloshchenkin to Ekaterinburg or play any further role in immediate events.

PART IV
The Aftermath

23. LONG LIVE MICHAEL

IN both London and Berlin the 'escape' of Michael was seen as of high importance, with both sides wondering how best to exploit that to their own advantage. Although the British, like the French, had withdrawn their ambassadors from Petrograd to the greater safety of Murmansk, on the White Sea, they still had a skeleton staff there, of whom the naval attaché Captain Francis Cromie was key to their intelligence sources. Just over two weeks after Michael's murder, and based on reports from a spy in the German general staff, he reported by telegram on June 29, 1918, that the Germans intended to follow up their seemingly successful offensive in the West by a new effort in Russia. Their aim was to 'break the Brest peace and declare a monarchy. Considerations will be more favourable than Brest Peace Conference, return of all territory to Russia, even Ukraine…Economic conditions will be onerous but less so than at present. Candidate for the throne is Grand Duke Michael and a high German Agent has already been sent to Perm to open negotiations, but Grand Duke has temporarily disappeared'.

The despatch to London, which fitted the facts as Cromie understood them, urged that since the Germans appeared bent on restoring the monarchy, albeit for their own interests, the best course for the British was to forestall them and back the monarchists first. 'In Ukraine there are 200,000 officers of whom 150,000 will at once join up, but only in support of monarchy', he said, adding that 'Grand Duke Michael is the most popular candidate'.[1]

The Germans had re-established an embassy in Moscow, with Count Joachim von Mirbach, a Russian expert, as ambassador; they also maintained an important consulate in Petrograd. Their messages to Berlin and to the Kaiser's brother Prince Henry, who was primarily responsible for questions relating to the Romanov dynasty, were also supportive of Michael as emperor. Prince Henry took the keenest interest in bringing the Bolsheviks to heel: his two sisters-in-law were Alexandra and Ella, both prisoners, and his wife, Princess Irene, was aunt to the five children in Ekaterinburg.

The question was how to rescue them, and the best hope of that might well prove to be Michael. On June 27, two weeks after his 'escape', *The Times* in London had reported rumours that 'he is at the head of an anti-revolution movement in Turkestan' and that 'he had issued a manifesto to the Russian people...leaving the decision as to the form of government to be adopted by the Duma which was to be convoked'.

This seemed to re-affirm Michael's manifesto on becoming emperor: that it was for the Russian people to decide its status, and that if he was to be emperor it was to be as a constitutional monarch not an autocrat. That being so, its authenticity seemed real enough. A week later, the newspaper had him 'at the head of the Siberian revolt'.[2]

On that same day, July 3, 1918, von Mirbach in Moscow advised Berlin that of all the Romanovs who might be restored to the throne the most popular was Michael, and that there was no support for ex-Tsar Nicholas whose cause he judged to be hopeless.

Of more immediate concern to von Mirbach was the news that Michael was not only leading the Siberian revolt but that he remained an ally of Britain and France and had published a 'manifesto' calling on all former Tsarist officers to support him. 'Effect of Michael Aleksandrovich's support for Entente on generals and officers, including those of groups who lean towards us, considerable according to impressions here. Groups here have shown themselves noticeably more restrained towards us during the last week.'[3]

A few days later came further confirmation to Berlin that Michael was the only possible candidate for the throne of a restored monarchy. For the Germans their evidence of that, in part, was the reaction of the people in Petrograd to news reports that Nicholas had been killed.

This wholly false story, spread by the Ural Soviet at the same time as they were announcing Michael's 'escape', was that while being evacuated by special train from Ekaterinburg because of the threat posed by advancing Czechs, Nicholas had become involved in a furious row with one of his guards, and the soldier had then killed him with a bayonet thrust. The object of all this was to test both public and foreign reaction to the death of Nicholas, while covering up the real murder of Michael.

The result from the Bolshevik standpoint was encouraging, as the German despatch from Petrograd to Prince Henry confirmed just over three weeks later. The report, passed on by Henry to the Kaiser, stated that although the 'murder' of Nicholas on the train was widely believed,

...the effect of this news on the masses was scarcely perceptible. Even the Russian church, whose interest can only be bound up with the imperial family, did not react in any way. Although the rumour was not retracted for almost two weeks, a requiem mass did not take place anywhere. This notoriously proved that the ex-Tsar has lost all sympathy from the people.

Grand Duke Michael is a different matter. The newspapers which carried the news of his flight and his alleged manifesto in Siberia were read feverishly and he is seen as the only possible source of deliverance from the unbearable circumstances. The famous Russian writers Kuprin and Amfiteatrov even attempted to publish a newspaper article about the Grand Duke, in which His Imperial Highness was characterised as the only Romanov not to have been discredited in any way. Both were, of course, immediately arrested.

The report, largely confirming Cromie's assessment of German intentions, concluded: 'only the restoration of the monarchy in Russia with German assistance…will guarantee Germany an alliance with Russia and the maintenance and support of German interests in East Europe'. What was needed was that 'a general Church Congress, presided over by the Patriarch, offers the Grand Duke the crown'.[4]

Here, it seemed, was proof that the Kremlin's dead-and-alive strategy was paying off. They had given the Germans an emperor for their planned monarchy but one who was set to go to war with them, while denying them the possibility that they could credibly find an alternative. If the Bolshevik leadership had been able to read the German diplomatic cables they would have been well pleased with themselves. The threat of a German-led counter revolution was real enough, but muddying the waters was better than going back to war with them, as the Socialist Revolutionaries wanted to do.*

What was more, their 'escape' story continued to be accepted at face value by the world at large. The man they had buried in a wood outside Perm was alive and well and in Siberia. Everyone knew that, because it said so in the newspapers.

But the newspapers were printing only what seemed to be credible reports from a number of sources. A Japanese diplomatic despatch to Tokyo was picked up by the British military attaché, who promptly cabled London on July 8, 1918 that 'a counter-revolutionary movement headed by Grand Duke Michael has started in Omsk…'[5] Four days later even a Moscow newspaper was reporting Michael's reappearance. 'Rumour has spread here', said a report from Vyatka, 'that the former Grand Duke Michael Romanov is in Omsk and has taken command of the Siberian insurgents. There are claims that he has issued a manifesto to the people calling for the overthrow of Soviet power and promising

---

* Von Mirbach was murdered in his Moscow embassy on July 6, 1918, by two Socialist Revolutionary members of the Cheka as part of a power struggle between the SRs and the Bolsheviks. The SRs were hoping to provoke a resumption of the war with Germany, in order to prevent a German-led counter-revolution.

to convene Assemblies of the Land to resolve the question of what regime there should be in Russia.'[6] The stories about Michael even reached Persia where Dimitri recorded in his diary the rumours that 'Misha is advancing on Moscow with Cossacks and has been proclaimed Emperor'.[7] The adage that a lie if repeated often enough becomes the truth was working well for the Kremlin.

What continued to trouble Berlin, however, were the reports that support for them was slipping away among the monarchists. As the German military attaché in Moscow observed on July 17, if Michael was leading a pro-Allied force 'then this would place Russian officers of a monarchist tendency in a difficult position'.[8] However, the hopeful news on July 17,1918, was that 'General Brusilov, formerly supreme commander,* has therefore sent a lieutenant-commander to the Grand Duke to prevent him aligning himself with the Entente'.[9] Nothing more would be heard of that, but next day came other news which, while not of any political significance in the struggle between revolution and counter-revolution, was not only to be believed but true.

It came in the form of a brief announcement by Comrade Sverdlov during a meeting of the Council of the People's Commissars in the Kremlin that 'at Ekaterinburg, by a decision of the Regional Soviet, Nicholas has been shot'. That was all, and after that, with no further comment, Lenin directed the comrades to continue their discussion of the draft of a new public-health law.[10] Unlike Michael, the Kremlin did not care if the world knew that Nicholas was dead, because they knew the world did not care either.

FIVE days earlier, on Friday July 12, Goloshchekin, the special envoy sent to Moscow to find out what the Kremlin wanted to do with the Romanovs in captivity, returned to Ekaterinburg to report that the answer was that the Ural Regional Soviet could do whatever it thought best. The situation was critical. Advancing

*Brusilov, Michael's former commander and friend, would later join the Red Army. He died in a a cramped Moscow apartment in 1924, but was given a state funeral.

Whites and Czechs were now so close that the city could fall in three days. The decision was quickly made and brutally simple: they would kill the whole family, and then next day they would kill the six Romanovs held in Alapaevsk. The executioner in the Ipatev House was to be Yacob Yurovsky, a local photographer turned secret policeman. He and a picked squad of other Cheka men would shoot Nicholas, Alexandra and the children, after which their bodies would be taken away, burned, and the remains hidden from any chance of discovery.

At midnight on Tuesday, July 16, the family was awakened by Yurovsky and told that because of the immediate military threat they were to be evacuated at once. Having dressed, they went quietly downstairs and were told to wait in a basement room while their transport was arranged. Yurovsky brought in three chairs, for Nicholas, Alexandra, and Alexis; the four girls stood in a row behind them. That done, Yurovsky re-entered the room with his Cheka death squad, and the firing began. It was pitiless slaughter, finished off with bayonet and rifle butt, and so horrific that when the truth came out it would revolt the world.[11]

The following day Grand Duchess Ella and the five male Romanovs at Alapaevsk were to face an even more terrible and deliberately cruel end. Taken in peasant carts to a disused mineshaft, they were then all buried alive, save for Grand Duke Serge who was shot after he tried to resist. Their killers shovelled earth and rubble on top of them, but later admitted under interrogation by the Whites who captured them shortly afterwards that they had heard hymn singing coming from the shaft for some time afterwards.[12]

As in Michael's case the Alapaevsk Romanovs were said to have been abducted by Whites and to have escaped. Apart from admitting the death of Nicholas, the rest of the family were said to have been evacuated to safety. The Bolsheviks also cynically continued in negotiations with the Germans for the release of Alexandra and the children, using the dead family as a bargaining tool.[13]

They did not bother to say more about Nicholas. The announcement of his death had no more effect on public opinion than the false story of him being killed by a Red Guard five weeks earlier. In Moscow the British diplomat Bruce Lockhart noted that 'I am bound to admit that the population of Moscow received the news with amazing indifference',[14] though that might not have been the case if they had known that five innocent children had also been murdered. When that did become known, revulsion at the massacre in Ekaterinburg — as well as the burying alive at Alapaevsk — would leave a stain on the Bolsheviks and their Soviet Union that would never wash away.

NOT knowing the truth, the Germans brushed aside the killing of Nicholas and persisted in their efforts to win over the invisible Michael. No one doubted that he was alive and in Omsk, 1,000 miles to the east of Perm, yet no one seemed to wonder why there were no reports or photographs of him actually in action — holding meetings, visiting troops, handing out medals, or sending telegrams to London, his ally in arms.

The first report of an actual 'sighting' of Michael was not until August 26, some ten weeks after his 'escape', when a British agent in Stockholm identified only as ST12 told London that 'a Swede arrived from Omsk reports that Grand Duke Michael Aleksandrovich is living in the Governor's House in Omsk with the Imperial Russian flag flying, with guards and procedures as in old regime days'.[15]

By then, however, the German armies in France were on the retreat. On August 8, 1918, a British counter-offensive had smashed their lines in what the German commander General Erich von Ludendorff would call 'a black day for the German army'. They would never recover. However, the hope in Berlin that they could at least secure an armistice which would allow them to carve out a new Russian empire was not yet entirely dashed, and in Russia itself the Germans would continue to think that it was still possible, persisting even unto the end in their aim of securing Michael's support and thus of his 'army' for the German cause.

Desperate to bring good news, on August 23, the German Ukraine Delegation in Kiev sent a positive cable to Berlin to say that Michael 'is by no means as pro-Entente as he is said to be…'[16] That seemed to confirm an earlier report that 'attention should be paid to news which has repeatedly come in recently that certain differences of opinion exist between Grand Duke Michael and the Omsk government about the Entente, as the Omsk government is pursuing solely Russian objectives, and in any case wishes to avoid a war with Germany'.[17]

By then the Germans in Russia had added reason for winning over Michael. An Allied Expeditionary Force had been sent to Murmansk on the White Sea, and although small, it had captured Archangel on August 2, 1918. The first aim of the British and French — joined later by Americans — had been to secure the stockpile of armaments sent in to supply Russia before their peace treaty in March and so that they did not fall into the hands of either the Bolsheviks or the Germans. The second aim was to re-open the war against Germany in Russia, for which they needed the support of Admiral Aleksandr Kolchak's advancing White Army in eastern Russia.

That was reason enough for the Germans to hope that somehow Michael could be persuaded to switch sides, and in their eagerness to win him over the Germans saw a new opportunity to earn his favour. After all, the Kaiser had already made sure that his precious son George had passed safely into family care in Denmark. Now the bait would be Natasha. They would save his beloved wife from the Bolsheviks, and the execution squad which surely otherwise awaited her in the next few weeks. Michael would then be further in their debt and that must surely bring him to accept that imperial Germany was his friend, not his foe.

NATASHA, who was then staying with her friend Maggie Abakanovich at her house on the Moika, had been told that

Michael had disappeared within hours of his being taken from the hotel. Colonel Znamerovsky had cabled her that 'Our friend and Johnny have vanished without trace'.[18] Seeking explanation she and Maggie had gone at once to the offices of Cheka boss Uritsky, who promptly arrested them both, sending them to the women's prison on the fourth floor of his headquarters at 2 Gorokhovyana Street.[19]

One of the last men to see her at the house on the Moika before her arrest was the German diplomat Armin von Reyer, a key figure in the secret negotiations between the German legation and the monarchist organisations in Petrograd. The fact that von Reyer knew where she was staying says much about German interest in Natasha. Afterwards he reported their conversation to Prince Henry in Berlin, emphasising Michael's popularity and recounting her story of the scenes at Easter when the people of Perm had overwhelmed them with flowers and gifts.[20]

Von Reyer was never in any doubt that Michael was alive, for there were too many reports to think otherwise. One of the first on his desk was that Michael had been 'brought by ship to Rybinsk', a river port on the Upper Volga, 200 miles north-east of Moscow and about 1,000 miles westwards by river from Perm.[21] The fact that this proved wholly wrong when more credible reports placed him some 1,600 miles to the east in Omsk, and behind friendly lines, did nothing to disturb the main point — that he had escaped his captors in Perm.[21]

In Petrograd, the question for the Germans was how Natasha would escape *her* captors. Her friend Maggie had been released, since even Uritsky could not think up any charge against her, except that she was Natasha's friend. That done, the threat for Natasha was that she would be shortly transferred to a proper prison in Moscow to stand trial for conspiracy.

German intervention was discreet, as it had to be if it was to be effective. In consequence, ten weeks later Natasha was still confined on the fourth-floor at Cheka headquarters. The reason was that she was said to be too ill to be moved to prison in

Moscow; she was suffering from tuberculosis — or so claimed a doctor who examined her.[22] Shortly afterwards, at the insistence of the doctor, she was removed to a nursing home, under guard. It was just in time. For on August 30 Lenin was shot and seriously wounded at a factory in Moscow by a Socialist Revolutionary, Fanya Kaplan, and coincidentally Uritsky was assassinated in Petrograd by a Jewish military cadet, Leonid Kanegisser, in revenge for the execution of a friend.

Coming as they did within hours of each other, the Kremlin reacted with ferocity, bringing in two decrees which inaugurated what would be known as the Red Terror. The first instituted the execution of hostages as reprisal for further attacks on Bolshevik leaders; the second commanded the execution of anyone 'with links to the White Guard organisations, conspiracies, and seditious actions'.[23] No one was to be spared, even those with diplomatic immunity, as was shown twenty-four hours after Uritsky's death when a Cheka squad forced its way into the British consulate in Petrograd and killed the resisting naval attaché Captain Cromie, shot down at the top of the staircase. His body was hung out of the window and left there for days.[24]

Hundreds of others would be killed in the coming weeks and months, and their number would doubtless have included Natasha; in the event, as a furious Cheka discovered a week later, she had vanished into the night. The guard at the nursing home knew she was in her bed when the lights were switched off, but in the morning she was no longer there.

The first her daughter Tata would know about that was when Gatchina Cheka chief Serov arrived at Nikolaevskaya Street on Saturday, September 7, 1918, and arrested her.[25] Kept overnight in the local Cheka office she was bundled onto a train next day and taken under escort to the same prison room which had been home to her mother since her arrest on June 13.

Told by Serov that she would be sent to a correction camp for young criminals, 'I burst into tears'.[26] The threat turned out to be a bluff. After interrogation it became clear that she was as much in the dark as the Cheka; she spent another frightened night sleeping on a tabletop, before being told that she was free.

It was pouring with rain that Tuesday morning, September 10, and she was drenched within minutes of getting outside. She had no money and had not eaten for two days. Knowing that she could not go back to Gatchina, she took her small suitcase and struggled with it on the long walk to the Fontanka, hoping to find refuge at the apartment of her 'Uncle Alyosha', Matveev. Climbing the stairs she reached his door only to discover that he was no longer there. The housekeeper refused to let her in, complaining that she had not been paid, and that she was tired of having the Cheka turn up every day in their hunt for Natasha. With that the door was slammed in her face.

She sat down on her suitcase on the landing and started to cry. Suddenly she heard a door open on the floor above and footsteps on the stairs. A voice called her name, and when she looked up, startled, it was to see 'a completely strange woman with flaming red hair'. It was Princess Vyazemskaya, disguised under a wig. Moments later Tata was running upstairs and into the arms of her mother. The apartment was her hiding place from the Cheka searching the floor below. It had been rented by the Germans.[27]

IN Perm, armed with the Red Terror decrees, Cheka chairman Malkov decided to combine those with an announcement that Michael and Johnson had been recaptured, thereby putting an end to the policy that he was leading a White army in Siberia. Since he would not have dared to do that without higher authority, it would appear that in the Urals at least there was increasing disquiet about propaganda which seemed to serve only the interests of the Whites. To dispose of Michael, Malkov issued a statement on September 18 that six days earlier a Cheka agent had arrested two men who, walking along a road, were 'behaving in a suspicious manner'.

One of these suspects, 'a tall man with a light-brown beard particularly drew attention to himself'. Taken to Cheka headquarters it was noted that the men were 'wearing make-up'; when this was removed 'they were identified as the former Grand Duke Michael Romanov and his secretary Johnson' and were immediately 'detained under close guard'.[28] To add substance to all of this, valet Chelyshev was passed off as Michael, and chauffeur Borunov as Johnson.

Two days later the Russian Telegraph Agency reported that 'Michael Romanov and his secretary have been detained by agents of Perm Provincial Cheka. They have been taken to Perm.'[29] The following day, under Warrant No. 3694, Chelyshev and Borunov were marched from their cells, and shot dead.[30]

A month earlier, Sverdlov, the 'Red Tsar', had cabled Perm to say that 'as to the Romanov servants, I give you permission to act as you see fit', which did not mean that Perm could use them to 'kill off' Michael. A furious Kremlin ordered a flustered Malkov to withdraw the story immediately. In consequence the announcement of Michael's 'recapture' appeared in only one newspaper and that was then blacked-out by being covered in printer's ink; in the regional newspapers the announcement was removed at the last moment from the presses.[31]

No further mention of this story appeared anywhere, and in consequence no attention was paid to it. The German report to Berlin which made reference to it dismissed it cynically as 'same as always'.[32] Michael was still in play, and the Germans were still intent on bringing him over to their side.

Nonetheless that would not save his 'accomplices' in Perm. After the killing of Chelyshev and Borunov, Colonel Znamerovsky and his wife were taken from the same prison and with others led to a sewage farm outside Perm, lined up, and shot.[33] Had Natasha remained in Perm instead of going off to Moscow as she did, there can be little doubt that she would also have been standing in that sewage farm alongside the others. Indeed, had she not escaped from her Cheka prison in Petrograd, she would have been in another line-up at some point, with the same result. She would have been murdered.

As it was, the Germans were in the process of passing her off as someone else, and more successfully than Perm had managed in the case of the unfortunate Chelyshev and Borunov. Natasha was to re-emerge as Frau Tania Klenow, with passport number 4594, issued by the Ukrainian consulate-general in Petrograd, and with a photograph showing her wearing the white head-dress of a nursing nun.[34] The outfit had been smuggled into her hideaway apartment on the Fontanka; with the photo in her passport, dated October 1, some three weeks after her escape, the Germans were ready for their next move: her removal to safety behind their lines.

Tata had already gone. After her reunion with her mother on September 10, she had been told to go back to Gatchina immediately in order not to arouse suspicion and to wait there until she received further instructions. They were not long in coming.

Tata would later remember that a 'strange man arrived…who he was I have never discovered, he vanished as silently as he appeared, leaving my passport; the tickets he would hand to me at the station next day'.[35] The passport was also forged, though under her real name of Nathalie Mamontov, it being thought safe enough since it was unlikely to be connected to the Brasova name of her mother in any routine checks at railway stations or at the border crossing into the Ukraine. The Germans had also arranged that she would travel with one of Natasha's friends, a Madame Yakhontova, who had property in the Ukraine and was travelling on a genuine passport.

So that Cheka eyes would have no reason to pay her more than a passing glance, Tata set off next morning with nothing to show that she would be gone for more than the day.* The 'strange man' had taken away her suitcase the day before saying

*The house would be subsequently destroyed in fighting between the Bolsheviks and the 'Whites' a year later, in October 1919. It is now a small apartment block. However, the adjacent 'guest house' which Michael bought is still there. The Soviets renamed it 'Uritskaya Street' in honour of the man who arrested Michael, but its original name has today been restored.

she would get it back, packed, along with her tickets when she got to Petrograd station.

He was there waiting for her, together with Madame Yakhontova, when she arrived and he had reserved seats for both of them in the train crowded with people trying to get out of Russia. Her suitcase was already on the rack above her seat, along with other cases belonging to her mother; there was also a kitbag filled with dirty clothes, under which were Natasha's sables as well as other valuables. The stranger thrust money into Tata's hands, waved goodbye, and disappeared back into the station.[36]

The route southwards out of Bolshevik Russia was through Vitebsk to the border crossing at Orsha on the Dnieper, a distance of some 420 miles.

At Orsha the next morning there was a long wait for examination of exit permits and luggage. It was a worrying prospect, given the valuables — including Natasha's pearl ear-rings 'the size of hazel nuts' — secreted inside a bar of soap hidden in their suitcases.[37] Madame Yakhontova found a man who assured her that the Bolshevik guards checking the luggage could be bribed; fortunately the man proved a genuine 'fixer' and to their relief the guards passed their luggage through with only casual scrutiny.

Across the border, Tata was 'struck by the look of order and tidiness that pervaded the territory occupied by the Germans...It was in such marked contrast to Bolshevik Russia...' There was also ample food to buy, and they purchased bread, butter, cold meat, cream cheese and bottles of *kvas*, a local beer. Across the border they boarded a new train which took them through the old *Stavka* town of Mogilev, then to Gomel and on to Kiev, a journey of 300 miles. At stations *en route* the locals on the platforms would offer for sale apples, pears, plums and watermelons. After Bolshevik Russia 'it seemed a land of plenty'.[38]

On arrival in Kiev they were met by Princess Vyazemskaya, who had left Petrograd the previous day with another German-forged passport; she had arranged accommodation for them with friends, and there they settled down to wait for Natasha. At last, in early October, there came a telegram from Gomel, the half-way point from the border crossing. Natasha would be with them in a few hours.

It did not take the Bolsheviks very long to work out that nurse 'Frau Klenow' in the white head-dress and the Countess Brasova were one and the same person, not only because once across the border she took off the head-dress but because of the fuss made of her by the Germans as she did so. The demure and humble nun crossing the border was no more; flanked by saluting Germans, with bowing flunkeys to carry her luggage into a reserved first-class carriage, it would be characteristic of her if Natasha had then given a mocking wave to the watching Cheka men on the other side of the line.

Certainly, the Russian Telegraph Agency realised who she was for it reported her crossing, saying that 'Brasova was greeted with great honour by the German local authorities...She was presented with an officer's carriage for her journey to Kiev'.[39] Reading that must have been a bitter moment in Gorokhovaya Street.

By then the Germans in Kiev were busy on the next part of their plan to make Michael even more grateful to them for their help: to send Natasha through Germany to be reunited with her eight-year-old son George in Denmark and bring him back. On October 21 the anxious message to Berlin was that 'as we are losing considerable ground with the monarchists...permitting the journey might be a suitable way to place the monarchic circles under an obligation to us. The precondition, though, would be that a political influencing of the Copenhagen court by the countess to our disadvantage is not to be feared.'[40] Natasha was not to be rude about the Germans.

King Christian X of Denmark was happy to extend an invitation to Natasha, though he raised his eyebrows when a subsequent request came into Copenhagen for permission to bring her daughter, Princess Vyazemskaya and two other companions. He agreed but later 'he did comment to the minister that he had not expected that she would appear with so many companions'.[41] Berlin signalled its approval for the journey on October 30, the *quid pro quo* being that she would bring little George back with her to the Ukraine, as bait for Michael. With a grateful Michael, something might yet be salvaged in Russia if the monarchists rallied to the Germans. It was a desperate last card, but what could they lose by trying?

Natasha, now Grafin von Brassow, posed once more for a passport photograph, this time wearing a hat and an elegant dress and completed the details for the exit visa. The young clerk typing out the paperwork looked up and asked her date of birth. Natasha told him it was June 27, 1888, and he duly filled in her age as thirty; her world might be falling apart, but Natasha was never going to admit that she was thirty-eight.[42] With the papers in her hand, bags packed, farewells made, and money organised, Natasha and the others gathered excitedly as they prepared to leave. Unfortunately, the date was November 11, 1918 and at eleven o'clock that morning the war ended. Natasha was holding a passport to nowhere.

WITH the war over, it was now the turn of the British to rescue Natasha. With German authority at an end it could only be a question of time before the Bolsheviks took control of Kiev and caught up with her. Knowing that, she and Tata together with her friend Princess Vyazemskaya fled to Odessa hoping to find some way to escape by sea. They found a room which they all shared at the *Hotel de Londres,* dreading the future. There was widespread looting and there were rumours that the only apparent exit route to safety, through Romania, had been closed.

As Odessa became blocked landward, and the sound of artillery fire could be heard in the distance, there came sudden and unexpected deliverance. A French battleship arrived and, after its marines and sailors stormed ashore, order was swiftly restored. However, the French showed no interest in evacuating anyone.

Then a British destroyer, *HMS Nereide* appeared in the harbour. Seeing it, Tata recalled, 'our hearts stood still'.[43] She ran up the gangway and asked permission to come aboard. Minutes later all three were being invited into the wardroom for tea with its captain, Lieutenant-Commander Herbert Wyld. *HMS Nereide*, just 772 tons, had a crew of only 72 including six officers. But having heard Natasha's story, 'they took us under their wing', as Tata put it. 'They came *en masse* for tea at our hotel, and we in turn were invited to meals on board.'[44] And when the time came for the destroyer to leave, the captain told them, to their immense joy, that they would not be left behind — that despite the cramped quarters they would be evacuated aboard the ship, on the first leg of a journey which would take them to Britain.

At the beginning of 1918 Natasha had thought, as Michael had done as he toasted the New Year, that the year ahead might bring an end to their torment. Now, on the deck of a British destroyer, as Odessa faded into the distance, she found herself facing the coming new year as a refugee, fleeing prison or worse, and with a husband who had been missing for more than six months. Yet hope was not lost. Natasha still believed that Michael was alive and that somehow soon they would be reunited.

As Michael had said in the last letter he had written to her from his desk in the *Korolev Rooms*, and which she would clutch to her for the rest of her life, *My dear soul...I will hope that God will allow us to be together again....*`

24. A FAMILY DIVIDED

THE massacre of Nicholas and his family at Ekaterinburg and the following day's massacre at Alapaevsk had been easily uncovered for the Whites had captured both towns relatively soon afterwards. Although they did not find the bodies of Nicholas and family, the bullet-marked walls and bloodstained scene in the basement of the Ipatev House told its own story, if not yet the whole story; at Alapaevsk they uncovered the mineshaft and removed the six bodies buried there. Interrogation of prisoners provided the evidence of what had happened and that in turn served to confirm that the Bolsheviks had also killed everyone in Ekaterinburg.

However, when the Whites reached Perm in December 1918 they found nothing which could solve the mystery of Michael. The Cheka men had fled, and the immediate witnesses to the abduction from the hotel room — Chelyshev and Borunov — were dead. There was no blood, no body, and no trace of where he had been taken, though there was no doubt that he had been forcibly abducted from the hotel by five men and taken away with Johnson in two carriages, for that much they could gather from servants at the *Korolev Rooms*. After what they had seen in the Ipatev House and the mineshaft, the presumption had to be that he was dead, though they could not be certain of that without finding his body, and as to that they had no idea where even to begin their search.

The Bolshevik story had never changed — that he had escaped — so could they have hidden him somewhere as hostage? The

Bolsheviks had taken four senior Grand Dukes as hostages and they were being held in a fortress on an island in the Neva some miles upstream from Petrograd. The Bolsheviks had thought that the four — Grand Dukes Paul, Dimitri Konstantinovich, Bimbo and his brother George — might be useful pawns at some point; any idea of that vanished on January 15, 1919, when the two leading German 'comrades', Rosa Luxemburg and Karl Liebknecht, were murdered after they attempted their own revolution in Berlin. In revenge for that, or such was the excuse, the four Grand Dukes were taken from their cells, shipped downriver to the Fortress of St Peter and St Paul, and on January 19 lined up against a wall and shot, their bodies thrown into a mass grave.

That brought the number of Romanovs known to have been murdered by the Bolsheviks to seventeen in the past six months. Michael would make it eighteen, but who was going to announce that without a body, and without a confession?

Nine months later, in September 1919, after a desperate letter from Natasha in London, Admiral Kolchak, signing himself as Supreme Commander of the White Army, replied that *all information I possess does not give any indication that the Grand Duke Michael Aleksandrovich is at present in Siberia or the Far East His destiny is quite unknown after he was taken away...and all attempts to find out where he is have not produced any results.*[1]

In short, Michael was to be 'presumed dead' but the Admiral chose not to say that directly. He was trying to be kind.

NATASHA'S journey back to Britain with Tata had taken many weeks. The *Nereide* took her down the Black Sea only as far as Constantinople where later she was given passage in a British battleship, *Agamemnon,* to Malta; from there she went by merchant ship to Marseilles; by rail to Paris, and finally on to London.

It was not therefore until March 1919 that she reached Wadhurst, in Sussex, and the large comfortable Tudor house, 'Snape', which with Paddockhurst no longer available had been leased in Michael's name in 1917 in expectation of his return at war's end. Michael had then transferred enough cash to secure it for two years, so at least Natasha had somewhere to go. Johnson's mother had gone there from Paddockhurst; like Natasha, she was desperate for news. Her son was also missing. Where Michael was, he must be. The arrival of Natasha raised her hopes that somehow all might yet be well.

Natasha still believed she would see Michael again. In Paris there had been the exciting news that the French Colonial Office had received a 'top secret' report that Michael was in French Indo-China, and asking for a visa. The French wanted photographs for identification. Bitterly, the man turned out to be a fraud. There were other false alarms. Michael was in Japan. Michael was in Siam. Each time, desperate hope was followed by despair.[3]

It was torture — and in all this, one comfort was that little George had been brought back by Miss Neame from Copenhagen, and that after a year of separation she at last had her two children safely back in her arms. '*Where is Papa?*' George had asked plaintively in a letter he had written in August 1918 on his eighth birthday;[4] it was still his question now, and there was still no answer.

The only moment of joy for Natasha was when Grand Duke Dimitri walked back into her life. Wearing British uniform he had been brought to Britain from Persia by the British ambassador there, Sir Charles Marling, in defiance of the rule that no male Romanov was to be allowed into the country. The ambassador would be rapped over the knuckles for that, but that was as far as it went. Dimitri would be the sole exception; the other surviving Grand Dukes would make France their home, for the door remained shut in Britain.

Dimitri would be a constant visitor for the first weeks and they teased each other as before. Thirty months had passed since their last meeting at Gatchina in October 1916, expecting that they would then meet again at Brasovo for Christmas, not as now in England — Dimitri penniless, his father Paul executed that

January by a firing squad, Natasha not knowing whether she was wife or widow. But although he was as flattering as ever, Natasha was so tormented by her fears for Michael that she could hardly talk about anything else. By the summer he had drifted away, trying to pick up the pieces of his own life.[5] As a sign of just how much the world had changed, on July 26, 1919, Natasha travelled up to London to Marlborough House to meet the Dowager Empress Marie. The British had sent a battleship to Odessa to rescue the Dowager Empress, her daughter Xenia and a swollen entourage of fellow refugees who had sheltered with her in the Crimea under German protection. Arriving in London she had gone to stay with her sister, the Dowager Queen Alexandra. The meeting was the first since she had given Natasha a dressing-down there six years earlier in 1913.

Nervous at the prospect, Natasha took Mme Johnson along with her as moral support, as well as little George, the grandson the Dowager Empress had never seen in Russia, nor had wanted to know about. Now the Dowager Empress made a great fuss of George; her beloved Michael's only son, and with looks that reminded her of his father at that age.[6]

As for Michael, she brushed aside Natasha's fears for him, adamant that he was alive and well; indeed she went much further than that: she refused to believe that anyone in her immediate family had been killed by the Bolsheviks. She would persist in so saying until her own death nine years later in Copenhagen. Natasha came away heartened, but vaguely disturbed. Everyone knew that Nicholas had been killed, except it seemed his mother. What value, then, her confidence that Michael was alive?

As the months went on, other worries crowded in. There had been some cash left in the Paris bank account set up when they left Russia in 1912, and £3,000 was transferred from Michael's Danish account to her London bank,[7] but her main asset was the jewellery she had smuggled out of Russia. Piece by piece she sold them to meet her bills, school fees for George and Tata, and her rental costs as she moved from Snape in 1920, firstly to a country house near Richmond, Surrey, and then to a smart apartment in West London. Natasha was beginning to worry about making ends meet.

There was nothing surprising in that. Europe was awash with poverty-stricken royals — Germans, Austrians, Greeks as well as Russians and others. The collapse of old Europe brought devastation in its wake as crowns were kicked into the gutter with no one to pick them up again. The Duke of Mecklenburg-Schwerin shot himself; so did the Kaiser's desolate youngest son Joachim. A British gunboat sent up the Danube rescued the ex-Austrian emperor Karl from mob revenge in Hungary, though he died shortly after being sent with his wife and eight children into exile in Portuguese Madeira, arriving with just £320 in his pocket. A British cruiser snatched Prince Andrew of Greece from a firing squad in Athens, after he was court-martialled as scapegoat for the humiliating defeat suffered by Greece in its war with Turkey; unwelcome in Britain, in 1944 he would die penniless in Monaco.*

In London, Dimitri's sister Marie was reduced to knitting sweaters for a living. When in desperation she wrote to Queen Mary for help, she received in reply a letter which did not contain the hoped-for cheque, but merely a list of people the Queen suggested might buy her sweaters.

Dimitri gave up on London as too expensive and went to Paris where he ended up in the arms of Coco Chanel, the famed perfumier. She kept him in style in the Ritz, though by chance he amply repaid her: testing out six new perfumes, she asked him to tell her which he liked most; he sniffed all six then pronounced the fifth to be the best. Chanel No 5 would prove to be one of the most successful brands of all time. Fortunately for Dimitri, he went on in 1924 to marry an American heiress, Audrey Emery of Cincinnati; their son — born in London and thereafter known

*Prince Andrew's only son Philip would marry in 1948 the future Queen Elizabeth, to become the Duke of Edinburgh. All he would inherit from his father would be some old suits, a silver hairbrush and some petty cash.

as Paul Ilyinski, would become a US marine, and end up as Republican mayor of Palm Beach, Florida.

Otherwise, the reality for those who had lost everything was that empty titles were matched by empty pockets. It also concentrated minds. Natasha's financial problems would go on, but inevitably there came a time when she had to face the fact that Michael was dead. Coming to terms with that was also a practical necessity: Michael's assets had to be recovered and his affairs sorted out while they still could be. To achieve that he had to be declared dead by a court, and six years after he had disappeared without trace, that was what happened. On July 5, 1924, the High Court in London granted her letters of administration of the English estates of the late Grand Duke Michael Aleksandrovich of Russia who 'died on or since the 12 day of June 1918, at a place unknown, intestate'.[8] The value of Michael's assets in England were given as only £95, but it was the order not the money which mattered.

Michael was legally dead. And nowhere was the news received more gladly than in a little fishing village across the Channel. For here at last was the opportunity Grand Duke Kirill had so long been waiting for, to take what he had not dared to take before. He would now become the next Emperor.

IN June 1917 Kirill had been given permission by Kerensky to go to Finland; he remained there with his family until 1920, when they all left for Germany. Later he and his German-born wife Ducky and their three children made their home in St Briac, on the Brittany coast. It was here on August 8, one month after the London High Court order, that Kirill tested the waters by issuing his first manifesto, declaring himself 'Guardian of the Throne'[9] — a title which confused everyone but which emboldened him a month later to issue a second manifesto in which he proclaimed himself 'Emperor of All the Russias', and thus as successor to the now legally-dead Michael.[10]

In this manifesto he stated that 'the Russian laws of succession... do not permit the Imperial Throne to remain vacant after the death of the previous Emperor and His nearest Heir have been established'.[11]

This was its own confirmation of the fact that he accepted that Michael had been Emperor; that he had not abdicated as had been claimed in March 1917, and that indeed he was still Emperor until pronounced dead in London in July. If 'the throne is never vacant', then the only person who had been filling it until then was Michael. Nicholas and Alexis were known to have been killed in 1918, so 'the previous Emperor and nearest Heir' did not refer to them. Accordingly Kirill, calling himself 'the senior member of the Tsarist House, and sole legal heir', was declaring himself Michael's successor in obedience to the *Fundamental Laws* governing the imperial house.[12]

No one was likely to say so, or even consider it, but the strategy of the Bolsheviks in denying the monarchists a 'live banner' by pretending that Michael was alive, not dead, now appeared to be vindicated six years later. That apart, the manifesto split the Romanov family, as it still divides them today.

Of the sixteen Grand Dukes who had been alive at the start of the war, only six lived long enough to get out of Russia. Of these, three — Kirill's two brothers, Boris and Andrew unsurprisingly recognised him as Tsar, as did Michael's brother-in-law Sandro. The three others — the 68-year-old former army supreme commander Nikolasha, his younger brother Peter, and Dimitri, did not. It also divided the huge numbers of monarchists then living in exile, in France, Britain, Germany, the Balkans and the United States, after the Red Army finally crushed the Whites in 1922 to become masters of all Russia.

The Dowager Empress was scathing in her condemnation. She protested to Nikolasha from her home in Denmark:

I was most terribly pained when I read Grand Duke Kirill Vladimirovich's manifesto proclaiming himself EMPEROR OF ALL THE RUSSIAS. To date there has been no precise information concerning the fate of My beloved Sons or My Grandson and, for this reason, I consider the proclamation of a new EMPEROR to be premature. There is still no one who could ever extinguish in me the last ray of hope.

I fear that this manifesto will create division. This will not improve the situation but, quite the opposite, will worsen it, while Russia is tormented enough without such a thing.

If it has pleased THE LORD GOD, as he acts in HIS mysterious ways, to summon My beloved sons and grandson to HIMSELF, then, without wishing to look ahead, and with firm hope in the mercy of GOD, I believe that HIS MAJESTY THE EMPEROR will be elected in accordance with Our Basic Laws by the Orthodox Church in concert with the Russian People...I am sure that, as the senior member of the HOUSE OF THE ROMANOVS, You are of the same opinion as Myself.

MARIA.[13]

Kirill had expected bitter opposition. He told Michael's sister Xenia that 'I know full well that I can expect no mercy from all the malicious attacks and accusations of vanity'.[14] The attacks on him were, however, founded on more than malice and charges of self-aggrandisement. The greatest practical objection to Kirill's action was that the 'White Russians' were united only in their opposition to the Bolsheviks and in their belief that their enemy would not rule for long, and come that day they would all return home.

Even among those who favoured a return to the crown, many wanted that to be a decision settled by a constituent assembly — in short, on the same terms as those set out in Michael's manifesto of March 1917. A constitutional monarchy might follow the downfall of the Bolshevik regime, and monarchists naturally hoped that it would, but the critical need was to overthrow the Bolsheviks, not divide the opposition.

Nikolasha, still widely respected as the former Supreme Commander, gave voice to that view when he issued his own manifesto in the wake of Kirill's. The aim, he said, was to re-establish the rule of law in Russia without stipulating the form of government[15] — in effect, another restatement of Michael's manifesto. Kirill had jumped the gun. In any case, why Kirill as Emperor? The so-called Supreme Monarchist Council, which claimed to represent majority monarchist opinion, favoured Dimitri[6] — and as it happened, so did the British government. Clinging to the small print of imperial laws, the high-minded Council held that Kirill — and his two younger brothers — were excluded from the succession because their German-born mother had not converted to Orthodoxy at the time of her marriage, as required by law.[16] It did not help that Kirill had married not only a divorcée but, contrary to the law of the Russian Orthodox Church, his first cousin.

Moreover there was also the abiding memory for many monarchists of the red flag on the tower of his palace in Petrograd in March 1917 and his arrival at the Tauride Palace wearing a red bow as he marched his marines to pledge their support to the Duma, in breach of his oath of allegiance. Kirill would never admit fault then, nor fault now as he named himself Emperor, and wife 'Ducky' as the Empress. He also promoted his son Vladimir from prince to 'Grand Duke' and 'Tsarevich'[17]— a move which would further cement the divisions in the Romanov family.

To be a Grand Duke under the imperial law meant that you were the son or grandson of a Tsar; Vladimir was a great-grandson of Alexander II and as such was entitled to be styled only as a prince. As for making him the Tsarevich and next-in-line to the throne — for many the door was then not only shut but slammed in his face. It has never been opened since.*

Kirill attempted to buy his place in the sun by handing out titles to those who did support him. At the same time, in hoping to placate Natasha he promoted her from 'Countess' — a title she had given herself since Nicholas would never have done so

---

*On Kirill's death in 1928, Vladimir called himself 'Head of the House of Romanov', not Emperor. He styled his daughter Marie as Grand Duchess, and her son George as a Grand Duke, though his father, then a banker in Madrid, was a Prussian prince, a great-grandson of the Kaiser. Maria now claims to be Head of the House of Romanov, and the true successor to the crown, with son George as heir. The other Romanov descendants treat that with scorn.

— to that of Princess Brasova. He also promoted son George from Count, the title which Nicholas had reluctantly conceded under pressure from Michael, to Prince Brasov.[18] Natasha simply shrugged. It was all now meaningless anyway, but so be it. She would call herself Princess, if only because of the satisfaction it gave her to have the Romanovs bidding for her favour.

AS Dimitri had done, Natasha moved to Paris in 1927 'since life in London is three times more expensive than in France'.[19] She had sent George to Harrow, one of the best-known public schools in Britain, and he completed his last year there in July of that year, just before his seventeenth birthday. In Paris, Natasha enrolled him in the exclusive, and equally expensive, École des Roches at Verneuil, fifty miles outside the capital; he would go on from there to the Sorbonne.

George brought with him to France his prized Norton motorcycle which he insisted on driving at high speed, much to the terror of Natasha. He had now grown to be as tall as his father, with the same slim figure. 'He was uncannily like Uncle Misha', thought Tata. He had the same look about him; his voice was similar; he even walked in much the same way.

Some émigrés within the divided Russian colony in Paris mentioned his name as the 'true successor' to the imperial throne in preference to the discredited and disliked Kirill but 'George treated the claims made on his behalf with indifference, tinged with amusement'.

It was in Paris that George, but not his mother, became the first beneficiary of the various interests which, on paper, sustained Natasha's hopes of financial security in the future. In 1928 the Dowager Empress died three years after the death of her sister, the Dowager Queen Alexandra. Hvidore, the Danish property which they jointly owned, was sold. King George V and his sisters waived their claims; the proceeds, amounting to the equivalent of $57,000 in the values of the day — some $500,000 today — were therefore divided equally between Michael's two sisters,

Xenia and Olga, and his son George. It was a very handsome legacy and a more-than-welcome windfall. For George, with almost $20,000 in his bank, he could feel himself a rather rich young man. He put some ten per cent of it immediately into the purchase of a brand-new Sports Chrysler motor car.[21] In July 1931, having finished his final examinations at the Sorbonne, he decided to celebrate with a holiday in the south of France. He and a Dutch friend planned to drive to Cannes, George promising Natasha that he would be back in two weeks, in time for his twenty-first birthday.

Having waved them goodbye, Natasha was playing bezique that afternoon with friends when the telephone rang in the hallway of her rented apartment at 5 rue Copernic, off the Place Victor Hugo. The Chrysler had skidded on the road near Sens, and crashed into a tree. The Dutch boy, who had been at the wheel, was killed; George was in hospital; both thighs were broken and he had severe internal injuries.

Distraught, Natasha took the first train southwards, arriving at the hospital in Sens just before midnight. She sat by his bedside all night, but there was no hope for him. George died without recovering consciousness at 11.30 a.m. on Tuesday, July 21, 1931. His body was brought back to Paris and buried in the fashionable cemetery at Passy, near the Trocadero. Hundreds attended the funeral, with Dimitri heading the procession behind the coffin, followed by a black-veiled Natasha.[22]

Natasha had bought two plots lying side by side at Passy, George was laid in one; the other she reserved for herself but not as the princess she had been styled three years earlier. On the cemetery receipt the name she gave was simply Mme De Brassow. So much for her view of Emperor Kirill.

THERE would be little left for Natasha after that. *'Oh Misha! Oh, Georgie!'* she would weep in private. At 51 she was still beautiful though her hair was snow-white, but her life was over. The end would come 20 years later, but even that in itself spoke volumes about its emptiness. Then penniless and living alone in the tiny attic room of an apartment at 11 rue Monsieur on the Left Bank, her landlady threw her out when it was discovered that Natasha had cancer. Taken to the Laënneck, the nearby charity hospital in the rue de Sevres in the 7th *arrondissement* she died at 3.50 pm on January 23, 1952.[24] The only clue to her identity among her pathetic effects was a faded Russian birth certificate dated 71 years earlier and naming her as plain Nathalie Sheremetevskaya — the name duly typed onto her death certificate.

However, as word spread in the dwindling band of Russian *émigrés* in Paris that Princess Brasova had died, they did what they could to give her burial the dignity denied her death. They took her to Passy to lie beside her beloved son George. Their grave is marked by a Russian cross of stone, above a chest-tomb of green-and-black marble, with the simple, gold-lettered inscription: *Fils et Epouse de S.A.I. Grand Duc Michel de Russie.*

And in far-away Perm they would not forget either. Although Michael's grave has never been found, a chapel to his memory and honour now stands in the wood where he was murdered, and there is a plaque to him on the wall of the hotel from which he was abducted. And interest increases: in 2010, the then Senator for St Petersburg, Viktor Yevtukhov — promoted deputy Minister of Justice in February 2011 — said: 'We should know more about this man and remember him, because this memory can give our society the ethical foundation we need'. Better late than never.

Many years ago, in 1927 when he was building a literary reputation in Riga, Vladimir Gushchik, the sometime Bolshevik commissar in Gatchina who had so admired Michael, wrote an epitaph for him in his book *Taina Gatchinskogo dvortsa*, and it is one which could well stand today:

And now, remembering this man, I wonder how You, Russia, will wash away his innocent blood? Will you ultimately be able to redeem the death of Michael the Last? [25]

How I wish for a 'wise government'
for my dear Russia, so that we could
boast of it to all European states...'
— *Michael letter, June 5, 1915*

Republic or monarchy — what
does it matter if only there
is order and justice in the land
— *Michael's diary, September 2, 1917*

Romanovs murdered by the Bolsheviks, 1918-1919

June 12/13, 1918, Perm

Grand Duke Michael Aleksandrovich (*Emperor Michael II*)

July 16/17, 1918, Ekaterinburg

Grand Duke Nicholas Alexandrovich (*Emperor Nicholas II*)
Grand Duchess Alexandra Fedorov (*Empress Alexandra*)
Grand Duke Alexis Nikolaeovich, aged 14 (*Tsarevich*)
Grand Duchess Olga, aged 23
Grand Duchess Tatiana, aged 21
Grand Duchess Marie, aged 19
Grand Duchess Anastasia, aged 17

July 17/18, 1918, Alapaevsk

Grand Duke Serge Mikhailovich, aged 64
Grand Duchess Elizabeth (*Ella*), aged 54
Prince Ioann Konstantinovich, aged 32
Prince Konstantin Konstaninovich *(brother)*, aged 27
Prince Igor Konstantinovich *(brother)*, aged 24
Prince Vladimir Paley *(son, Grand Duke Paul below)*, aged 21

January 19, 1919, Fortress St Peter & St Paul

Grand Duke Paul Aleksandrovich, aged 58
Grand Duke Dimitri Konstantinovich, aged 58
Grand Duke Nicholas Mikhailovich (*Bimbo*), aged 60
Grand Duke George Mikhailovich, aged 55

ACKNOWLEDGEMENTS

AT the 90th anniversary of Michael's death in Perm, in June 2008, I went there to join in the ceremonies to mark that day, little knowing what to expect. I was both astonished and delighted at the scale of the events, and by the thousands who turned out to honour his memory. Forgotten? Clearly not in Perm, where he was murdered in 1918 but is still revered by many. It was those three days of marches, of church services, of concerts, and of an academic conference to discuss his life, which seemed its own proof that Michael was dead but not gone. And that the more Russia knows about him, the greater the hope that it can bridge that gap between the Soviet version of history, and the reality. Hence this book.

However, this would not have been possible without the long research that had gone into a prior book, of which I was co-author with my wife Rosemary, *Michael & Natasha*. And as then, the many people and institutions we thanked deserve thanks again.

In Russia, I remain enormously grateful to all those at the State Archive of the Russian Federation in Moscow who gave us such enormous help over many months — the director, Sergei Mironenko, the deputy director Alya Barkovets, and the historian Vladimir Khrustalev, in particular. As ever, I also remain in the debt of Dr Aschen Mikoyan, of Moscow University, whose grandfather was chairman of the Supreme Soviet, and who spent many months editing some 3,000 pages of letters and documents about Michael. I shall always remember her blurting out — *'how could we have done this to him!'* — and I know that many other Russians now feel the same. I must also pay tribute to the unfailing 'detective work' of Dr Aleksandr Ushakov, who found documents that added considerably to an understanding of Michael and his times, as did Dr Sergei Romanyuk in researching documents in other Moscow archives. The staff at the Russian State Historical Archive in St Petersburg were equally helpful as were those at Gatchina Palace, as well as in the Perm archives.

In England, Richard Davies, archivist at the Leeds Russian Archives at the University of Leeds, is someone to whom I shall ever remain grateful, for his archive possesses a wealth of personal documentation on Michael, generously given to it by Natasha's grand-daughter by her first marriage, Pauline Gray.

In the United States, there are several institutions which have invaluable source material on the period covered here, including the Hoover Institution at Stanford University, and the Houghton Library, Harvard University. At Columbia University, we had Michael's war diaries 1915-1918 translated for the first time.

In Europe, given the amount of time that Michael spent there, the trail inevitably follows in his footsteps — Paris, Vienna, Cannes, Berlin, Copenhagen, Switzerland. A great many people helped in tracing him, not least Professor Dr Ferdinand Opll at the *Stadt-und Landsarchiv* in Vienna, who provided more information about Michael's marriage than the embarrassed and out-witted *Okhrana* managed to do afterwards in 1912. Again, each and everyone is to be thanked.

Finally, I should pay tribute to Dr Vladislav Krasnov, born in Perm, but now a senior American academic, for his enthusiasm in promoting the memory of Michael in his home city and beyond. It was he and his committee who erected a memorial plaque to Michael on the walls of the hotel in Perm from which he was abducted in June, 1918 — still now much as it was then — and since then they have taken their cause to St Petersburg and Moscow. It is to their credit. No one loved his country more than Michael. If one day his country will come to embrace him also, then his brutal death in a dark wood might prove not to be the end of his story.

Chapter Notes

MA = Michael
NS= Natasha
MA's diary — Michael's diary 1915-1918
N = Nicholas II (letters) or in 'N's diary'
AF = Empress Alexandra
DE = Dowager Empress Marie Federovna
GAPO = State Archive Perm District
GARF = State Archive, Russian Federation, Moscow
LRA = Leeds Russian Archive, University of Leeds
PRO = Public Record Office, London
RA = Royal Archives, Windsor
Vienna SLA = *Wiener Stadt-und Landsarchiv*

Dates are according to Russian calendar, unless shown in *italics*

1. Love and Duty

1. Vassili, p 105
2. Alexander, *Once a Grand Duke*, p 78
3. Witte, *Memoirs* p 19
4. Alexander, p 80
5. *Ibid* p 168-9
6. Nicholas II, *Journal Intime.* (hereafter N's diary) p 125
7. Vassili, p 105
8. Alexander p 161
9. Nicholas of Greece, p 181
10. Polovtsov, pp 126-7
11. Melgunov, p 229
12. Mossolov, p 95
13. *Ibid*
14. Grand Duke Konstantin K's diary, February 26, 1904, cited Maylunas/ Mironenko p 240
15. Dillon, p 41
16. Buxhoeveden, p 92
17. Mossolov, p 33
18. Witte, p 194
19. *Ibid*
20. Chavchavadze, p 107, Radziwill, *Secrets*, pp 44-6
21. Sullivan, p 181
22. Gelardi, pp 91-3.115
23. Chavchavadze, p 235
24. *Ibid*, 242
25. Radziwill, *Secrets*, p 60
26. *Ibid*, pp 69-70; Chavchavadze, p128
27. Kleinmichel, pp 66-8
28. N to DE , October 20, 1902, p 170
29. Vorres, p 115
30. *Observer*, London, *October 7*, 1906. The story also appeared in *The Sunday Times*, and *Reynold News*, London.
31. *The Times*, London, *November 5, 1908*

2. A Scandalous Exile

1. State Archive of the Moscow Region, f. 2170-8-1-64;.*Vsya Moskva;* Moscow Historical Archive, f.179-24-237-15
2. Natasha's father was still registered as living in the Vozdvizhenka apartment eighteen years later in 1924
3. 13. MA to NS, November 3, 1909, GARF 622/12

4. MA to NS, July 28, 1909, GARF 622/09
5. Letter to Natasha's granddaughter Pauline Gray, December 17, 1973, LRA MS 1363/136
6. Trubetskoi, 4, p 110
7. NS to MA, August 8, 1911, GARF 668/76
8. Radziwill, *Secrets*, p 92
9. Trubetskoi 4, p 110
10. *Ibid*
11. Majolier, p 35
12. Trubetskoi, 4, p 117
13. Okhrana report, September 6,1911, cited Maylunas/Mironenko, p 345
14. *Ibid,* December 17, 1912, pp 364-5
15. MA to N, October 6, 1912, GARF 601/1301
16. MA to N, October 14, 1912, GARF *ibid*
17. St Savva marriage register, No 35, 1912, Vienna SLA
18. Paléologue, *February 10,* 1916, Vol II, p 172
19. Marriage register, Vienna SLA
20. *Ibid*
21. *Ibid*
22. *Okhrana* Paris report December 17, 1912, cited Maylunas/Mironenko pp 364-5
23. N to DE, November 21, 1912 cited Maylunas/Mironenko, p 363
24. N to DE November 7 1912, *Letters,* p 283-4
25. *Ibid*
26. The ten-point memorandum is undated andunsigned, but was clearly written in early November 1912; Fredericks was the court minister responsible for matters relating to the Grand Dukes. GARF 601/1301 f.175-6
27. MA to N, November 16, 1912, GARF 601/1301. MA's 'terms' were attached to this letter.
28. N to DE, November 21, 1912, *Letters,* p 285
29. George V to N, *December 16,* 1912, cited Maylunas/Mironenko p 363
30. British ambassador to Sir Edward Grey, January 16, 1913, PRO/FO 371/1743
31. *Ibid*
32. *Ibid January 4,* 1913
33. *Ibid January 16,* 1913
34. Mossolov, p 65
35. Radziwill, *Secrets,* p 94
36. MA to N, November 1, 1912, GARF 601/1301
37. Majolier, p 81
38. MA to N, April 23, 1914, *f. ibid*
39. Polovtsov, p 115
40. Natasha's documents, LRA 1363/72
41. Majolier, p 46

3. A Brief Peace

1. Vorres, p 64
2. Queen Victoria's Journal, *October 8,* 1899, RA
3. Majolier, p 82
4. Xenia's diary July 12, 1913, cited Maylunas/Mironenko p 379
5. *Ibid*
6. *Ibid*
7. DE to N, July 27, 1913, *Letters,* pp 287-8
8. Knebworth House archive
9. Majolier, p 43
10. MA to N, March 8, 1914, *f. ibid*
11. MA accounts, 1914-1916, Paddockhurst Estate Office
12. Chavchavadze, p 178
13. George V to N, 6, 1912, GARF 601
14. *The Times,* London, *December 30, 1913, January 10, 1914, May 13,1 1914.*
15. Natasha continued to use her coronet notepaper when she returned to Russia, notwithstanding that she had no title.GARF 668/77-8

16. *The Times,* London, *January 10, 1914*
17. *Ibid, December 2, 1913*
18. On *May 9, 1914,* LRA 1363/39
19. *May 19, 1914, ibid*
20. *Ibid,* 1363/386
21. Majolier, p 47
22. Gray, p 38
23 *The Times,* London, *July17, 1914*
24 Majolier, p 49
25. *Ibid,* p 42
26. George V's diary, RA, although for security reasons the departure was not recorded in the Court Circular until *August 20, 1914*
27. Yousoupoff, *Lost Splendour,* p 180
28. Poutiatine
29. Majolier, p 53

4. War Hero

1. The Times, London, *January 17,* 1913
2. Lincoln, p 76
3. *Ibid,* p 83
4. Kournakoff, p 55
5. Polovtsov, p 115
6. *Ibid,* p 127
7. Kournakoff, p 80
8. Polovtssov, pp 116-7
9. Kournakoff, p 55
10. Polovtsov, pp 126-7
11. Paléologue, Vol 1 p 302
12. N to AF, *Letters,* October 27, 1914, p 10
13. Polovtsov, p 138
14. Paléologue, *February 10,* 1916. Vol II p 172
15. MA to N, November 15, 1914, GARF 601/1301
16. Polovtsov, p 134
17. *Ibid,* p 132
18. Poutiatine
19. MA's Diary, January 2, 1915
20. MA to NS, January 16, 1915, GARF 622/20
21. *Ibid* January 15, 1915

22. *Ibid,* January 20, 1915
23. *Ibid,* January 22, 1915
24. N to AF, November 19, 1914, p 14
25. MA to NS, January 22, 1915, GARF 622/20
26. *Ibid,* February 16, 1915
27. *Ibid,* February 4, 1915
28. *Ibid,* January 22, 1915
29. MA's Diary, January 21-2, 1915
30. *Ibid,* February 9, 1915
31. MA to NS, February 16, 1915, GARF 668/78
32. Polovtsov, p 135
33. *Ibid,* p 138
34. *Fund of the Imperial Russian Cavalry,* Hoover Institution archives
35. Krylov, 'Istoricheskie miniatyury', *Moskva,* Moscow, 3, 1990
36. Radziwill, Secrets, p 96
37. Alexander, p 303
39. Polovtsov, p 138
39. Gushchik, pp 12-13
40. *Ibid,* pp 28-9
41. MA's diary, April 17, 1915
42. N to AF, March 3, 1915, p.32
43. AF to N, *Letters,* p 54
44. MA to N, March 14, 1915, *f. ibid*
45. Imperial ukase of March 26, 1915, cited Jaques Ferrand, *Il est toujours des Romanov!* Paris, 1995, p 25
46. MA's Diary, April 10, 1915
47. AF to N, April 4, 1915, p 62

5. Alexandra The Great

1. MA's Diary, April 19, 1915
2. NS to MA, June 10, 1915, GARF 668/78
3. MA to NS, June 14, 1915, GARF 622/20
4. *Ibid,* June 20, 1915
5. NS to MA, June 10, 1915, *NS f. ibid*
6. MA to NS, April 7, 1915, *MA f. ibid*
7. Washburn, pp 261-2
8. MA to NS, June 10,1915, *f. ibid*
9. NS to MA, June 20,1915, *f. ibid*
10. MA to NS, June 5, 1915, *f. ibid*

11. MA's Diary, July 30, 1915
12. *Ibid*, August 7, 15, 1915
13. MA to NS, June 20, 1915, *f. ibid*
14. Grand Duke Andrew's diary, cited Golder (ed) p 239
15. Knox, p 332
16. Paléologue, *August 17*, 1915, Vol II, p 60
17. Brusilov, p.180
18. AF to N, August 22, 1915, p 14
19. N to AF, August 25, 1915, pp 71-2
20. AF to N, August 28, 1915, p 125
21. Vyrubova, p 100
22. Grand Duke Konstantin's diary, August 25, 1902, cited Maylunas/ Mironenko, p 219
23. Xenia's diary, August 29, 1902, *ibid*, p 217
24. Paléologue, October 12, 1915, Vol I, p 83
25. Bruce Lockhart, pp 128-9
26. Knox, p 334
27. Paléologue, *April 27*, 1915, Vol 1 pp 333-4
28. Grand Duke Andrew's diary, cited Golder, p 240
29. *Ibid*
30. Paléologue, *September 2*, 1915, Vol II, pp 66-67
31. Buchanan, p 238
32. N to AF, August 25, 1915, p 72
33. *Ibid*, August 26, 1915, p 73
34. *Ibid*, August 27, 1915, p 74
35. AF to N, August 31, 1915, p 132
36. *Ibid*, September 6,1915, p 143
37. N to AF, September 11, 1915, p 87
38. *Ibid*, September 14, 1915, p 89
39 AF to N, September 16, 1915, p 168
40. *Ibid*, September 11, 1915, p 158
41. N to F, September 17, 1915, pp 90-1
42. AF to N, September 9, 1915, p 153
43. Paléologue, June 15, 1915, Vol II. pp 13-14
44. AF to N, June 25, 1915, p 110
45. *Ibid*, August 30, 1915, p 131
46. Lincoln, p 159
47. AF to N, September 11,1915, p157
48. *Ibid*, September 12, 1915, p 159
49. *Ibid*, September 14, 1915, p 168
50. N to AF, September 16, 1915, p 90
51. AF to N, September 17, 1915, p 176

6. Rival Courts

1. Majolier, p 84
2. Gushchik, p 44
3. *Ibid*, p 29
4. Majolier, p 83
5. Gushchik, p44
6. Abrikossow, p 234
7. MA Diary, October-December 1915
8. NS to MA, December 10, 1914, GARF 668/77
9. Dimitri to NS, January 20, 1916, GARF 622/28
10. MA's Diary, October 18, 1915
11. *Ibid*, August 10, 1915
12. *Ibid*, October 18/November 25, 1915
13. Paléologue, *February 10*, 1915, Vol II, p 173
14. Abrikossow, p 235
15. *Ibid*, p 234
16. Kerensky, *Memoirs*, p 143
17. *Ibid*, p 147
18. Abrikossow, p 236
19. *Ibid* p 233
20. Bruce Lockhart, p 160
21. Abrikossow, p 237
22. AF to N, January 7, 1916, p 256
23. Paléologue, February 6, 1916, Vol II, p 166
24. Rodzyanko, *Rasputin*, p 175
25. Paléologue, *September 15*, 1915, Vol II, p 74
26. *Ibid, February 22*, 1916, p 188
27. MA's Diary, February 9, 1916
28. Rodzyanko, *Rasputin*, p 177-8
29. *Ibid*
30. MA's Diary, February 9, 1916
31. AF to N, February 5, 1916, p 276

7. War On Two Fronts

1. Knox, p 435
2. MA's diary, December 11-27, 1915
3. NS to MA, February 29, 1916, GARF 668/79
4. *Ibid,* May 9, 1916
5. *Ibid,* July 1, 1916
6. *Ibid,* March 11, 1916
7. *Ibid,* June 20, 1916
8. *Ibid,* July 9, 1916
9. Paléologue, *February 10,* 1916, Vol II, p 171
10. *Ibid*
11. NS to MA, July 16, 1916, *f. ibid*
12. MA to NS, August 5, 1916, GARF 622/21
13. NS to MA, March 21, 1916, *f. ibid*
14. *Ibid,* March 25/March 11, 1916
15. MA to NS, March 20, 1916, *f. ibid*
16. NS to MA, July 19, 1916, *f. ibid*
17. *Ibid*
18. MA to NS, August 2, 1916, *f. ibid*
19. MA's diary, June 29, 1916
20. MA to NS, June 23, 1916, *f. ibid*
21. Brusilov, cited Lincoln, p 255
22. MA's diary, December 1, 1916; the award was made on November 23, citation *Fund for the Museum of Russian Cavalry,* Hoover Institution archive
23. MA's diary, August 23, 1916
24. *Ibid*, September 2, 1916
25. N to AF, April 4, 1916, p 166
26. AF to N, May 25, 1916, p 339
27. Ibid, September 13, 1916, p 398
28. MA's diary, September 30, 1916
29. MA to N, November 11, 1916, GARF 601/1301

8. Murder Most Fair

1. AF to N, March 12, 1916, p 297
2. Knox, p 412
3. Sazonov, p 292
4. MA to NS, July 20, 1916, GARF 622/21
5. Grand Duke George Mikhailovich to N, November 24, 1916, cited Golder, p 248
6. Yousoupoff, p 199
10. *Ibid* p 211
11. Paléologue, November 19, 1916, Vol III, p 96
12. Yousoupoff, p 205
13. *Ibid,* p 212
14. *Ibid,* p 223
15. Buchanan, Meriel, p 147
16. Yousoupoff, p 230
17. *Ibid,* p 232
18. Pares, p 408
19. Paléologue, *December 30,* 1916, Vol III, p 131
20. Yousoupoff, p 242
21. *Ibid,* p 245
22. Paléologue, *January 3,* 1916, Vol III, p 136
23. Pares, p 410
24. MA's diary, December 19, 1916
25. Poutiatine
26. AF to N, August 16, 1916, p 383
27. Dimitri to NS, January 16, 1917, GARF 622/28
28. *Ibid,* February 6, 1916

9. Palace Plotters

1. Pares, p 416
2. Paléologue, *January 12,* 1917. Vol III p 162
3. *Ibid, January 9,* 1917, p 157
4. Paley, p 38; Marie, p 279
5. Paléologue, *January 152,* 1917. Vol III p 167
6. *Ibid, January 21,* 1917, pp 170-1
7. Rodzyanko, *Rasputin,* pp 246-7
8. Buchanan, Vol II, p 43
9. Knox, p 515
10. Rodzyanko, *Rasputi*n, pp 248-50; *Memoirs,* cited Golder,pp 117-8
11. Mme Rodzyanko to Prince Yusopov's mother, January 7, 1917, cited Vulliamy (ed) p 122
12. Rodzyanko, *Rasputin,* pp 253-4; *Memoirs,*pp 118-9

13. MA's diary, January 29. 1917
14. *Ibid,* January 28-9, 1917
15. Brusilov, pp 287-8
16. *Ibid*
17. MA's diary, January 29. 1917
18. Sttankevich, p 31
19. AF to N, September 2, 1915, p 135
20. Paléologue, *April 2,* 1916, Vol II, p 227
21. Guchkov, p 205
22. *Ibid,* p206
23. *Ibid*
24. Pipes, p 269; Katkov, p 277
25. Rodzyanko, pp 244-5
26. Pares, p 428

10. 'Make Yourself Regent'

1. Alexander, p 312
2. Vyrubova,, cited Maylunas/ Mironenko, p 530
3. Alexander, p 316
4. Rodzyanko, Rasputin, p 259
5. Ibid, p 260
6. Sandro to his brother Bimbo, February 14, 1917, cited Maylunas/ Mironenko, p 530
7. AF to N, February 22, 1917, cited Maylunas/Mironenko, p 536
8. N to AF, February 23, 1917, *ibid,* 537
9. MA's diary, February 25, 1917
10. Buranov/Khrustalev. Doc. 7, p 34
11. MA's diary, February 26, 1917
12. *Okhrana* report, February 24, 1917, Steinberg/Khrustalev, Doc 9, pp 36-7
13. Rodzyanko to N, February 26, 1917, *ibid,* Doc 11, p 40
14. Pares, p 443
15. Knox, p 516
16. Pares, p. 444
17. MA's diary, February 27, 1917
18. AF to N, February 26, 1917, GARF 601/115
19. N to AF, February 26, 1917, GARF 601/115
20. *Ibid*, February 26,7, 1917
21. Belyaev to N, Febuary 27, 1917, cited Steinberg/Khrustalev, Doc 9, p 81
22. Pares, p 441, Buranov/Khrustalev, 15, p 42
23. Shulgin, Dni, p 178-9
24. *Ibid*, p 171
25. Matveev's diary, February 27, 1917
26. MA' diary, February 27, 1917
27. Pares, p 451
28. MA's diary, February 27, 1917
29. Rodzyanko, cited Buranov/ Khrustalev, 17, p 42
30. *Ibid*
31. Milyukov, *Vospominaniya,* Vol II, p 275
32. MA to General Alekseev, Buranov/ Khrustalev, 72, p 86-7
33. *Ibid*
34. *Ibid*
35. MA's diary, February 27, 1917
36. N to Prince Golitsin, February 27, 1917, GARF 601/2089
37. MA's diary, February 27, 1917
38. *Ibid*
39. *Ibid*
40. Poutiatine

11. Address Unknown

1. Karkov, p 310
2. Nz's diary, February 28, 1917, cited Maylunas/Mironenko, p 541
3. Gen. Alekseev to Pskov,,February 27, 1917, Buronov/Khrustalev, 70, p 85
4. *Ibid,* February 28,1917, 73, p 89
5. N to AF, telegram, February 28, 1917, GARF 640/108
6. Pares, p 456
7. Dehn, p172
8. Benckendorff, pp 2-3
9. *Ibid*, pp 14-15
10. Buxhoeveden, p 255
11. Dehn, p 156
12. Katkov, p 312
13. Pares, p 459
14. N's diary, March 1,1917 cited Maylunas/Mironenko, p 541

15. Vyrubova, p 209, Bykov, p 32
16. Nabokov, p 45-6
17. Shulgin, pp 170-1
18. Ibid, 189-91, Pares, p 454
19. Kerensky, Catastrophe, pp 36-7
20. *Ibid*, p 21
21. Nabokov, p 43
22. MA's diary, February 28, 1917
23. *Izvestia*, No 3 March 1, 1917, BuranovKhrustalev Doc 31, p 52
24. Paléologue, *March 13*, 1917, Vol III, pp 229-30
25. Kschessinska, p 164
26. Buchanan, Meriel, p 168
27. MA's diary, February 28, 1917
28. Poutiatine
29. Matveev's Diary, March 1, 1917
30. MA to NS, February 28, 1917, GARF 622/22
31. Grand Duke's manifesto, March 1, 1917, GARF 5881/36732.
32. AF to N, March 2, 1917, Steinberg/Khrustalev, Doc 24, p 94
33. MA to NS, March 1, 1917, GARF 622/22
34. Buchanan to Foreign Office, London, March 14, 1917, PRO/FO 371/2459
35. Polovtsov, pp 151-2
36. Cyril, p 209
37. Grand Duke Paul to Kirill, March 2, 1917, Paley, pp 55-6
38. Kirill to Paul, *ibid*, p 56
39. Gen. Dubensky, cited Lincoln p 337
40. Shulgin, p 269
41. BuranovKhrustalev Doc 89, p 102
42. Rodzyanko to Ruzsky, March 2, 1917, *ibid*, Doc 78, pp 92-3

12. Poisoning The Chalice

1. Alekseev to Pskov, March 2, 1917, Buranov/Khrustalev, Doc 79, p 94
2. Alekseev to army commanders, March 2, 1917, *ibid* Doc 80, p 94
3. Ruzsky, cited Lincoln, p 340
4. Grand Duchess George, *Memoirs,* p 182
5. Alekseev to N, March 2, 1917, GARF 601/2100, cited Steinberg/Khrustalev, Doc 20, pp 89-90
6. Lincoln, p 341
7. N to Rodzyanko, March 2, 1917, Buranov/Khrustalev, Doc 86a, p 98
8. Ruzsky, cited *ibid,* Doc 89, p 103
9. *Ibid*
10. Lincoln, p 341
11. George V's diary, *March 15*, 1917, RA
12. MA's diary, March 1, 1917
13. Alexander, p 168, Chavchavadze p 173
14. Paléologue, Vol III, mutiny 2nd Brigade, *September 1,* 1916, p 17; Petrograd mutiny, *October 16, November 9,* 1916, pp 74-5, p 83
15. Sukhanov, p 116
16. *Ibid,* pp 120-2; Milyukov, p 34
17. Sukhanov, p 122
18. *Ibid,* pp 153-4
19. *Ibid,* pp 154
20. *Ibid,* p 155

13. 'A Father's Feelings'

1. Shulgin, pp 238-9
2. *Ibid*, pp 266-7
3. *Ibid*
4. *Ibid*
5. Guchkov, GARF 601/2099. cited Steinberg/Khrustalev, Doc 25, p 97
6. Nicholas, *ibid*
7. Mossolov, p 124; Benckendorff, p 46
8. Gen Boldyrev, p 198
9. Protocol of talks, Steinberg/Khrustalev, Doc 25, p 97
10. Katkov, p 343
11. Gen. Dubensky, cited Lincoln, p 344
12. N's diary, March 2, 1917; Pipes p 469
13. Milyukov, *Revolution*, p 36
14. *Ibid*, p 37
15. Kerensky, p 214
16. *Ibid*

17. Kerensky, Catastrophe, p 67
18. Rodzyanko to Ruzsky, March 3, 1917, Buranov/Khrustalev, Doc 95, 110-11
19. Alekseev to army commanders, March 3, 1917, *ibid*, Doc 97, pp 112-3
20. Matveev's diary, March 3, 1917

14. Emperor Michael

1. Melgunov, p 230
2. Marie, p 230
3. Cantacuzène, p 122
4. Almedingen, p 195
5. Ibid
6. Shulgin, Dni, pp 263-4
7. *Ibid*, p 265; Bykov p 27
8. *Ibid*, pp 266-9
9. Nabokov, p 46
10. Matveev's Diary, March 3, 1917
11. Paley, p 59
12. *Ibid*, p 61
13. Kerensky, *Catastrophe*, p 68
14. Majolier, p 99
15. Matveev's diary, Wednesday, March 1, 1917
16. Poutiatine
17. Kerensky, *Catastrophe*, p 69
18. Shulgin, *Dni*, p 277
19. Matveev's diary. March 3, 1917
20. Kerensky, *Catastrophe*, p 59

15. Playing For Time

1. N's diary, March 2, 1917, GARF 601/265, cited Steinberg/Khrustalev. Doc 30, p 107
2. Nabokov, p 49
3. Kerensky, *Memoirs*, p 207
4. Shulgin, *Dni*, p 272
5. Ibid, p 274
6. Rodzyanko, *Archiv russkoi revolyutsii*, p 61
7. Milyukov, *Revolution*, p 38
8. Shulgin, *Dni*, p 196
9. Milyukov, *Vospominaniya*, Vol II, p 17, cited Katkov, p 408
10. Shulgin, Dni, pp 263-74
11. *Ibid*, p 274
12. Paléologue, *March 17*, 1917, Vol III, p 240
13. Kerensky, *Catastrophe*, p 69
14. *Ibid*, p 70
15. Paléologue, *March 17*, 1917, Vol III, p 241
16. Rodzyanko to Alekseev, March 3, 1917, Buranov/Khrustalev Doc 98, pp 111-2
17. Nabokov, pp 35-6
18. Baron Nolde, *Nabokov*, p 19
19. Poutiatine
20. Shulgin, *Dni*, pp264-74
21. Petrograd Soviet Executive Committee, March 3, 1917, Buranov/Khrustalev Doc 142, p 177
22. Shulgin, *Dni*, p 277
23. Matveev's diary, March 3, 1917
24. Wonlar-Larsky, pp 166-7, 171
25. N's diary, March 3, 1917, cited Maylunos/Mironenko, p 551
26. Nicholas's telegram, LRA MS/1363/141
27. Nabokov, pp 48-9
28. *Ibid*, p 53
29. Michael's manifesto, GARF 668/131
30. Nabokov, p 54
31. Nolde, *Nabokov*, p 19
32. *Ibid*, p 10
33. Nabokov, p 54
34. *Ibid*, p 53
35. Nolde, *Nabokov*, p 20
36. Shulgin, *Dni*, p 279
37. Paléolog MA's due, *March 17*, 1917, Vol III, p 241
38. Nolde, Nabokov, p 20.
39. Lomonosov, cited Melgunov p 236
40. Ibid, p 237
41. N's diary, March 3, 1917, cited Maylunos/Mirenenko, p 551
42. Alexander p 320
43. MA's diary, March 3, 1917

16. Retreat to Gatchina

1. MA to NS, March 3, 1917, GARF 622/22
2. Poutiatine
3. MA's diary, March 4, 1917
4. *Ibid*
5. Poutiatine
6. Grand Duchess George, p 179
7. Russian newspapers, LRA MS 1000/5
8. Paléologue, *March 17*, 1917, Vol III, p 243
9. Buchanan, Vol Ii, p 71
10. *The Times*, London, *March 19*, 1917
11. Cantacuzène, p 122
12. Grand Duchess George, p 180
13. Maklakov, cited Katkov, p 411
14. Paley, pp 60, 67
15. Mossolov, p 69
16. Dimitri to Yusupov, April 23, 1917, *Red Archives*, p 127
17. Grand Duchess George, p 182
18. MA's diary, April 5, 1917
19. *Ibid*, April 5, 1917
20. Grand Duchess George, p 183
21. Pipes, p 307
22. Hanbury-Williams, p 179
23. Knox, p 613
24. MA letter, May 5, 1917, LRA MS 1407
25. Kournakoff,, p 317
26. Grand Duchess George, p 184-5
27. *Ibid*, p 185
28. Majolier, p 83
29. Gilliard, p 217-8
30. Rose, p 212, *April 6,* 1917
31. *Ibid*, pp 212-3
32. *June 4, 1917*, cited Rose, p 216
33. Ibid, p 215

17. Farewell My Brother

1. Majolier, p 100
2. Grand Duchess George, p 182
3. MA's diary, May 5, 1917
4. *Ibid,* May 5-14, 1917
5. Polovtsov, pp 207-8
6. Kerensky, p 120
7. MA's diary, July 31, 1917
8. Polovtsov, p 292
9. MA's diary, July 31, 1917
10. Benckendorff, p 107
11. Wilton, p 184 (Kobylinski deposition)
12. Kerensky, Catastrophe, p 257
13. Benckendorff, p 107
14. MA's diary, July 31, 1917

18. Kerensky's Captive

1. MA's diary, August 21, 1917
2. Ibid, August 22, 1917
3. Pipes, p 447
4. Polovtsov, p 208
5. Kerensky, *Murder,* p 138
6. *Ibid*, p 195, *Catastrophe*, pp 137-9
7. MA's diary, August 25, 1917
8. *Ibid*, August 29, 1917
9. Pipes, p 441
10. Lincoln,, p 415
11. Kerensky, Catastrophe, p 318
12. Pipes, p 441
13. *Ibid,* p 467
14. *Ibid,* p 460
15. *Ibid,* p 41
16. Lincoln, p 423
17. MA's diary, August 29, 1917
18. *Ibid,* August 31, 1917
19. *Ibid,* September 4, 1917
20. Buchanan to Lord Stamfordham, September 7, 1917 RA GV P 284 A/26
21. MA's diary, September 6, 1917
22. Telegram to Balfour, PRO FO/371/3015, circulated to 'King and Cabinet'
23. MA's diary, September 13/15, 1917
24. *Ibid,* September 2, 1917
25. Dimitri's diary, October 1917

19. Citizen Michael

1. Kerensky, Catastrophe, pp 333-4
2. Pipes, p 489
3. MA's diary, October 19/25, 1917
4. *Ibid*, October 26, 1917
5. *Ibid*, October 27, 1917
6. *Ibid*, October 30, 1917
7. Majolier, p 118
8. MA's diary, October 31, 1917
9. Wonlar-Larsky pp 172-3; in Russian, her married name was Vonlyarlyarskaya
10. *Ibid*
11. MA's diary, November 1, 1917
12. *Ibid*, November 4, 1917
13. Poutiatine
14. *Ibid*
15. MA's diary, November 7, 1917
16. Ibid, November 13, 1917
17. Ibid, November 15, 1917
18. Majolier, p 112
19. MA's diary, November 15, 1917
20. Buranov/Khrustalev, *Gibel imperatorskogo doma* 1917-19 p 91
21. Gushchik, p 22
22. *Ibid*
23. *Ibid*
24. MA's diary, December 25/31, 1917
25. Oliver H. Radkey, T*he Election to the Russian Constitutent Assembly,* Harvard University Press, Cambridge, Mass., 1950, pp 20-21
26. Miss Neame, letter to her family in Brighton, England, May 16, 1918 (*private collection*)
27. MA's diary, March 4, 1918
28. Miss Neam letter *ibid*
29. Poutiatine
30. *Ibid*
31. *Ibid*
32. Commissar order, GARF 130/10, cited *Gibel* Buranov/Khrustalev, p 93
33. Poutiatine
34. MA to NS, March 10, 1918, LRA MS 1363/36-4
35. Poutiatine

20. Prisoner of Perm

1. MA to NS, telegram, March 14, 1918, LRA MS 1363/37-1
2. Letter from Johnson, cited Poutiatine
3. Khrustalev/Lykov, p 89
4. Poutiatine
5. MA to NS, March 10, 1918, LRA MS 1363/36-4
6. Johnson to Lenin, telegram, March 15. 1918, GARF 130/1109
7. MA to NS, telegram, March 19, 1918, LRA MS 1363/37-2
8. *The Times*, London, March 22, 1918
9. MA to NS, telegram, March 19, 1918, LRA Ms 1363/37-3
10. MA to Bonch-Bruevich, March 20, 1918, GARF 130/1109
11. Chelyshev to Natasha, March 26, 1918, LRA MS 1363/37-4
12. MA to NS, telegram, March 19, 1918, 1363/37-3
14. *The Times*, London, April 6, 1918
15. Mirkina/Khrustalev, p 153
16. Khrustalev/Lykov, pp 108-9
17. MA to NS, April 10, 1918, LRA MS 1363/36
18. Poutiatine
19. Miss Neame letter
20. *Ibid*
21. Majolier, p 132
22. March 25, 1918, GARF 130/1109
23. 'Prisoner of Perm' photo, LRA MS 1363/268
24. Krumnis, cited Mirkina/Khrustalev, p 153
25. *Ibid*
26. Wilton, p 120
27. MA to NS, telegram, April 19, 1918, LRA Ms 1363/37-6
28. *Ibid,* April 25, 1918, 1363/26
29. MA's diary, May 11, 1918, Mirkina/Khrustalev, p 159
30. Shamarin, GARF 539/2765
31. Myasnikov, p 83
32. MA's diary, May 16, 1918, cited *ibid*

33. *Ibid*, May 12-17, 1918
34. *Ibid* May 17, 1918
35. *Ibid*, May 18, 1918
36. Alexandrov, p 221
37. Poutiatine
38. Wilton, p 121

21. Either Him Or Us

1. Khrustalev/Likov, p 92
2. Buranov/Khrustalev, p 96
3. MA's diary, May 21,1918, cited Mirkina/Khrustalev (*hereafter MK*) p 160
4. MA to NS, June 3, 1918, LRA MS, 1363/31
5. MA's diary, May 19-23, 1918, MK *ibid*
6. Krumnis, GARF 5881/414
7. MA's diary, May 25, 1918, MK p 161
8. Wilton, p 121
9. Unsigned and undated note, LRA MS 1363/22
10. MA's diary, May 29, 1918, MK *ibid*
11. MA to NS, June 3, 1918, LRA MS 1363/22
12. *Ibid*, June 3, 1918
13. MA's diary, June 7, 1918, MK p 163
14. Myasnikov, p 63
15. Biographical note, Myasnikov
16. Kerensky, *Murder*, p 255
17. Myasnikov, p 31
18. *Ibid*, pp 69-70
19. MA's diary, June 7, 1918, MK *ibid*
20. *Ibid*, June 8-9, 1918
21. *Ibid*, June 10-11, 1918
22. Myasnikov, p 116
23. Malkov statement, GAPO 90/M-60
24. Mikov, GAPO 90/2/M-22b

22. Death in the Woods

1. Myasnkov, p 59
2. Ibid
3. Ibid,, pp 82-4
4. British Meteorological Office,, Bracknell, Berkshire
5. Myasnikov, p 59
6. *Ibid*, p 87
7. *Ibid*, pp 94-5
8. *Ibid*, p 95
9. Biographical note, Introduction, Myasnikov
10. Myasnikov, p 95
11. Khrustalev/Lykov, p 118
12. Statement by Znamerovsky, *ibid* cited pp 118-9
13. Statement by Chelyshev, *ibid*, cited p 109
14. Krumnis, cited Mirkina/Khrustalev, pp 152-3
15. Statement by kitchen maid, cited Khrustalev/Lykov, pp 114-5
16. Statement by Chelyshev, *ibid*, p 109
17. Markov, Mirkina/Khrustalev, pp 152-3
18. *Ibid*
19. Wilton, p 123
20. *Ibid*
21. Krumnis, cited Mirkina/Khrustalev, pp 153
22. Chelyshev statement, Khrustalev/Lykov, p 109; Markov, Mirkina/Khrustalev, pp 152-3
23.Myasnikov, p 98
24. *Ibid*, pp 98-100
25. *Ibid*, p 105
26. *Ibid*, pp 105-8
27. *Ibid*, p 111
28. Markov, Mirkina/Khrustalev, pp 152-3
29. *Ibid*
30. Myasnikov, p 112
31. Markov, Mirkina/Khrustalev, pp 152-3
32. Myasnikov, p 113

33. *Ibid*
34. *Ibid*
35. Resolution Perm Provincial Executive Committee, June 13, 1918, cited Khrustalev/Lykov, p 90
36. Wilton, p 240
37. *Izvestya*, Perm., June 15, 1918, cited Mirkina/Khrustalev, p 149
38. V. F. Sivkov, Perm Provincial Executive Committee, cited Buranov/Khrustalov, p 107
39. Vera Karnaukhova, in evidence to Sokolov, *RTiKhIDNI 588/8*, cited Khrustalev/Lykov pp 138-40
40. Krumnis, cited Mirkina/Khrustalev, pp 152-3
41. Myasnikov, p 119
42. *Ibid*, p 114
43. Alexandrov, pp 81-3
44. *Ibid*

23. Long Live Michael

1. Telegram no 551, June 29, 1918, PRO/ADM 137/883
2. *The Times*, London, June 27, 1918,
3. *Ibid*, July 3, 1918
4. *Ibid*, July 6, 1918
5. July 8, 1918, PRO WO 106/1220/44
6. *Nasha rodina*, Moscow, July 21, 1918 cited Mirkina/Khrustalev, p 141
7. Dimitri's diaries 1918
8. Moscow to Berlin, July 17, 1918, PRO GFM 6/139 A3097
9. July 1, 1918, PRO GFM 6/140 A30977
10. Bykov, p 82
11. Investigations which established the essentials of the murder were begun after the Whites captured Ekaterinburg on July 25, 1918.
12. Sinolin; it was Sinolin who recovered the bodies and carried out the first investigations of the murders.
13. Pipes, pp 780-3
14. Bruce Lockhart, p 304
15. Stockholm, August 26, 1918, PRO WO 106/1219/815
16. Kiev, August 23, 1918, PRO GFM, 6.140/AS 4034
17. July 22, 1918,
18. Majolier, p 129
19. GARF 439/8780, cited Mirkina/Khrustalev, p 156
20. June 15, 1918, PRO GFM6/139 A29471
21. Ibid
22. Majolier p 153
23. *Ibid*, p 142
24. Bruce Lockhart, p 321; 'hung out of window' Paley, 244
25. Majolier p 145; the evidence dates her arrest as September 7, 1918
26. *Ibid*, p 153
27. *Ibid*, pp 158-60
28. *Izvestia*, Perm, cited Mirkina/Khrustalev p 156
29. Russian Telegraph Agency, September 20, 1918, *ibid* p 156
30. O'Connor, p 256
31. Mirkina/Khrustalelv p 156
32. September 21, 1918, PROGFM 6/140/A39669
33. Wilton, p 129
34. LRA Ms 1363/82
35. Majolier, p 142
36. *Ibid*, p 161
37. *Ibid*, p 170
38. *Ibid* pp 166-9
39. GARF 391/161, cited Buranov/Khrustalev, p 111
40. Kiev, October 24, 1918, PRO GFM, 16/140 A44463
41. Copenhagen, November 2, 1918, *ibid*, A46412
42. Berlin, October 30, 1918, *ibid*, A45995
43. Majolier, p177
44. *Ibid*, p 179

24. A Divided Family

1. Kolchak telegram, September 15, 1919, LRA MS 1363/98
2. Majolier, p 191
3. LRA MS 1363/101, Gray, 138
4. Ibid, 1363/119
5. Majolier, p 192
6. August 2, LRA MS 1363/103-3
7. LRA MS 1363/69
8. *The Times,* London, July 6,, 1924
9. Cyril, p 220
10. *Ibid,* p 248
11. *Ibid,* p 247
12. *Ibid,* p 222, 248
13. Letter, October 4, 1924, kindly provided by Prince Nicholas Romanov, great-nephew of 'Nikolasha'
14. Cyril, p 222
15. *Ibid,* p 165
16. *Ibid,* p 232
17. *Ibid,* p 248
18. *Almanac de Gotha,* 1936
19. Gray, p 146
20. Majolier, p 226
21. Ibid, p 230
22. *Illyustrirovannaya Rossiya,* Paris, August 1, 1931. LRA MS 1363/123
23. Natasha grand-daughter Pauline Gray to author
24. Death certificate: copy to author from Natasha's grand-daughter Pauline
25. Gushchik, p 46

BIBLIOGRAPHY

SOURCES AND WORKS CITED

ORIGINAL SOURCES

MICHAEL ALEKSANDROVICH, GRAND DUKE, EMPEROR MICHAEL II
— *Letters,* 1908-1918: State Archive of the Russian Federation, Moscow
— Letters, 1909-1910: Russian State Historical Archive, St. Petersburg
— *Diaries,* 1915-1918: Forbes Collection, New York
— *Letters, telegrams:* Leeds Russian Archive, University of Leeds
— *Legal papers, miscellanea*: Knebworth House archive, England
— *Personal photograph album:* School of Slavonic and East European
Studies, University of London

NATHALIE SERGEYEVNA BRASOVA ('NATASHA')
— *Letters,* 1909-1916: State Archive of the Russian Federation, Moscow
— *Telegrams,* 1909-1913; miscellanea 1919-1934: Leeds Russian Archive,
University of Leeds

GEORGE MIKHAILOVICH, COUNT BRASOV
— *Letters* 1918: Leeds Russian Archive, University of Leeds

DIMITRI PAVLOVICH, GRAND DUKE
—*Diaries*, Houghton Library, Harvard University
—*Letters,* 1915-1917: State Archive of the Russian Federation, Moscow

Other Archives consulted:
Moscow Historical Archive
Moscow Archive of Scientific and Technical Documentation
Public Record Office, London (PRO)
Royal Archives, Windsor (RA)
Royal Archives, Copenhagen
State Archive of the Moscow District
State Archive of the Perm District (GAPO)
Wiener Stadt-und Landsarchiv, Vienna

SELECTED WORKS

ALEXANDER Mikhailovich, Grand Duke ('Sandro'): *Once a Grand Duke*, Cassell, London 1932
— *Always a Grand Duke*, Farrar & Rinehart, New York, 1933
ABRIKOSSOW, Dimitri I., *Revelations of a Russian Diplomat*, University of Washington, Seattle, 1964
BING, Edward J (ed.) *The Secret Letters of the Last Tsar: The Confidential Correspondence between Nicholas II and His Mother, Dowager Empress Marie Feodorovna*, Nicholson & Watson, London 1937
BROWDER, R P and KERENSKY A F: *The Russian Provisional Government 1917*, Stanford University Press, 1961
BRUCE LOCKHART, R H: *Memoirs Of A British Agent*, Macmillan, London, 1932
BRUSILOV, General Alexei: *A Soldier's Note-Book*, Macmillan, London, 1936
BUCHANAN, Sir George: *My Mission To Russia*, Cassell, London, 1923
BUCHANAN, Meriel, *The Dissolution of an Empire*, John Murray, London, 1932
BUXHOEVEDEN, Baroness Sophie: T*he Life and Tragedy of Alexandra Feodorovna, Empress of Russia*, Longmans, London, 1928
BYKOV, P M: *The Last Days of Tsardom*, Martin Lawrence, London, 1934
CANTACUZÈNE, Princess: *Revolutionary Days,* Chapman & Hall, London, 1920
CHAVCHAVADZE, Prince David: *The Grand Dukes,*
Atlantic International Publications, N.Y., 1990
CLARKE, William: *The Lost Fortunes of the Tsars*, Weidenfeld & Nicolson, London, 1994
CYRIL, Grand Duke (Kirill Vladimirovich): *My Life in Russia's Service,* Selwyn & Blount, London, 1939
DEHN, Lili: *The Real Tsaritsa*, Thornton Butterworth, London, 1922
DOBSON, Christopher: *Prince Felix Youssoupoff,* Harrap, London, 1965
GELARDI, Julia: *Born to Rule, Granddaughters of Queen Victoria, Queens of Europe,* Headline Book Publishing, London, 2005
GEORGE, Grand Duchess (Marie Georgievna): *Memoirs*, Atlantic International Publications, N.Y., 1988
GRAY, Pauline: *The Grand Duke's Woman*, Macdonald, London, 1976
KATKOV, George: *Russia 1917: The February Revolution,* Longmans, Green, London, 1967
KERENSKY, Alexander and BULYGIN, Paul: *The Murder of the Romanovs,* Hutchinson, London, 1935
KERENSKY, Alexander: *The Catastrophe*, Appleton, N.Y., 1927
— *Memoirs,* Cassell, London, 1966

KNOX, Major-General Sir Alfred: *With the Russian Army,* Hutchinson, London, 1921

KOURNAKOFF, Sergei: *Savage Squadrons,* Harrap, London, 1936

KSCHESSINKA, Mathilde (Romanovsky-Krassinsky, Princess): *Dancing in Petersburg,* Victor Gollancz, London, 1961

LETTERS of the Tsar to the Tsaritsa, 1914-1917 Bodley Head, London 1929

LETTERS of the Tsaritsa to the Tsar, 1914-1916, Duckworth, London 1923

LINCOLN, W. Bruce: *Passage Through Armageddon,* Simon & Schuster, N.Y., 1986

LUCKETT, Richard, *The White Generals,* Routledge & Kegan Paul, London, 1971

MAJOLIER, Nathalie: *Stepdaughter to Imperial Russia,* Stanley Paul, London, 1940

MAYLUNAS, Andrei, and MIRONENKO, Sergei: *A Lifelong Passion,* Weidenfeld & Nicolson, London, 1996

MILYUKOV, Paul N: *History of the Russian Revolution,* Academic International Press, Florida, 1978

MOSSOLOV, A A: *At the Court of the Last Tsar,* Methuen, London, 1935

(NABOKOV V D:) *V D Nabokov and the Russian Provisional Government 1917,* Yale University Press, 1976

Nicholas II, *Journal Intime.* Translated by A. Pierre, Paris, Bayor, 1925.

NICHOLAS, Prince of Greece: *My Fifty Years,* Hutchinson, London 1926

NICOLSON, Harold: *King George the Fifth,* Constable, London, 1952

O'CONNOR, John (ed.): *The Sokolov Investigation,* Souvenir Press, London, 1972

PALÉOLOGUE, Maurice: *An Ambassador's Memoirs,* Doran, N.Y., 1925

PALEY, Princess: *Memories of Russia,* Herbert Jenkins, London, 1924

PARES, Sir Bernard: *The Fall of the Russian Monarchy,* Jonathan Cape, London, 1939

PIPES, Richard: *The Russian Revolution,* 1899-1919, Collins Harvel, London 1990

POLOVTSOV, General P A: *Glory and Downfall,* Bell, London 1935

RADKEY, Oliver H: *The Election to the Russian Constituent Assembly,* Harvard University Press, 1950

RADZIWILL, Princess Catherine: *Secrets of Dethroned Royalty,* Cassell, London, 1920

— *Nicholas II: The Last of the Tsars,* Cassell, London, 1931

RODZYANKO M V: *The Reign of Rasputin,* Philpot, London, 1927

ROSE, Kenneth: *King George V,* Weidenfeld & Nicolson, London, 1983

SAZONOV, Serge: *Fateful Years,* Jonathan Cape, London, 1928

STEINBERG, Mark D and KHRUSTALEV, Vladimir M: *The Fall of the Romanovs,* Yale University Press, 1995

SUKHANOV N N: *The Russian Revolution,* Princeton University Press, 1984

SULLIVAN, Michael John: *A Fatal Passion: The Story of the Uncrowned Last Empress of Russia*, Random House, 1997

VASSILI, Count Paul: *Behind the Veil at the Russian Court*,
Cassell, London, London, 1913

VORRES, Ian: *The Last Grand Duchess*, Scribner, N.Y., 1965

VULLIAMY, C E (ed.): *The Red Archives*, Geoffrey Bles, London, 1929

VYRUBOVA, Anna: *Memoirs of the Russian Court*, Macmillan, London, 1923

WALKER, Stanley: T*he Russian Campaign, 1915*, Andrew Melrose, London, 1916

WILTON, Robert: *The Last Days of the Romanovs*,
Thornton Butterworth, London, 1920

WITTE, Count Sergei: *Memoirs*, Doubleday, Page, N.Y., 1921

WONLAR-LARSKY, Nadine: *The Russia That I Loved*, MacSweeney, London, 1937

WRANGEL, General Peter: *Memoirs*, Williams & Northgate, London, 1929

YOUSSOUPOFF, Prince Felix: *Rasputin: His Malignant Influence*,
Jonathan Cape, London, 1927

— *Lost Splendour*, Jonathan Cape, London, 1953

RUSSIAN WORKS

ARTEMOV, S: Mikhail Romanov: "Poberg"i ego posledstviya, *Zerkalo*, 9 & 12, 1990

BURANOV, Yu. and KHRUSTALEV, V: *Gibel imperatoskogo doma 1917-1919 gg*, Progress, Moscow, 1992

(GUCHKOV A I:) 'Aleksandrr Ivanovich Guchkov rasskazyvaet',
Voprosy istorii, Moscow 7-8, 1991

GUSHCHIK, Vladimir: *Taina Gatchinskogo dvortsa*, Literature, Riga, 1927

ISAKOV, S G: *Russkie v Estonii, 1918-1940*, Kompu, Tartu, Estoniam, 1996

KHRUSTALEV V M and LYKOV I A: *Skorbnyi put Mikhaila Romanova: Ot prestola do Golgofy*, Pushka, Perm, 1996

Kratkii ocherk Brasovskogo imeniya ego Imperatorskogo Vysochestva...Georgiya Aleksandrovicha, Orlovskyhvestnik, Orel, 1895

KRYLOV, A: *Istoricheskie miniatyury*, Moscow, 3, 1990

MATVEEV, A.S: 'Vel. knyaz Mikhail Aleksandrovich v dni perevorota',
Vozrozhdenie, Paris, 24, 1952

MELGUNOV, S P: *Martovskie dni 1917 goda*, Editeurs réunis, Paris, 1961

MILYUKOV, P N: *Istoriya vtoroi russkoi revolyutsii*,
Rossiisko-bolgarskoe izdatelstvo, Sofia, 1921

MYASNIKOV, G: 'Filosofiya ubiistva, ili pochemu I kak ubil Mikhaila Romanova',
Minuvshee, Atheneum & Feniks, Moscow & St. Petersburg, 18, 1995

MIRKINA, I A and KHRUSTALEV V M: 'Sudba Mikhaila Romanova',
Voprosy istorii, Moscow, 1990

PLATONOV, Oleg: 'Tsareubiitsy', *Literaturnaya Rossiya*,
Moscow, 38, September 1990
RODZYANKO M V: 'Godsudarstvennaya Duma I fevralskaya 1917 goda
revolyutsiya', *Arkhiv russkoi revolyutsii*, Berlin, 6, 1922
SHULGIN, V V: *Dni,* Novoe Vremya, Belgrade 1925; Sovremennik, Moscow,
1989
STANKEVICH, V B: *Vospominaniya 1914-1919,*
Ladyzhnikov, Berlin, 1920; Moscow 1994
TOROPOV, S A: 'Samosud', *Vechernyaya Perm*, Perm, January 15, 1990
TRUBETSKOI, V: 'Zapiski kirasira', *Nashe nasledie*, Moscow, 2-4, 1991

FRENCH

Journal intime de Nicolas II, Payot, Paris, 1925
Enache, Nicholas, La Descendance de Pierre le Grand. Sedopols, 1983
Poutiatine, Princess Olga, 'Les Derniers Jours du Grand-Duc Michel
Alexandrovich', *Revue des Deux Mondes*, Paris, November 1 & 15, 1923

INDEX

OCT 1 8 2012

CPSIA information can be obtained at www.ICGtesting.com
Printed in the USA
LVOW110938071012

301811LV00001B/7/P

9 781466 445000